Eating Disorders Review
Part I

Edited by

Stephen Wonderlich
James E Mitchell
Martina de Zwaan
Howard Steiger

Foreword by

Michael J Devlin

RADCLIFFE PUBLISHING
OXFORD • SEATTLE

Radcliffe Publishing Ltd
18 Marcham Road
Abingdon
Oxon OX14 1AA
United Kingdom

www.radcliffe-oxford.com
Electronic catalogue and worldwide online ordering facility.

British Library Cataloguing in Publication Data

A catalogue record for this book is available from the British Library.

ISBN 1 85775 634 7

Coventry University

Typeset by Advance Typesetting Ltd, Oxford
Printed and bound by TJ International Ltd, Padstow, Cornwall

Contents

Foreword

One of the most challenging tasks for healthcare professionals in the twenty-first century is keeping up with the rapid developments in our understanding of the mechanisms of illness and in our approaches to treating and preventing illness. In the case of eating disorders, the multidisciplinary nature of our field presents a particular challenge, since no one conference or journal can hope to bring together the many contributions of psychologists, psychiatrists, dieticians, nurses, social workers, primary care physicians and adolescent medicine specialists, educators, epidemiologists, basic researchers and all of the many others who are dedicated to moving our field forward.

The Academy for Eating Disorders (AED), from its inception, has sought to bring together researchers and clinicians from these various disciplines to educate the professional community, to advocate for our patients, and to work toward the eventual elimination of eating disorders worldwide. The book you now hold represents a new and pioneering approach to this enterprise. The idea of an AED Annual Review was inspired by the need for a high quality resource that was both comprehensive and up to date. Textbooks, whilst comprehensive, are typically obsolete even as they are published, and journals, whilst up to date, rarely present the reader with a comprehensive overview of the field. Drs Wonderlich, Mitchell, de Zwaan and Steiger have effectively filled this gap by assembling a panel of experts in eating disorders and commissioning them to produce, on a very rapid timetable, overviews of progress in various aspects of eating disorders research and practise during the period 2002–2003, looking ahead to projects that will come to fruition in the years ahead. This volume includes reviews of diverse areas such as classification, comorbidity, trauma, family issues, psychobiology, prevention, and treatment of anorexia nervosa and binge eating disorder. The companion volume, to be published next year, will cover the period 2003–2004, and will include a variety of topics that complement this year's selection. Taken together, each two-year set will cover all of the major areas of eating disorders research, and will provide the reader with thoughtful summaries of, and commentaries on, the latest research.

As this year's President of the Academy for Eating Disorders, I would like to personally commend the editors for initiating this important project and, despite significant challenges, bringing it out on time. It is an exciting and informative volume and sets a high standard for a series that will surely be an important resource in the years ahead, not only for eating disorder specialists, but for all healthcare professionals and individuals in the community who wish to access the latest and best information on the biology, treatment, and prevention of these devastating disorders.

Michael J Devlin, MD
President, Academy for Eating Disorders
September 2004

Preface

Welcome to the first of what we hope will be an ongoing series of reviews of the area of eating disorders, published by the Academy for Eating Disorders, for clinicians and researchers. This project, sponsored by the Academy, began in response to a perceived need for up-to-date, thorough and practical reviews of current literature in the area of eating disorders. All of us know that busy clinicians and researchers alike rarely have time to read all of the new literature in this area. And even when they do have time to read the literature, the clinical implications are not always obvious. Therefore the editors of this volume identified 20 topics covering the major aspects of eating disorders, from prevention to treatment, as well as many areas in between, and decided, with AED support, to publish this annual review. The current plan is that one volume will be published every year, and each volume will cover 10 of these 20 topics, so that each topic will be covered every other year. Authors of the individual chapters were asked to focus on the developments of the last two years, linking these to earlier findings of relevance. As can be seen, each of the chapters is also written so that the clinical implications of the work are highlighted, and key references that may be of particular interest to clinicians are designated in the reference list. This volume is not designed to provide a detailed retelling of the recently published studies in the field, but instead to summarize this information critically for practitioners and researchers so that they can access the most up-to-date information in a concise and useful form.

Because this is the first year of this endeavor, we hope that readers of this volume will find it informative. However, since it is our first volume, we are particularly interested in feedback from readers regarding the format, the topics covered and the amount of detail included.

We hope that this review will develop into a volume that clinicians and researchers alike will anticipate as a means of surveying the most important recent findings in our field in a concise, user-friendly and clinically useful way.

Stephen Wonderlich
James E Mitchell
Martina de Zwaan
Howard Steiger
September 2004

List of editors

Stephen Wonderlich, PhD
Neuropsychiatric Research Institute and Department of Neuroscience, University of North Dakota School of Medicine and Health Sciences, Fargo, USA

James E Mitchell, MD
Neuropsychiatric Research Institute and Department of Neuroscience, University of North Dakota School of Medicine and Health Sciences, Fargo, USA

Martina de Zwaan, MD
University of Erlangen, Erlangen, Germany

Howard Steiger, PhD
Douglas Hospital, McGill University, Montreal, Canada

List of contributors

Timothy D Brewerton, MD
Department of Psychiatry and Behavioral Sciences, Medical University of South Carolina, Charleston, USA

Scott Crow, MD
Department of Psychiatry, University of Minnesota Medical School, Minneapolis, USA

Michael J Devlin, MD
New York State Psychiatric Institute, College of Physicians and Surgeons, Columbia University, New York, USA

Sarah E Fischer, BA
New York State Psychiatric Institute, College of Physicians and Surgeons, Columbia University, New York, USA

Daniel le Grange, PhD
Department of Psychiatry, University of Chicago, Chicago, USA

James I Hudson, MD, ScD
Biological Psychiatry Laboratory, McLean Hospital, Belmont, and Department of Psychiatry, Harvard Medical School, Boston, USA

Rebecca A Hudson
Biological Psychiatry Laboratory, McLean Hospital, Belmont, USA

Corinna Jacobi, Dipl. Psych.
Clinical Psychology and Psychotherapy Technical University, Dresden, Germany

Kathryn B Miller, PhD
Eating Disorders Research Program, Department of Psychiatry, University of Minnesota, Minneapolis, USA

Sarah Perkins, BSc
Section of Eating Disorders, Institute of Psychiatry, London, UK

Carol B Peterson, PhD
Eating Disorders Research Program, Department of Psychiatry, University of Minnesota, Minneapolis, USA

Harrison G Pope Jr, MD, MPH
Biological Psychiatry Laboratory, McLean Hospital, Belmont, and Department of Psychiatry, Harvard Medical School, Boston, USA

Dana A Satir, BA
College of Physicians and Surgeons, Columbia University, and New York State Psychiatric Institute, New York, USA

Ulrike Schmidt, MD, PhD
Section of Eating Disorders, Institute of Psychiatry, London, UK

C Barr Taylor, MD
Department of Psychiatry and Behavioral Sciences, Stanford University School of Medicine, Palo Alto, USA

B Timothy Walsh, MD
College of Physicians and Surgeons, Columbia University, and New York State Psychiatric Institute, New York, USA

1

Update on the prevention of eating disorders

C Barr Taylor

Abstract

Objectives of review. This chapter reviews studies published in the last two years related to universal and targeted prevention of eating disorders. Universal prevention programs attempt to reduce risk factors in entire populations. Targeted prevention programs focus on reducing risk factors in individuals who are not yet, but are at high risk of becoming, 'subclinical' or clinical cases.

Summary of recent findings. The evidence now suggests that targeted prevention interventions may reduce potential risk factors in older adolescent and college-age women. Universal prevention interventions have not yet been shown to have strong or lasting effects on eating disorder attitudes and behaviors in elementary- and middle-school populations. Prevention programs do not appear to be harmful.

Future directions. The base of preliminary evidence is substantial enough to merit more definitive studies, including ones that would determine whether a reduction in risk factors could lead to a reduction in the incidence of eating disorders. Other important questions include the following. How can programs related to weight control be combined with programs to reduce the incidence of eating disorders? How can universal prevention interventions have stronger and longer-lasting effects on risk factors, particularly in elementary-school children and early adolescents? How should environmental/system and family factors be included in interventions? Should programs be provided for both boys and girls in the same setting? And if so, how should this be done?

Introduction

In this chapter, we review studies published in the last two years relating to issues of eating disorder prevention. We include articles related to both universal prevention, which attempts to reduce the incidence of a disease by eliminating or reducing risk factors that are prevalent in a population, and targeted prevention interventions (sometimes called selected interventions) that focus on reducing risk factors in individuals who are not yet, but are at high risk of becoming, 'subclinical' or clinical cases.

Literature review

Both universal and targeted interventions require identification of risk factors, and a number of potential risk factors have been identified in longitudinal studies (Stice 2002; McKnight Investigators 2003; Jacobi *et al.* 2004). However, the ultimate test of a risk factor is to demonstrate that its reduction leads to a reduced incidence of the disorder, and no risk factor for eating disorders has yet passed this test. Many researchers have argued that prevention activities should also focus on 'protective' factors (e.g. building higher levels of self-esteem), which might reduce the probability that an individual who is at risk goes on to develop the disorder. However, no such protective factors have been identified in prospective risk-factor studies. The effort to develop targeted prevention programs is also complicated by the need to accurately identify high-risk individuals. In theory, a highly sensitive and specific screen could partition a population into no risk, high risk or case, and high-risk individuals would be provided with targeted prevention interventions (or monitored), while cases could be referred for treatment. Unfortunately, no screen has been developed that has been demonstrated to accurately partition individuals into these groups (Jacobi *et al.* 2004). Despite these issues, several recent studies provide new hope for prevention interventions.

Reviews

Two recent and somewhat contradictory reviews provide an important insight into the status of prevention programs. Pratt and Woolfenden (2002) examined randomized controlled trials with a major focus on eating disorder prevention programs for children and adolescents. Trials needed to include a control group and at least one objective outcome measure (e.g. BMI) or a standardized psychological measure used with the intervention and control group pre- and post-intervention. Of 1379 potential studies identified, eight met these selection criteria. Only one of eight pooled comparisons of two or more studies used similar measures and similar intervention types, and demonstrated statistically significant effects on outcomes related to eating disorder risk factors. Combined data from two eating disorder prevention programs based on a media literacy and advocacy approach indicated a reduction in the internalization or acceptance of societal ideals relating to appearance at a three- to six-month follow-up.

However, the authors concluded that there was insufficient evidence to support the effect of prevention programs designed to address eating attitudes and behaviors, and other adolescent issues and attitudes, behaviors or psychopathology. Stice and Shaw (2004) provided a more optimistic review, perhaps because of the inclusion of more recent studies than were available for Pratt and Woolfenden (2002). They focused on prevention programs that were evaluated in controlled trials using controlled effect sizes to compare across studies for outcomes. The outcomes needed to be used in at least 10 of the trials. Their literature search identified 51 published and unpublished studies that met the inclusion criteria. The weighted average effect sizes across the various trials at post-treatment were 0.38 for knowledge, 0.19 for thin-ideal internalization, 0.13 for body dissatisfaction, 0.11 for dieting, 0.14 for negative affect and 0.12 for eating pathology (effect sizes of 0.20–0.40 are considered to be moderate). The average effect sizes were 0.05 to 0.29 at follow-up. However, 32 (53%) of the interventions resulted in significant reductions in at least one established risk factor for eating pathology (such as body dissatisfaction) and, even more impressively, 15 (25%) of the interventions resulted in significant reductions in eating pathology. Stice and Shaw note that the more recent prevention trials have been more effective than the earlier ones, and the inclusion of these trials partly explains the difference in results between their analysis and that of Pratt and Woolfenden (2002). Exploratory analyses of potential moderators suggested that targeted programs provided to higher-risk individuals produced significantly larger effects than did universal programs, that interactive programs seemed to be more effective than didactic ones, and that interventions were more effective for older adolescents and college-age women.

Recent trials

As noted above, recent trials have provided evidence for prevention effects, at least in older students and in higher-risk populations. Table 1.1 summarizes the sample, design, intervention and findings for studies focusing on elementary- and middle-school boys and girls. Of note, all of these samples were universal interventions. Overall, the results have been mixed. McVey and Davis (2002) found no significant differences in the intervention compared with the control group at post-test or follow-up. In a replication, there were significant effects for body dissatisfaction, diet and negative affect at post-test and follow-up, and for bulimic symptoms at post-test but not at follow-up (McVey et al. 2004). In a study of middle-school boys and girls, Kater et al. (2002) found no significant pre–post effects between intervention and assessment-only students for an 11-lesson curriculum with similar goals to those of the curriculum used in the studies by McVey and Davis (2002) and McVey et al. (2004). McVey et al. (2003a) looked at the effectiveness of school-based, 10-session peer support groups facilitated by public health nurses. There was a significant increase in body esteem and a significant decrease in dieting from pre- to post-intervention and at 3-month follow-up for the intervention. Unfortunately, these results were not replicated in a follow-up study, which found no significant group × time effects

Table 1.1 Description of the sample, design, intervention and findings for studies focusing on universal elementary and middle-school samples

Study	Sample	Design	Intervention	Findings
McVey and Davis (2002)	263 sixth-grade girls	4 schools assigned to I or C; pre-post 6 months, 12-month follow-up	6 weekly, 1-hour, interactive multimedia sessions with life skills focus: ML, SE, BI, BSA, HWR, SM, PR	No significant differences between I and C
McVey et al. (2004)	258 sixth-grade girls	As above	As above	I, compared with C, improved on BI, SE and dieting attitudes post; no significant differences at follow-up
Kater et al. (2002)	415 fourth- to sixth-grade boys and girls	375 received I and 79 served as C (assessment only); pre-post only	11-lesson 'Healthy Body Image' curriculum with focus on BI, NG&D, PR	Girls in I scored significantly higher on knowledge at post than did C; no other measures were significant
McVey et al. (2003a)	214 seventh- to eighth-grade girls	7 I schools matched with 5 C schools; 3-month follow-up	10-session peer support group, facilitated by public health nurse: ML, BI, SE, SM, PR	Significant effects for I compared with C on BI and dieting
McVey et al. (2003b)	282 seventh- to eighth-grade girls	8 I schools matched with 8 C schools; 2-month follow-up	As above	No significant I vs C effects
Withers et al. (2002)	242 seventh-grade boys and girls	104 I girls compared with 114 C (assessment only); 1-month follow-up	1 session, psychoeducation video	Knowledge increase post-test and at 1-month follow-up, I compared with C, but no differences for BI, dieting
Wade et al. (2003)	86 eighth-grade boys and girls	Students assigned to SE program, ML program, or C, 3-month follow-up	SE and ML provided in five, 1-hour class settings	ML group had lower levels of weight concerns at post; no differences at follow-up
Steiner-Adair et al. (2002)	499 seventh-grade girls	16 schools randomized to I or C, 6-month follow-up	8 weekly 45- to 90-minute sessions, SE, BSA, PR, other	I vs C, significant differences at post and 6-month follow-up on knowledge, weight-related body esteem

I, intervention; C, control; ML, media literacy; SE, self-esteem; BI, body image; BSA, body size acceptance; HWR, healthy weight regulation; SM, stress management; PR, positive relationships; NG&D, normal growth and development.

with the same program and a similar number of students (McVey *et al.* 2003b). McVey and her colleagues are to be commended for this careful programmatic research. Two other universal interventions also found minimal or no effects (Withers *et al.* 2002). These studies, taken together with the modest or negative effects reported from previous large controlled prevention studies (e.g. Killen *et al.* 1993; O'Dea and Abraham 2000), suggest that psychoeducation programs focusing on healthy weight regulation and improved body image have minimal and short-lived universal prevention effects. However, in a study with somewhat more encouraging results, Steiner-Adair *et al.* (2002) evaluated the effectiveness and feasibility of a primary prevention program for risk factors for eating disorders in adolescent girls aged 12–14 years at baseline. The program, called 'Full of Ourselves: Advancing Girl Power, Health and Leadership,' addresses eight topics delivered in weekly sessions of 45–90 minutes. The program was implemented in 24 schools in two regions of the USA. Sixteen of the 24 sites randomized assigned subjects to a participant or control group. Pre, post and six-month data were obtained for 411 of 499 subjects who completed the study, and about 83% of subjects also provided follow-up data six months later. Significant differences were found between participants and controls on measures of knowledge and weight-related body esteem (but not other aspects of 'body esteem') which were maintained at the six-month follow-up. Eating-related behaviors, including skipping meals and dieting, appeared to be unaffected by program participation. The authors note that the program was feasible and safe, and that it has been packaged for delivery in most school settings. The results of Steiner-Adair *et al.* (2002) are encouraging but modest. For instance, on the Body Esteem Scale weight scale, the means for pre, post and follow-up were 2.6, 2.7 and 2.6, respectively, for participants and 2.6, 2.4 and 2.4 respectively, for controls, suggesting that the program helped participants to maintain, but not to improve, body esteem, while the latter decreased in control patients.

Table 1.2 summarizes studies in high-school and older populations. With the exception of the study by Bruning Brown *et al.* (2004), all focused on selected or opportunistic populations. The results of studies by Stice *et al.* (2003), Stice and Ragan (2002), Bearman *et al.* (2003) and Zabinski *et al.* (in press) suggest that prevention interventions might have a significant effect on reducing some potential risk factors, at least in targeted populations. The study by Bruning Brown *et al.* (2004) also suggested some universal effects, at least in the short term. In a novel aspect of this study, parents of students in the study (both treatment and waiting list) were invited to participate in a separate study of an Internet program combined with a handout designed to encourage parents to accept variations in weight and shape and to discourage negative attitudes and behaviors that might affect their daughters. Parents in the intervention group significantly decreased their overall critical attitudes toward weight and shape compared with those in the control group.

Table 1.2 Description of the sample, design, intervention and findings for studies focusing on high-school and older students

Study	Sample	Design	Intervention	Findings
Stice et al. (2003)	148 high-school and college-age women; self-selected for BI concern	Students randomized to DI, HWR or control; 3, 6-month follow-up	3 weekly, 1-hour group sessions; DI: students critiqued thin body ideal; HWR: promoted healthy weight regulation	DI, HWR compared with C: significant improvement in affect, reduction in bulimic symptoms at 3 months
Bruning Brown et al. (2004)	All tenth-grade girls in a private school	I = 102, C = 53 (assessment only); 3-month follow-up	8-week, Internet-delivered, psychoeducation program with discussion group	I had significantly greater increase in knowledge and reduced eating restraint at post; no significant differences at follow-up
Bearman et al. (2003)	74 college women; self-selected for BI concern	Randomized: I = 38, C = 35; 1 and 3-month. follow-up	4-session CBT intervention for BD	I vs C effects for BD and NA at post-test and 3 months; no effects for dieting or bulimic symptoms
Stice and Ragan (2002)	66 college women	I = 17 women in eating disorders course; C = 49 matched students	15-week, twice-weekly 1.5-hour psychoeducational class	I vs C effects for thin ideal internalization, body dissatisfaction, dieting, eating disorder symptoms, pre–post treatment
Zabinski et al. (in press)	60 college women with high level of weight/ shape concerns	Subjects randomized to I = 30 or C = 30; 10-week follow-up	8 weekly, 1-hour synchronous online chat sessions plus psychoeducation	I significantly reduced eating pathology and improved SE over C post and at follow-up

I, intervention; C, control; ML, media literacy; SE, self-esteem; BI, body image; BSA, body size acceptance; HWR, healthy weight regulation; SM, stress management; PR, positive relationships; NG&D, normal growth and development; BD, body dissatisfaction; NA, negative affect; DI, dissonance intervention.

Are prevention interventions harmful?

Several years ago, Mann *et al.* (1997) examined the effects of having classmates who had recovered from eating disorders describe their experiences and provide information about eating disorders to their peers. At follow-up, intervention participants had slightly more symptoms of eating disorders than did controls, and the authors argued that the intervention might actually be harmful. In the same year, Carter *et al.* (1997) found that a school-based eating disorder prevention program provided to 46 schoolgirls aged 13–14 years at baseline resulted in an increase in knowledge and a decrease in target behavior and attitudes. However, the effects had disappeared six months later and there was an increase in dietary restraint compared with baseline. The authors concluded that 'school-based prevention programs may do more harm than good.' Recent studies provide little evidence to support these findings. Pratt and Woolfenden (2002) concluded that there was no evidence that prevention interventions could be harmful, and none were reported in the review by Stice and Shaw (2004). In a related issue, some human subjects' committees have been concerned that asking students about 'eating disorder behaviors' might be problematic (e.g. asking about behaviors such as vomiting might inadvertently 'normalize' the behavior). Common sense argues against such questions having harmful effects in the context of the considerable media coverage of eating disorders that is available to students, but Celio *et al.* (2003) provided some data on this issue. The authors compared the responses to eating disorder attitudes and behaviors of 115 sixth-grade girls, who completed a questionnaire at baseline and one year later, with an additional 107 girls who had not been part of the baseline and who only provided data at follow-up. No evidence of a negative effect in the twice-assessed group was found, and all rates decreased from baseline to follow-up.

Combined weight loss/maintenance and eating disorder interventions

In the last few years there has been discussion of the issues related to combining weight loss/maintenance and eating disorder prevention and intervention programs (e.g. Irving and Neumark-Sztainer 2002; Neumark-Sztainer 2003). Historically, the eating disorder and obesity prevention experts have recommended conflicting and contradictory public health messages. For instance, in commenting on the limitations of weight loss programs in the context of messages to lose weight, Marcia Angell, then editor of the *New England Journal of Medicine,* wrote in an editorial that 'countless numbers of our daughters ... are suffering immeasurable torment in fruitless weight-loss schemes and scams, and some are losing their lives' (Kassirer and Angell 1998). On the other hand, Schwartz and Puhl (2003) stated that 'fear of inadvertently inducing more eating disorders should not keep people from addressing childhood obesity.' Story *et al.* (2002) found that 17% of registered dietitians and 10% of pediatricians felt that concerns about eating disorders were barriers to the treatment of overweight children. Some of the controversy is related to very different definitions of dieting, which is considered to be a risk factor for eating disorders but also a necessary component of healthy weight regulation. In reality, except for students who are obese (BMI > 95%) or at risk of overweight with obesity-related complications and who may need special programs, the recommendations for both overweight and at-risk students are similar, namely to adopt healthy weight regulation practices, including eating regular meals and exercising regularly (Barlow and Dietz 2002). In theory, an integrated obesity and eating disorder prevention program would sort students into risk categories and provide interventions that are appropriate and tailored to each risk level (Taylor *et al.* 2002). This task requires separate and distinct messages that are appropriate for both risk groups, as well as messages for students who are at risk for both, and general messages that are appropriate for those with minimal risk. For instance, students with a healthy weight, but with very high levels of concern about weight and shape, might need a program that emphasizes acceptance of body weight and healthy and moderate physical activity and dietary practices. For students who are overweight or at risk of becoming overweight, a program that emphasizes weight loss or weight maintenance is likely to be more appropriate.

In a study related to the issue of combined interventions, Presnell and Stice (2003) examined an intervention to promote a low-calorie diet for non-obese college women with high levels of concern about weight and shape. Non-obese women ($n = 82$) were randomized to either a six-week, low-calorie diet or a waiting-list control condition. The diet intervention resulted in significant weight loss and, contrary to the restraint model which hypothesizes that dieting would increase eating pathology, dieting resulted in significant decreases in bulimic symptoms relative to the control condition. The study by Luce *et al.* (2004) described below also provides data relevant to this issue.

Special populations

Studies have shown that certain populations are at particular risk for eating disorders (e.g. dancers, models), but surprisingly few studies have focused on prevention within such populations. Olmsted *et al.* (2002) screened 212 young women attending a pediatric diabetes clinic who were screened for signs of eating disturbance. Of these women, 130 individuals passed the screening and were invited to participate in the intervention phase of the study, of whom 85 girls were randomized to the intervention or treatment-as-usual group. There were significant reductions following treatment on the Restraint and Eating Concerns subscales of the Eating Disorder Examination (EDE) and on the Drive for Thinness and Body Dissatisfaction subscales of the Eating Disorder Inventory (EDI), but there was no improvement in the frequency of purging by insulin omission or hemoglobin A_{1c} levels. Moreover, of the 130 girls who were initially identified as candidates for the program, only 85 (*c.* 65.5%) expressed an initial interest, and only 36 (*c.* 28%) completed the psychoeducational program. We could not find any studies published in the last few years that have focused on such high-risk populations.

Delivery issues

Based on evidence that an Internet-delivered program could help to reduce eating-disorder risk factors in at least high-risk populations, the Stanford research group has undertaken a number of studies to examine some of the issues related to delivering such a program. As was mentioned earlier, preliminary evidence suggested that an Internet program can be effective, at least in the short term, for improving eating disorder attitudes, and that a program designed to educate parents about issues related to eating disorders/weight criticism can also be effective, at least in reducing criticism related to risk factors (Bruning Brown *et al.* 2004). Since a number of studies have shown that peer teasing about weight may be a risk factor for eating disorders, Abascal *et al.* (2004) examined the impact of mixing 'higher'- and 'lower'-risk students in the same online discussion, on the assumption that higher-risk students might do better in groups that addressed their needs only. A total of 78 tenth-grade female students were provided with an online eating disorder prevention program and randomized to participate in a higher-risk *and* highly motivated group, a lower-risk *or* less motivated group, or a combined group. The students in the first group made significantly fewer negative comments and more positive comments in the online group discussion than the higher-risk and highly motivated participants in the combined group. However, there were no differences among groups on outcome measures. The results suggest that, since it is relatively easy to provide interventions with separate groups, it seems appropriate to do so, if for no other reason than to minimize the few very negative comments that were posted by students that might have created an adverse environment for the higher-risk participants who the intervention specifically targets.

In a step towards the development of population-based interventions to simultaneously prevent eating disorders and excessive weight gain, a computer-based algorithm was developed to sort female high-school students into one of four risk groups, namely no eating disorder risk/no overweight risk (NR), high eating disorder risk/no overweight risk (EDR), no eating disorder risk/high overweight risk (OR) or high eating disorder risk/high overweight risk (EDOR). Participants completed an online assessment of their weight and shape concerns and entered their self-reported weight and height. Tailored feedback about risk status for developing an eating disorder and/or obesity and a corresponding recommendation for enrollment in a tailored intervention was given to each student. The algorithm identified 111 NR, 36 EDR, 16 OR and 5 EDOR students. In total, 56% of the EDR group and 50% of the OR group elected to receive the recommended targeted curricula. Among the EDOR group, four (80%) selected both, and one student elected to complete the universal core curriculum only. Significant improvements in weight and shape concerns were observed. This study suggests that it is feasible to apply an Internet-delivered algorithm to a population of young women and to simultaneously provide universal and targeted interventions in a classroom setting. The authors also examined the effects of feedback on mood. There were no significant differences in pre–post mood ratings in the core feedback group. A slight increase in 'Shameful' was observed within the EDR participants' ratings (from $M = 1.42$ to $M = 1.67$) after receiving feedback. Among the 20 students who accepted the Body Image Enhancement group recommendation, 'Shameful' increased from $M = 1.15$ to $M = 1.40$, with an effect size of 0.68. Among the 16 students who rejected the group recommendation, 'Shameful' increased from $M = 1.75$ to $M = 2.00$, with an effect size of 0.19. For the 15 participants who received overweight or risk for overweight feedback and a corresponding recommendation for the targeted Weight Management group, the opposite effect was found. Scores on 'Shameful' decreased, with an effect size of 0.12. Because the combined Body Image Enhancement and Weight Management feedback groups consisted of only five participants, interpretations based on these data are considered unreliable, and therefore the mood data for this group were not reported. These data suggest that much more information is needed about how weight and weight/shape messages should be combined, and how those messages affect students' mood, body image, sense of stigmatization and motivation (Luce *et al.* 2004).

System/setting interventions

It is difficult to change attitudes and behaviors related to eating disorders because they are strongly reinforced by a variety of family, peer, medical and other cultural factors. Consequently, some prevention researchers have argued for the need to change the ecology of children and adolescents, notably the school environment (Neumark-Sztainer 1996; Piran 1999; Levine and Piran 2001; Levine and Smolak 2005). However, we cannot find recent studies that have evaluated these issues.

Summary of important findings

Taken together, these studies suggest that targeted (selective) prevention interventions may reduce potential risk factors in older adolescents and college-age women. Universal prevention efforts that promote healthy weight regulation, discourage unhealthy dieting, and address developmental, cultural and social factors relating to body image and eating have not yet been shown to be effective for middle-school students. In general, the outcomes have been modest and inconsistent. Prevention programs do not appear to have harmful effects. However, the study by Mann *et al.* (1997) does suggest that programs which include 'recovered' patients in seminars might inadvertently normalize eating disorder pathology. Much more work is needed to determine how weight loss/maintenance messages and programs can be incorporated into universal and targeted prevention programs.

Future directions

The evidence base is certainly substantial enough to merit more definitive studies, including ones that would determine whether a reduction in risk factors could lead to a reduction in the incidence of the disorders, at least in older adolescents and college students. The results identify promising prevention programs and delineate sample, format and design features that are associated with larger effects, but they also suggest the need for improved methodological rigor and statistical modeling of trials and enhanced theoretical rationale for interventions. Other important questions include the following. How can universal preventions have stronger and longer-lasting effects on risk factors? What is the best age for such interventions and how long should they last? What are the advantages and disadvantages of combined interventions that focus on, for example, healthy weight regulation plus increasing social competence plus changing norms and behaviors with regard to weight- and shape-related teasing? How should environmental/system and family factors be included in interventions? Should programs be provided for both boys and girls in the same setting? And if so, what is the best way to accomplish this?

It is also important to determine how programs related to weight control can be combined with programs to reduce eating disorders. The rising level of obesity in adolescents is an overwhelming public health emergency, but interventions to reduce weight gain and interventions to reduce eating disorder risk must be developed in ways that do not offset each other. For all of these questions, studies first need to demonstrate that significant and important changes in the putative risk factors or protective factors can be achieved and maintained.

Although targeted interventions have proved effective, their effects are generally short-lived and specific to a few dimensions. Thus the same major questions are applicable. In addition, the challenges in delivering such interventions, particularly to populations, are substantial. For example, in school settings, how can high-risk individuals be identified and motivated to participate in interventions in ways that are not stigmatizing? There are several other important developments that bear monitoring and study. The Internet is a major source of information/discussion. Discussion groups devoted to eating disorders are common. Much has been written in the lay press about the possible impact of 'pro-anorexia' websites – that is, websites which promote unhealthy weight regulation practices. However, the actual impact of these sites on increasing rates of eating disorders is not known, nor is the way in which information and programs on the Internet can be used for positive purposes. Although such studies are difficult to undertake, an understanding of the impact of the Internet is extremely important.

Corresponding author: C Barr Taylor, MD, Department of Psychiatry and Behavioral Sciences, Room 1326, Stanford University School of Medicine, Stanford, CA 94305-5722, USA. Email: btaylor@stanford.edu

References

Abascal L, Bruning Brown J, Winzelberg AJ, Dev P and Taylor CB (2004) Combining universal and targeted prevention for school-based eating disorder programs. *Int J Eat Disord*. **35**: 1–9.
> To determine whether high-risk students might do better in discussion groups with other high-risk students, rather than with low-risk students who might be more critical of others' weight/shape, 78 tenth-grade female students were provided with an online eating disorder prevention program and randomized to participate in (1) a higher-risk *and* highly motivated group, (2) a lower-risk *or* less motivated group, or (3) a combined group. The students in the first group made significantly fewer negative comments and more positive comments in the online group discussion than the higher-risk and highly motivated participants in the combined group. However, there were no differences among groups on outcome measures. The results suggest that, since it is relatively easy to provide interventions with separate groups, it seems appropriate to do so, if for no other reason than to minimize the few very negative comments that were posted by students that might have created an adverse environment for the higher-risk participants who the intervention specifically targets.

Barlow SE and Dietz WH (2002) Management of child and adolescent obesity: summary and recommendations based on reports from pediatricians, pediatric nurse practitioners, and registered dietitians. *Pediatrics*. **110**: 236–8.

Bearman SK, Stice E and Chase A (2003) Effects of body dissatisfaction on depressive and bulimic symptoms: a longitudinal experiment. *Behav Ther*. **34**: 277–93.

Bruning Brown J, Winzelberg AJ, Abascal LB and Taylor CB (2004) An evaluation of an Internet-delivered eating disorder prevention program for adolescents and their parents. *J Adolesc Health*. **35**: 290–6.

Carter JC, Stewart DA, Dunn VJ and Fairburn CG (1997) Primary prevention of eating disorders: might it do more harm than good? *Int J Eat Disord*. **22**: 167–72.

Celio AA, Bryson S, Killen JD and Taylor CB (2003) Are adolescents harmed when asked risky weight control behavior and attitude questions? Implications for consent procedures. *Int J Eat Disord*. **34**: 251–4.

Irving LM and Neumark-Sztainer D (2002) Integrating the prevention of eating disorders and obesity: feasible or futile? *Prev Med*. **34**: 299–309.

Jacobi C, Hayward C, de Zwaan M, Kraemer HC and Agras WS (2004) Coming to terms with risk factors for eating disorders: application of risk terminology and suggestions for a general taxonomy. *Psychol Bull*. **130**: 19–65.

Jacobi C, Abascal L and Taylor CB (2004) Screening for eating disorders and high risk behavior: caution. *Int J Eat Disord*. **36**: 273–88.

Kassirer JP and Angell M (1998) Losing weight – an ill-fated New Year's resolution. *NEJM*. **338**: 52–4.

Kater KJ, Rohwer J and Londre K (2002) Evaluation of an upper elementary school program to prevent body image, eating and weight concerns. *J School Health*. **72**: 199–204.

Killen JD, Taylor CB, Hammer LD *et al*. (1993) An attempt to modify unhealthful eating attitudes and weight regulation practices of young adolescent girls. *Int J Eat Disord*. **13**: 369–84.

Levine MP and Piran N (2001) The prevention of eating disorders: towards a participatory ecology of knowledge, action and advocacy. In: R Striegel-Moore and L Smolak (eds) *Eating Disorders: new directions for research and practice*. American Psychological Association, Washington DC, pp. 233–53.

Levine MP and Smolak L (2005) *The Prevention of Eating Problems and Disorders*. Lawrence Erlbaum Associates, Mahwah, NJ.

Luce KH, Osborne MI, Winzelberg AJ and Taylor CB (2004) Application of an algorithm-driven protocol to simultaneously provide universal and targeted prevention programs. *Int J Eat Disord.* **37**: 1–7.
This study examined the feasibility and acceptability to 188 female high-school students of using an Internet-delivered program to assess, recommend and provide both universal and targeted interventions for eating disorders and weight gain prevention. The algorithm identified 111 students in the no-risk (NR category), 36 with eating disorder risk (EDR), 16 with overweight risk (OR) and five with both risks. In total, 56% of the EDR group and 50% of the OR group elected to receive the recommended targeted curricula. Significant improvements in weight and shape concerns were observed in all groups. An Internet-delivered program can be used to assess risk and to provide simultaneous universal and targeted interventions in classroom settings.
McKnight Investigators (2003) Risk factors for the onset of eating disorders in adolescent girls: results of the McKnight Longitudinal Risk Factor Study. *Am J Psychiatry.* **160**: 248–54.
McVey G and Davis R (2002) A program to promote positive body image: a 1-year follow-up evaluation. *J Early Adolesc.* **22**: 96–108.
McVey GL, Lieberman M, Voorberg N, Wardrope D and Blackmore E (2003a) School-based peer support groups: a new approach to the prevention of disordered eating. *Eat Disord.* **11**: 169–85.
McVey GL, Lieberman M, Voorberg N, Wardrope D, Blackmore E and Tweed S (2003b) Replication of a peer support program designed to prevent disordered eating: is a life skills approach sufficient for all middle-school students? *Eat Disord.* **11**: 187–95.
McVey G, Davis R, Tweed S and Shaw BF (2004) Evaluation of a school-based program designed to improve body image satisfaction, global self-esteem, and eating attitudes and behaviours: a replication study. *Int J Eat Disord.* **36**: 1–11.
Mann T, Nolen-Hoeksema S, Huang K, Burgard D, Wright A and Hanson K (1997). Are two interventions worse than none? Joint primary and secondary prevention of eating disorders in college females. *Health Psychol.* **16**: 1–11.
Neumark-Sztainer D (1996) School-based programs for preventing eating disturbances. *J School Health.* **66**: 64–71.
Neumark-Sztainer D (2003) Obesity and eating disorder prevention: an integrated approach? *Adolesc Med.* **14**: 159–73.
O'Dea J and Abraham S (2000) Improving the body image, eating attitudes and behaviors of young male and female adolescents: a new educational approach which focuses on self-esteem. *Int J Eat Disord.* **28**: 43–57.
Olmsted MP, Daneman D, Rydall AC, Lawson ML and Rodin G (2002) The effects of psychoeducation on disturbed eating attitudes and behavior in young women with type 1 diabetes mellitus. *Int J Eat Disord.* **32**: 230–9.
Piran N (1999) Eating disorders: a trial of prevention in a high-risk school setting. *J Prim Prev.* **20**: 75–90.
Pratt BM and Woolfenden SR (2002) Interventions for preventing eating disorders in children and adolescents. *Cochrane Database Syst Rev.* **2**: CD002891.
Presnell K and Stice E (2003) An experimental test of the effect of weight-loss dieting on bulimic pathology: tipping the scales in a different direction. *J Abnorm Psychol.* **112**: 166–70.
Schwartz MB and Puhl R (2003) Childhood obesity: a societal problem to solve. *Obesity Rev.* **4**: 57–71.
Steiner-Adair C, Sjostrom L, Franko DL *et al.* (2002) Primary prevention of eating disorders in adolescent girls: learning from practice. *Int J Eat Disord.* **32**: 401–11.
This study evaluated the effectiveness and feasibility of a primary prevention program for risk factors for eating disorders in adolescent girls. Nearly 500 seventh-grade girls participated in the program, called 'Full of Ourselves: Advancing Girl Power,

Health and Leadership.' They were assessed at baseline, immediately after program completion, and 6 months later on several self-report measures of knowledge, body image, and eating and weight-related behaviors. Significant differences were found between participants and controls on measures of knowledge and weight-related body esteem, which were maintained at the 6-month follow-up. Eating-related behaviors, including skipping meals and dieting, appeared to be unaffected by participation in the program. The authors note that the program was feasible and safe, and that it resulted in positive and maintained changes in knowledge and weight satisfaction for adolescent girls.

Stice E (2002) Risk and maintenance factors for eating pathology: a meta-analytic review. *Psychol Bull*. **128**: 825–48.

Stice E and Ragan J (2002) A preliminary controlled evaluation of an eating disturbance psychoeducational intervention for college students. *Int J Eat Disord*. **31**: 159–71.

Stice E and Shaw H (2004) Eating disorder prevention programs: a meta-analytic review. *Psychol Bull*. **130**: 206–27.

This meta-analysis found that intervention effects ranged from none to moderate, with some effects persisting for as long as 2 years over minimal intervention and control conditions. Larger effect sizes occurred for targeted, interactive and multi-session programs. The authors note the need for more methodological rigor and enhanced theoretical rationale for interventions.

Stice E, Trost A and Chase A (2003) Healthy weight control and dissonance-based eating disorder prevention programs: results from a controlled trial. *Int J Eat Disord*. **33**: 10–21.

Story MT, Neumark-Sztainer DR, Sherwood NE *et al.* (2002) Management of child and adolescent obesity: attitudes, barriers, skills, and training needs among health care professionals. *Pediatrics*. **110**: 210–14.

Taylor CB, Cameron R, Newman M and Junge J (2002) Issues related to combining risk factor reduction and clinical treatment for eating disorders in defined populations. *J Behav Health Serv Res*. **29**: 81–90.

Population-based psychotherapy considers the provision of services to a population at risk for or already affected by a disease or disorder. Using existing data on prevalence, incidence, risk factors and interventions (both preventive and clinical) for eating disorders (anorexia excluded), this paper examines issues related to integrating and providing risk reduction and treatment to a population of female college students.

Wade TD, Davidson S and O'Dea JA (2003) A preliminary controlled evaluation of a school-based media literacy program and self-esteem program for reducing eating disorder risk factors. *Int J Eat Disord*. **33**: 371–83.

Withers GF, Twig K, Wertheim EH and Paxton SJ (2002) A controlled evaluation of an eating disorders primary prevention videotape using the Elaboration Likelihood Model of Persuasion. *J Psychosom Res*. **53**: 1021–7.

Zabinski M, Wilfley DE, Calfas KJ, Winzelberg AJ and Taylor CB (in press) An interactive psychoeducational intervention for women at risk of developing an eating disorder. *J Consult Clin Psychol*.

2
Family issues and eating disorders

Daniel le Grange

Abstract

Objectives of review. This review set out to scrutinize the literature pertaining to family issues in eating disorders for the years 2002–2003.
Summary of recent findings. The literature has devoted much attention to the crucial role that family dynamics play in the development and outcome of eating disorders. In most instances, the family with an offspring who has an eating disorder has been cast in a negative light, because of either specific interactional patterns or parental psychopathology that are believed to play a causative role in the development of eating disorders. In keeping with the unfavorable sentiments expressed in the past, most of the studies reviewed ascribed a negative and/or causative quality to family issues with regard to eating disorders. Compared with control families, eating-disorder families were depicted as more conflictual, less cohesive, and lower in emotional expressiveness. Also, parents of eating-disorder patients were found to report higher rates of psychopathology than their control counterparts.
Future directions. Although methodological shortcomings plague many studies, and conclusions should be drawn with caution, the real question still remains whether eating disorders follow or precede reported family dynamics. Longitudinal prospective inquiries may resolve our decades-old 'chicken-or-egg' debate.

Introduction

The association between family functioning and family pathology on the one hand and disordered eating on the other has received a great deal of attention over the years. Clinicians and researchers alike have alluded to the impact, mostly negative, that familial factors might have on the development of eating disorders. In this chapter I shall review the available studies as well as conference presentations during 2002–2003 that have examined family issues and eating disorders. This review will include both clinical and non-clinical studies across the eating-disorder diagnostic spectrum and age range.

Examination of family issues in eating disorders is, of course, not new. The earliest descriptions of anorexia nervosa (AN), in both the English and French literature, ascribed a crucial role to the way in which patients and their families interact and the way in which this interaction influences the development and outcome of the illness. In 1868, Sir William Gull described the family of AN patients as the 'worst attendants', while Charcot went a step further in 1889 when he described the influence of the parents as 'particularly pernicious.' On the other hand, Charles Lasegue had a more positive view of family influences when he stated in 1873 that he always considered the 'preoccupations of the parents side by side with that of the patient.'

It is perhaps fair to say that these disparate views of the family are reflected in a continuing divide today, on one side of which the family is either seen as pathological and a hindrance that should be excluded from treatment (e.g. 'parentectomy'), or it is believed that it should be included, but that pathological family interaction should be modified through treatment (Palazzoli 1974; Minuchin et al. 1978). On the other side of the divide is the view that it is premature to refer to a 'typical' eating-disorder family, but rather that the family is a resource and part of the solution (Eisler et al. 2000).

Consequently, family dynamics have for many decades now been implicated in the development (e.g. psychosomatic families) and perpetuation (e.g. family praise for slenderness and self-discipline) of eating disorders. In particular, Minuchin et al. (1978) described the family with an anorexic child as typified by four structural, transactional characteristics, namely enmeshment, overprotectiveness, rigidity and lack of conflict resolution. In his view, changing these characteristics is a prerequisite for treatment to be successful. There is also a rich literature on parental and family disturbance and the impact that these have on the index patient (Morgan and Russell 1975; Humphrey 1989). More recent examples have described eating-disorder families as overconcerned with parenting (Shoebridge and Gowers 2000), while eating-disorder patients have described their families as critical and coercive in terms of parental control (Haworth-Hoeppner 2000).

For this chapter, articles were identified through MEDLINE and PsycINFO for the years 2002 and 2003. Keywords entered were *eating disorders, family dynamics* and *family interaction*. In addition, conference presentations and abstracts for this same time period were scrutinized for relevant information. A total of 20 journal articles, book chapters or conference presentations were identified for this review, and these are divided into two parts, namely *family functioning/dynamics* and *attachment and eating disorders*.

Literature review

Family functioning/dynamics

The majority of the articles yielded by this search focus on family functioning or family dynamics and eating disorders. The present discussion first views the controlled studies that investigated clinical or non-clinical samples (eight studies), before turning to studies without a control comparison group, also using clinical and non-clinical samples (seven studies).

Controlled studies

Clinical samples

The first study evaluated family dynamics among three adult groups, namely 17 subjects with bulimia nervosa (BN), 18 clinical controls and 20 non-clinical controls (Benninghoven *et al.* 2003). The Core Conflictual Relationship Theme method was applied to narrative material for all three groups. There were no differences between the two clinical groups, but these groups showed low levels of cohesion and degree of expressiveness, and more conflict compared with the normal controls.

Three studies investigated parental characteristics and their relationship to eating disorders. Davis *et al.* (2002) compared family physical activity patterns in 139 female adolescents hospitalized with AN and their parents (78 mothers and 48 fathers) with 94 age-matched controls and their parents (88 mothers and 61 fathers). Physical activity data were based on retrospective recall during structured interviews for child and parent. There were no differences in activity between case and control parents for the six years prior to assessment. The only positive finding was that both the patient's activity at the age of 10 years and the mother's activity when her child was this age positively predicted the child's activity in the year prior to hospitalization. De Amusquibar and De Simone (2003) compared the characteristics of 50 mothers of patients with an eating disorder with a control group of 30 mothers of non-clinical adolescents. On the Eating Attitude Test-26 (EAT-26), among others, patients' mothers had higher scores for eating-disorder symptoms and depression, and a higher incidence of bottle-fed daughters, provoked abortions, and poor mother–daughter relationships with their own mothers. Espina (2003) investigated alexithymia among 73 parents of daughters with an eating disorder (AN and BN) as well as the parents of 72 normal female controls. Comparisons were made using the Toronto Alexithymia Scale (TAS-20), the Eysenck Personality Questionnaire (EPQ), the Beck Depression Inventory (BDI) and the Self-Rating Anxiety Scale (SRAS). Parents with a daughter with an eating disorder reported higher scores on the TAS-20, which were associated with neuroticism, anxiety and depression.

The significance of parental relationships in the development of eating disorders was addressed by Solomon *et al.* (2003). These authors investigated perceived relationships between parents and their daughters with AN from both the parent's and the child's perspective. The participants consisted of 31 women with AN, 31 control women, and the parents of both groups. The Parental Environment Questionnaire (PEQ) showed no differences between the eating disorder and control groups, and when there were differences, they were not specific to families with a daughter with AN. Comparing fathers with mothers, the results revealed that there were no differences for the fathers and daughters. However, the daughters perceived significantly less involvement with their mothers than their mothers did, and had less regard for their mothers than their mothers had for them.

Non-clinical samples

In one of only two studies using a non-clinical sample, McGrane and Carr (2002) evaluated the relationship between perceived family dysfunction and parental psychological problems and the risk of eating disorders in young women. A total of 27 subjects 'at risk' of developing an eating disorder (using the Eating Disorder Inventory-2 (EDI-2) to define 'at risk') and 27 control subjects completed the Family Assessment Device (FAD) and the Symptoms Checklist-90 (SC-90). The 'at risk' group scored significantly higher than the control group for family problems in general functioning as well as roles, affective responsiveness and problem solving. The 'at-risk' group also reported that their mothers had more problems with depression, anxiety and sensitivity (among other areas) than the control group, and their fathers had more anger–hostility and depression.

Fonseca et al. (2002) looked at the familial correlates of extreme weight control behaviors among 9042 adolescents aged 12–18 years, who participated in a statewide health survey. Participants were divided into two groups, namely 'extreme dieters' and a control group of non-extreme dieters. Using logistic regression, male 'extreme dieters' reported significantly more 'parental supervision' and sexual abuse, and significantly less 'parental expectations', 'connectedness with adults, friends' and 'maternal presence in the home' than the control group. Female 'extreme dieters' reported significantly more sexual abuse and significantly less 'parental supervision' and 'maternal presence' than the control group.

Quasi-controlled study

Finally, a quasi-controlled study was undertaken by McDermott et al. (2002), in which 80 children and adolescents with AN, BN or eating disorder not otherwise specified (ED-NOS) and their parents completed the Family Assessment Device-General Functioning Scale (FAD-GFS). There were no differences in scores for the parents and their children. 'Community norms' were established by examining the Western Australian Child Health Survey. Subjects in this study had significantly higher scores for in family dysfunction than the norm. There was no significant difference in the total scores of family functioning for all eating disorder groups, although the BN groups reported more difficulty in the areas of family activity planning, decision making and family interactions compared with the other eating-disorder groups.

Uncontrolled studies

Clinical samples

Okon *et al.* (2003) used experience sampling methodology to consider the extent to which family interaction was a predictor of symptom variation in 20 girls diagnosed with BN. Perceived family environment was established using the Family Environment Scale (FES) and the Conflict Behavior Questionnaire (CBQ). The authors found that 'potent family hassles' were positive predictors of bulimic behaviors in those adolescents who perceived their families as having high levels of conflict or low levels of emotional expressiveness. To investigate whether parents see their families as dysfunctional as their daughters with eating disorders do, Dancyger *et al.* (2003) examined the clinical records of 236 girls with an eating disorder. Using the Family Adjustment Device (FAD), Schedule of Affective Disorders and Schizophrenia-Lifetime (SADS-L), Eating Disorders Inventory (EDI) and BDI, no differences were reported between mothers and fathers. Overall, parents also reported significantly 'healthier and less chaotic' family functioning than did the children (Dancyger *et al.* 2003).

Only one study examined overweight children who were seeking weight loss treatment (Decaluwe and Braet 2003). The authors examined parental influence on eating psychopathology and psychological problems in overweight and normal weight controls using the Symptom Behavior Checklist (SBC) and the child version of the Eating Disorder Examination (EDE). Parental psychopathology was measured using the SCL-90 and the Ghent Parental Behavior Scale (GPBS). Parents of the overweight children reported more psychopathology and less positive parental behavior compared with the normal weight control group. For the overweight group, parental psychopathology was associated with emotional and behavioral problems as well as disordered eating in the children.

Von Ranson *et al.* (2003) determined whether maternal eating disorder or parental substance use/misuse was associated with elevated levels of disordered eating in the offspring. The study participants were 674 adolescent female twins and their biological parents. The twins completed the Minnesota Eating Disorder Inventory (MEDI), all female subjects completed the Eating Disorder Questionnaire (EDQ), and all subjects completed the Substance Abuse Module of the Composite International Diagnostic Interview (CIDI). Female subjects were split into 'Bulimic Eating Disorder' and 'Restricting Eating Disorder' groups, the parents were split into 'Substance Use Disorder (SUD) Yes' and 'Substance Use Disorder (SUD) No' groups, and the daughters were split into 'Substance Use (SU)' and SUD groups. Daughters' disordered eating correlated significantly with maternal eating disorder, but there was no association between eating disorders and SUD across generations.

Wisotsky *et al.* (2003) explored the relationship between self-reported family functioning, comorbid psychopathology and current comorbid psychological symptom status in a group of 51 eating disorder patients (aged 12–26 years). All patients attended a day treatment program and completed the Family Adaptability and Cohesion Evaluation Scale (FACES)-II, SCL-90, EDI-2, BDI and TAS-20. These authors found that when patients perceived family functioning to be more dysfunctional, the level of self-reported eating pathology and current comorbid psychological symptoms were also more severe.

Non-clinical samples

Worobey (2002) investigated the interpersonal and intrafamilial predictors of maladaptive eating attitudes in young women. The study group consisted of 258 female undergraduates attending a marriage and family class, and all participants completed the Love Attitudes Scale (LAS), the Childhood Family Mealtimes Questionnaire (CFMQ) and the Eating Attitude Test (EAT)-26. These authors found that family attitude towards physical appearance when based on weight, rather than on romantic interpersonal relationships, showed stronger associations with maladaptive eating attitudes. In a related study by Keery et al. (2003), the relationship between teasing by parents and siblings and body dissatisfaction and eating disturbance was investigated in a large study group of 325 female adolescents. Participants reported that 18% of fathers and 12% of mothers teased them about their appearance. Controlling for BMI, teasing by a father significantly predicted thin-ideal internalization, social comparison, body dissatisfaction, depression, low self-esteem, and restrictive and bulimic eating behaviors. Maternal teasing was found to predict restricting behaviors.

Attachment and eating disorders

Although attachment theory is beyond the scope of this review, some authors have looked at the association between attachment style and eating disorders. A cursory view of this association might shed further light on family issues and eating disorders. Since the late 1950s, when Bowlby started to prepare the foundation of attachment theory, there has been some suggestive evidence linking Bruch's theory of abnormal mother–child interactions and eating disorders with attachment insecurity in later life. Several recent studies have found that attachment processes are abnormal in eating-disorder populations, and that insecure attachment is common in this group (Ward et al. 2000). In their review, Ward and Gowers (2003) argue more forcefully when they say that, the 'overwhelming message from the research literature is of abnormal attachment patterns in eating-disordered populations' (p.115). They go on to say that, clinically, anorexic women appear avoidant, whereas bulimic women are more angry and chaotic. This fits with the way in which insecure attachment can be defined – as either anxious/avoidant/dismissive or angry/preoccupied/enmeshed. However, as is the case in much of this work, family dysfunction could be secondary to the presence of an ill family member, rather than it being causative in nature.

Ward and Gowers (2003) have evaluated the relationship between attachment and childhood development on the one hand, and eating disorders on the other. These authors state that it is widely accepted that parent–child relationships play a central role in children's psychological development. The quality and form of these relationships are thought to predict later interpersonal relationships and to have a profound influence on personality development and psychological functioning in later life. However, they do concede that there is only a modest body of evidence to support these assumptions.

In the only article addressing the issue of attachment that could be identified, Latzer *et al.* (2003) looked at attachment style and family functioning as discriminating factors in eating disorders. They compared 25 AN cases, 33 BN cases, and 23 female control subjects in order to evaluate family environment, individual attachment styles and the interaction between family environment and attachment style. Subjects completed the FES and the Adult Attachment Scale (AAS). No significant differences were found between the eating disorder groups, but control subjects reported better family relationships, independence and expressiveness. Control subjects also reported more cohesiveness, leisure and encouragement with regard to personal growth than female subjects with BN. The control group had significantly more secure attachment than the eating-disorder groups, while the latter scored significantly higher on avoidant attachment than the controls.

Summary of important findings

Findings from most of the studies reviewed here emphasize the importance of family dynamics and interpersonal relationships among family members with regard to the causation or maintenance of eating disorders. For the most part, families with an eating-disordered offspring are cast in a negative light – that is, more conflictual, with low levels of expressiveness and parents presenting with high rates of psychopathology when compared with normal controls. Moreover, some studies have suggested that parental psychopathology or a 'negative family environment' exacerbate eating disorder symptom severity, or that there is an association between parental psychopathology (e.g. parents with an eating disorder) or parental attitude (e.g. teasing or comments about a child's weight) and disordered eating in the offspring. In contrast, the families of control subjects are characterized by cohesiveness and the encouragement of personal growth.

However, these findings are far from conclusive. Some of the pathological family attributes were not specific to eating disorders. For instance, Benninghoven *et al.* (2003) found that the eating disorder group and non-eating disorder clinical group in their study shared many similarities compared with a normal control group. In other instances, there were no differences between the eating disorder and normal control groups (e.g. Solomon *et al.* 2003). Finally, in some studies parents tended to perceive their families in a more favorable light than did their offspring, whether or not their child had an eating disorder (Davis *et al.* 2002; Dancyger *et al.* 2003).

The pressing question remains as to whether these elevated scores on measures of psychopathology in families with an eating-disordered offspring precede the onset of the eating disorder, or whether these family issues are a consequence of the eating disorder. The methodological design of most of the studies reviewed here hampers our ability to answer this question with any certainty. A large number of the studies are cross-sectional. Therefore the most obvious shortcoming is that it is difficult to establish whether family issues contribute to eating disorders, whether eating disorders contribute to family dysfunction, or whether a common factor contributes to both. Secondly, in many studies the role of family dysfunction was ascertained by retrospective recall and self-report, further undermining any certainty about the role that family dynamics play in eating disorders. Thirdly, several studies did not include a control group, which removes any certainty that these family issues are unique to families with an eating-disordered offspring.

Clinical implications

Given the apparent importance of family issues, it would seem prudent to include the family in the assessment and treatment of eating-disorder patients, particularly in the case of adolescents. Involving the family in these processes seems especially appropriate when considered from the viewpoint that family pathology plays a causative role in eating disorders, and that this underlying pathology needs to be addressed in treatment. However, the notion that families or parents of eating-disorder patients are characterized by a greater degree of psychopathology than controls is not borne out by the Maudsley family-based treatment (Le Grange *et al.* 2003). This treatment does not assume that family pathology underlies eating disorders, nor is 'changing family pathology' a prerequisite for a successful outcome of treatment. Quite the contrary is true in that this family-based treatment assumes that parents or families constitute a vital resource and strength. This apparent disconnection between research observation on the one hand and clinical reality on the other underscores the distance that we still need to travel in order to fully understand family issues in eating disorders, and how best to address these in treatment.

Future directions

Answers to the dilemmas posed above, still elude us. Although family issues are among the putative causal factors that contribute to the development of eating disorders, the main obstacle in our search for answers, as articulated by Polivy and Herman (2002), is the challenge to conduct true experimental research in which alleged causal factors can be manipulated. According to those researchers, a large number of studies among eating-disorder patients attempt to isolate correlates of eating disorders in the hope that this can be turned into a persuasive argument of *causes*. As it is not always possible to identify a suitable sample of eating-disorder patients, many researchers have turned to the study of correlates of eating-disorder symptoms, as they exist in large samples of non-clinical subjects (e.g. college students). Retrospective recall and self-report assessments characterize these inquiries, which leads to the confusion of correlation and causation and extrapolations into examinations of the causes of eating disorders (Polivy and Herman 2002). These authors urge tolerance of these shortcomings, given the significant obstacles to conducting meaningful research in this area of inquiry.

Although many studies have aimed to examine the possible impact of the family on the development of eating disorders, little has been done in terms of the potential impact that an eating disorder can have on the family. A case in favor of studying non-clinical samples has been put forward in that clinical samples can be a significant confounding factor, as families are assessed *after* the eating disorder has developed (Mazzeo and Espelage 2002). Therefore the study of non-clinical samples could further add to our understanding of the association between family functioning and disordered eating.

Finally, one potentially fruitful avenue of inquiry is longitudinal study designs. Such research may clarify the reported role that family pathology/interaction/ dynamics plays in the development of eating disorders. Prospective investigation of the potentially different influences that parents with or without an eating disorder might have on the development of their offspring has already been embarked upon (Agras *et al.* 1999; Whelan and Cooper 2000).

Acknowledgement

The author wishes to thank Lydia Kruge for her assistance in compiling the articles for this review.

Corresponding author: Daniel le Grange, PhD, Department of Psychiatry, University of Chicago, 5841 S Maryland Avenue, MC3077, Chicago, IL 60637, USA. Email: dlegrang@uchicago.edu

References

Agras WS, Hammer L and McNicholas F (1999) A prospective study of the influence of eating-disordered mothers on their children. *Int J Eat Disord.* **25**: 253–62.

Benninghoven D, Schneider H, Strack M, Reich G and Cierpka M (2003) Family representations in relationship episodes of patients with a diagnosis of bulimia nervosa. *Psychol Psychother Theory Res Pract.* **76**: 323–36.

Dancyger I, Fornari V, Scionti L, Wisotsky W and Mandel FS (2003) Do parents see their families as dysfunctional as their daughters with eating disorders do? *Int J Eat Disord.* **34**: 8.

Davis C, Blackmore E and Kirsh C (2002) *Family physical activity patterns in hospitalized females with anorexia nervosa: a case–control study.* Paper presented at the 2002 Academy for Eating Disorders International Conference on Eating Disorders, Boston, MA. April 25–28.

De Amusquibar AMG and De Simone CJ (2003) Some features of mothers of patients with eating disorders. *Eat Weight Disord.* **8**: 225–30.

Decaluwe V and Braet C (2003) Parental influence on eating psychopathology and psychological problems in overweight children. *Int J Eat Disord.* **34**: 9.

Eisler I, Dare C, Hodes M, Russell GFM, Dodge E and Le Grange D (2000) Family therapy for adolescent anorexia nervosa: the results of a controlled comparison of two family interventions. *J Child Psychol Psychiatry.* **41**: 727–36.

Espina A (2003) Alexithymia in parents of daughters with eating disorders. Its relationships with psychopathological and personality variables. *J Psychosom Res*. **55**: 553–60.

Fonseca H, Ireland M and Resnick MD (2002) Familial correlates of extreme weight control behaviors among adolescents. *Int J Eat Disord*. **32**: 441–8.

Haworth-Hoeppner S (2000) The critical shapes of body image: the role of culture and family in the production of eating disorders. *J Marriage Fam*. **62**: 212–27.

Humphrey LL (1989) Observed family interactions among subtypes of eating disorders using structural analysis of social behavior. *J Consult Clin Psychol*. **57**: 206–14.

Keery H, Boutelle KN, Van den Berg P and Thompson K (2003) The impact of appearance-related teasing by family members. *Int J Eat Disord*. **34**: 49.

Latzer Y, Zipora H, Eitan B and Laura C (2003) Attachment style and family functioning as discriminating factors in eating disorders. *Contemp Fam Ther Int J*. **24**: 581–99.

Le Grange D, Loeb K, Walsh BT and Lock J (2003) Family-based outpatient treatment for adolescent anorexia nervosa: a clinical case series. *Int J Eat Disord*. **34**: 8–9.

McDermott BM, Batik M, Roberts L and Gibbon P (2002) Parent and child report of family functioning in a clinical child and adolescent eating disorders sample. *Aust N Z J Psychiatry*. **36**: 509–14.

McGrane D and Carr A (2002) Young women at risk for eating disorders: perceived family dysfunction and parental psychological problems. *Fam Ther*. **24**: 385–95.

Mazzeo SE and Espelage DL (2002) Association between childhood physical and emotional abuse and disordered eating behaviors in female undergraduates: an investigation of the mediating role of alexithymia and depression. *J Counsel Psychol*. **49**: 86–100.

Minuchin S, Rosman BL and Baker BL (1978) *Psychosomatic Families: anorexia nervosa in context*. Harvard University Press, Cambridge, MA.

Morgan HG and Russell GFM (1975) Value of family background and clinical features as predictors of long-term outcome in anorexia nervosa: four-year follow-up study of 41 patients. *Psychol Med*. **5**: 355–71.

Okon DM, Greene AL and Smith JE (2003) Family interactions predict intra-individual symptom variation for adolescents with bulimia. *Int J Eat Disord*. **34**: 450–7.

Palazzoli MS (1974) *Self-Starvation: from the intrapsychic to the transpersonal*. Chancer Press, London.

Polivy J and Herman CP (2002) Causes of eating disorders. *Annu Rev Psychol*. **53**: 187–213. **This is a very thorough review that details the causes of eating disorders. Attention is paid to sociocultural factors, familial influences and individual risk factors (e.g. interpersonal experiences, affective influences, self-esteem, body dissatisfaction, cognitive factors and biological factors).**

Shoebridge P and Gowers S (2000) Parental high concern and adolescent-onset anorexia nervosa. *Br J Psychiatry*. **176**: 132–7.

Solomon JW, Klump KL, McGue M, Iacono W and Elkins I (2003) Parent and child perceptions of the parental relationship in anorexia nervosa. *Int J Eat Disord*. **34**: 7–8.

Von Ranson KM, McGue M and Iacono WG (2003) Disordered eating and substance use in an epidemiological sample. II. Associations with families. *Psychol Addict Behav*. **17**: 193–202.

Ward A and Gowers S (2003) Attachment and childhood development. In: J Treasure, U Schmidt and E Van Furth (eds) *Handbook of Eating Disorders*. John Wiley & Sons, Chichester, pp. 103–20.

Ward A, Ramsay R, Turnbull S, Benedettini M and Treasure J (2000) Attachment patterns in eating disorders: past in the present. *Int J Eat Disord*. **27**: 279–87.

Whelan E and Cooper PJ (2000) The association between childhood feeding problems and maternal eating disorder: a community study. *Psychol Med*. **30**: 69–77.

Wisotsky W, Dancyger I, Fornari V *et al.* (2003) The relationship between eating pathology and perceived family functioning in eating disorder patients in a day treatment program. *Eat Disord J Treat Prev*. **11**: 89–99.

Worobey J (2002) Interpersonal versus intrafamilial predictors of maladaptive eating attitudes in young women. *Soc Behav Pers*. **30**: 423–34.

3

Treatment of binge-eating disorder

Michael J Devlin and Sarah E Fischer

Abstract

Objectives of review. We reviewed the literature from the period 2002–2003 in order to identify studies of medication, psychological/dietary and combined treatments for binge-eating disorder (BED). We focused on studies that targeted binge eating as the primary outcome.

Summary of recent findings. There is now further evidence that anti-depressant medications are more effective than placebo for binge-frequency reduction and possibly weight loss. The appetite suppressant sibutramine and the anticonvulsants topiramate and zonisamide also appear promising for both binge reduction and weight reduction, at least in the short term. Relatively few new psychotherapy studies were published, but one large-scale study reported a marked and equal beneficial effect of group cognitive behavioral therapy (CBT) and interpersonal therapy (IPT) on binge eating, with limited effect on weight.

Future directions. Studies of specialized eating disorder-based treatments vs standard behavioral weight management and studies of the natural history of BED are crucial to answering fundamental questions about the utility of the BED diagnosis and the long-term impact of treating BED.

Introduction

Since the initial description of binge-eating disorder (BED) in the early 1990s (Spitzer *et al*. 1992, 1993), the treatment of this disorder, particularly in obese samples, has been an area of active research interest. By 2001, the following had been established. First, a variety of psychological and dietary treatments are moderately effective in treating BED, yielding an impressive short-term and in some cases long-term reduction in binge eating, but only limited weight loss. Secondly, medications, primarily antidepressants, produce marked short-term binge suppression, with a variable weight response. Thirdly, minimal interventions, such as self-help and guided self-help, are effective in some patients. Fourthly, the course of binge eating in BED is often unstable, leading to high short-term placebo response rates in some studies. Excellent reviews of the research on pharmacotherapy (Carter *et al.* 2003) and psychosocial treatments (Wonderlich *et al.* 2003) for BED have recently been published.

At the beginning of the period covered by this review, namely 2002–2003, several important questions regarding medication treatment and psychological and dietary treatment, as well as overarching questions, remained unanswered. These included the following.

- **Psychological/dietary treatments**. How specific is the response to psychosocial approaches – that is, do some forms of psychotherapy yield better results than others? Are there factors that predict the overall or treatment-specific response? Do obese patients with BED benefit from specialized eating-disorder-based treatment approaches, or do standard behavioral weight loss treatments produce similar or better results?
- **Pharmacological treatments**. What are the long-term response and relapse rates for BED patients treated with medication? Are certain classes of medication more effective for binge reduction or weight loss than others? Can we predict which patients will achieve long-term success with medications only?
- **Overall treatment issues**. Do combined psychotherapy/medication treatments offer additional benefits compared with either form of treatment alone? What, if any, are the long-term benefits of binge cessation? Specifically, is there a long-term weight benefit associated with binge cessation? Are there gender differences in response to treatment for BED? Based on the state of the field, are placebo/no-treatment control groups scientifically justified?

This review will summarize BED treatment research during the period 2002–2003. It will discuss the degree to which the above questions have been answered, the further research that is needed to answer the remaining questions, and new questions that have arisen in the context of research carried out during this time.

Literature review

Pharmacological treatments

Studies of medication for BED have, for the most part, enrolled overweight or obese individuals and have thus included weight together with binge-eating frequency as important outcome measures. Medications studied during the period of review have included three distinct classes, namely antidepressants, appetite suppressants and anticonvulsants.

Antidepressants

Several recent studies have addressed the utility of antidepressants, particularly selective serotonin reuptake inhibitors (SSRIs), in the treatment of BED. Arnold *et al.* (2002) conducted a six-week, double-blind, flexible-dose study of fluoxetine 20 to 80 mg daily for BED. Notably, subjects were not required to be overweight or obese, although the mean BMI was in the Class II obese range. Of the 60 subjects who entered the study, there were 10 dropouts prior to the first post-baseline visit, and 35 study completers. Intent-to-treat analysis for the 50 subjects with post-baseline data revealed a significantly greater reduction in binge eating and weight for subjects taking fluoxetine. Just under 50% of subjects who were receiving fluoxetine reported at least a marked reduction in binge frequency, and 45% reported binge cessation. Fluoxetine-treated subjects showed a mean weight loss of 3.3 kg in six weeks. In comparison, placebo-treated subjects showed a mean weight gain of 0.7 kg.

The utility of another SSRI, citalopram, was recently studied in another clinical trial conducted by the same group (McElroy *et al.* 2003c) using similar methodology. The design employed was again a randomized, double-blind, placebo-controlled, flexible-dose (20–60 mg daily) clinical trial, with 38 outpatients randomized to receive treatment for six weeks. As in the fluoxetine study, the mean BMI of subjects was in the obese range. However, in this study there was a significant baseline BMI difference between groups, with placebo subjects in the Class I obese range and citalopram subjects in the Class III obese range. Completion rates were relatively high, with 31 of 38 patients completing the study. There was a demonstrated advantage for citalopram compared with placebo in binge-frequency reduction, with 47% of patients randomized to citalopram achieving binge remission. Citalopram-treated subjects lost an average of 2.1 kg in six weeks, while placebo-treated subjects gained an average of 0.2 kg.

Pearlstein *et al.* (2003) conducted a small-scale ($n = 20$), 12-week, randomized, double-blind, placebo-controlled, flexible-dose study of fluvoxamine up to 300 mg daily for BED. Both fluvoxamine and placebo groups showed a marked improvement in binge frequency, with more than 50% of subjects reporting full remission, and several psychological features of BED also showing improvement in both groups. Although the inability to detect differences between treatment groups may have been due in part to the small enrollment and limited power of the study or to the context of treatment, which included self-monitoring and frequent clinical contact, the finding of a substantial placebo response is reminiscent of earlier findings.

One further retrospective study examined the utility of the serotonin and norepinephrine reuptake inhibitor (SNRI) antidepressant venlafaxine in the treatment of BED (Malhotra *et al.* 2002). The authors reviewed the medical charts of 35 consecutive outpatient women who were treated with venlafaxine alone ($n = 29$) or in combination with other antidepressants ($n = 6$) at a weight management program that included behavioral dietary counseling for most patients along with medication treatment. The median duration of treatment was 120 days, and the mean dosage was 222 mg daily. A reduction of at least 50% in binge-eating frequency was noted in 88% of the patients, and 43% of patients experienced a medically significant weight loss of at least 5%. Although these results are promising, it is not possible to determine whether the observed improvements were due to the behavioral or the medication treatment, or to a combination of the two.

In all of the above trials, antidepressant medications were generally well tolerated, with few patients withdrawing for medication-related reasons. Although treatment was in most cases associated with an improvement in depressive and other psychological symptoms, most studies did not detect differential effects of active medication vs placebo in this regard. It is also worth noting that patients with severe psychiatric comorbidity, including substance use disorders, significant suicidality, or lifetime psychosis, mania or hypomania, were in most cases excluded. This may affect the degree to which the reported results can be generalized to clinical populations.

Appetite suppressants

The use of appetite suppressants in the treatment of obese individuals with BED was pioneered by Stunkard et al. (1996) in a dexfenfluramine study that was notable for its high placebo response rate, high remission rate (80%) at the end of treatment, and lack of beneficial effect on weight. Following the removal of dexfenfluramine from the market due to its association with cardiac valvulopathy and pulmonary hypertension, attention shifted to the newer agent sibutramine, a serotonin and norepinephrine reuptake inhibitor that is structurally similar to venlafaxine.

Following an open trial of sibutramine for obese patients with BED (Appolinario et al. 2002b), the same group conducted a randomized, double-blind, controlled clinical trial of this agent in 60 outpatients with BED (Appolinario et al. 2003). After a two-week single-blind placebo lead-in, during which approximately 25% of subjects dropped below threshold binge frequency, the remaining 60 patients were randomly assigned to treatment for 12 weeks with sibutramine 15 mg daily or placebo. An impressive feature of the study is that although 20% of the patients did not complete the trial, all patients were followed up. The reduction in binge frequency for sibutramine-treated patients was superior to that for placebo-treated patients. Interestingly, the groups diverged most dramatically during the first two weeks on medication. Following that point, the decrease in binge eating was nearly parallel in the two groups. In total, 12 of 23 sibutramine-treated patients (52%) who completed the trial vs eight of 25 placebo completers (32%) reported binge remission. The mean weight loss in the sibutramine group was an impressive 7.4 kg, compared to a mean weight gain of 1.4 kg in the placebo group. The medication was generally well tolerated, with only one sibutramine-treated patient withdrawing for a probable drug-related reason (insomnia). There was a small increase in resting heart rate (from 79.8 to 87.1 beats per minute) attributable to sibutramine, but there was no significant effect on blood pressure. Interestingly, sibutramine treatment was associated with a greater reduction in depressive symptoms compared with placebo.

An interesting mechanistic counterpart to this study was provided by Mitchell *et al.* (2003), who studied the effect of sibutramine treatment on binge eating, hunger and fullness in a laboratory feeding paradigm. Seven adult binge eaters were assigned to receive treatment with sibutramine and placebo, each for a four-week period, in a double-blind crossover design. At baseline and at weeks one and four of each treatment period, subjects consumed a fixed-size single-item midday meal and a multiple-item late afternoon/early evening binge meal, consisting of three of the subject's typical binge foods. Sibutramine treatment was associated with an overall decrease in hunger ratings, an increase in fullness ratings, and a decrease in the amount consumed in a laboratory binge meal. Strikingly, although all seven subjects were able to engage in a typical binge meal in the laboratory following placebo treatment, only three subjects were able to do so following sibutramine treatment. These results parallel the results of the clinical trial reviewed above, and highlight the direct effects of this medication on appetite, satiety and binge size in this population.

Anticonvulsants

The newest category of medication to enter the BED treatment arena is the anticonvulsant medications. Although most anticonvulsants are associated with weight gain, two newer anticonvulsants, namely topiramate and zonisamide, are instead associated with appetite decrease and weight loss, making them appealing candidates for BED treatment. Topiramate has several mechanisms of action, including enhancement of gamma-aminobutyric acid (GABA) transmission, blockade of voltage-dependent sodium channels, antagonisms of α-amino-3-hydroxy-5-methylisoxazole-4-propionate (AMPA)/kainate glutamate receptors, and carbonic anhydrase activity. The mechanism(s) that account for its activity in psychiatric disorders and appetite/weight regulation are unclear. Zonisamide, in addition to several of the above effects, also modulates serotonin and dopamine function, which suggests that it may have effects distinct from those of topiramate.

Following earlier case reports suggesting that topiramate may suppress binge eating in patients with comorbid mood disorders (Shapira *et al.* 2000; Schmidt do Prado-Lima and Bacaltchuck 2002), two prospective studies, one open and one randomized, have been reported. The first (Appolinario *et al.* 2002a) included 8 patients who were assigned to a 16-week period of treatment with topiramate at a daily dosage of 150 mg. Of the six patients who completed the trial, four patients had complete remission of binge eating, and the other two markedly reduced their binge frequency. The mean weight loss was 4.1 kg. The most definitive study to date of topiramate for BED was reported by McElroy *et al.* (2003a). In this 14-week, randomized, placebo-controlled, double-blind, flexible-dose (50–600 mg daily, median dose 212 mg) study, 61 obese outpatient women and men were entered. Almost all randomized patients had at least one post-randomization outcome measure and were included in the intent-to-treat analysis, but 26 patients did not complete the study. As predicted, the topiramate group experienced a greater reduction in binge frequency than the placebo group, and there was a remission rate of 64% in the active medication group, compared with 30% in the placebo group. The mean weight loss for topiramate-treated patients was 5.9 kg, compared with a mean gain of 1.2 kg in the placebo group. A preliminary report of a 42-week open-label extension of this study (McElroy *et al.* 2003b) suggests that there is good maintenance of improvements in binge eating and continued weight loss during this period of continued treatment. Notably, topiramate has also been reported to be effective in the treatment of normal-weight patients with bulimia nervosa (Hoopes *et al.* 2003) and obesity (Fitchet 2002). Despite concerns about the tolerability of topiramate, studies have generally reported relatively high tolerability. In the study by McElroy *et al.* (2003a), side-effects that were more common in the topiramate group than in the placebo group included paresthesias, taste perversion and confusion, and in the open-label extension the commonest side-effects were paresthesia, dry mouth, cognitive problems and headache. Rare but serious side-effects of topiramate, including nephrolithiasis, acute narrow angle glaucoma, and hyperchloremic non-anion-gap metabolic acidosis, were not observed. The low starting dosage and gradual escalation schedule used in this study may have limited the cognitive side-effects.

Most recently, the utility of the anticonvulsant zonisamide for BED was assessed in a small, open-label, 12-week, flexible-dose study (McElroy *et al.* 2004). A total of 14 women and 1 man with a mean BMI of 40.0 kg/m^2 were treated with zonisamide 100–600 mg (mean dosage 513 mg) daily. Eight of the 15 subjects completed the protocol, with four subjects discontinuing due to adverse events, including one for presumed nephrolithiasis, which was considered to be a serious adverse event. The most common side-effects were altered taste, fatigue, dry mouth and cognitive problems. In an intent-to-treat analysis, the mean weekly binge frequency decreased from 8.0 to 1.1, and the average weight loss was 6.0 kg. Consistent with topiramate studies, 8 out of 15 (i.e. just over half) of the subjects achieved binge cessation, and 13 out of 15 (86%) showed a reduction in binge frequency of at least 75%. These results, although preliminary, are quite promising, and further study is warranted.

Psychological and dietary treatments

Research on psychotherapy for BED during the period under consideration in this review has been most notable for increasingly sophisticated studies of specialized treatments for BED and for the investigation of new treatment components that may improve the long-term outcome, including healthy eating, weight management and self-acceptance.

Specialized psychotherapies for BED

The most notable study of psychotherapy reported during the period under review was a large-scale randomized comparison of group cognitive–behavioral therapy (CBT) and interpersonal therapy (IPT) in overweight and obese women and men with BED (Wilfley *et al.* 2002). A total of 162 patients participated in

20 group sessions held at weekly intervals over a period of five months. The underlying theories of the two treatments were quite distinct, with CBT focusing on dysregulated dietary restraint and dysfunctional automatic thoughts, whereas IPT focused on the interpersonal context of binge eating. Importantly, the fidelity of both treatments was insured by rigorous monitoring and rating of group sessions. A notable feature of the study was its success in patient retention, with 158 of 162 randomized patients completing post-treatment assessments, and 133 patients completing all three follow-up assessments conducted at four-month intervals over the 12 months following treatment. Binge-eating remission rates were high and roughly equivalent for the two treatment groups, with 79% of CBT patients and 73% of IPT patients reporting binge cessation following treatments. Deterioration over the 12 months following treatment was minimal. Although patients on average did not lose a clinically significant amount of weight with either treatment, individuals who were abstinent at the end of treatment and remained in remission at the 12-month follow-up assessment lost an average of 2.4 kg during the follow-up year, while those who relapsed gained an average of 2.1 kg during this period. A preliminary analysis of predictors revealed that CBT was more effective for binge abstinence than IPT for older patients, and that IPT was more successful for weight loss than CBT among patients with higher levels of reported interpersonal problems (Saelens et al. 2002).

Preliminary results from an additional randomized clinical trial of group CBT and group psychodynamic interpersonal therapy have recently been reported (Tasca et al. 2002). The study design differed from that of the study by Wilfley et al. (2002) in that it included a waiting-list control group. Both active treatments appeared to confer a significant and similar benefit in the reduction of binge eating. The preliminary analysis suggested that patients with greater cognitive distortions and interpersonal problems responded more favorably to CBT, while those with fewer cognitive distortions and interpersonal problems responded more favorably to psychodynamic interpersonal therapy.

A newer form of psychotherapy that has been studied in the treatment of eating disorders, including BED, is dialectical behavioral therapy (DBT), a treatment originally developed for borderline personality disorder patients that is based on an affect regulation model of binge eating. The use of DBT in eating disorders has recently been well summarized (Kotler et al. 2003). Following an earlier study demonstrating the efficacy of a 20-session weekly course of group DBT for BED (Telch et al. 2001), the authors went on to examine the predictors of relapse at six-month follow-up (Safer et al. 2002). A total of 32 women who had achieved remission following a course of DBT were assessed using a wide variety of psychological and eating-related measures. The strongest predictors of relapse were an early onset of binge eating at age 16 years or younger and a high level of dietary restraint. The authors speculate that the mindful eating and distress tolerance taught in DBT may help patients to step back from the restrictive 'dieter's mindset' and thereby break the cycle of dieting and binge eating.

Novel adjunctive interventions

One of the unique challenges in designing treatment interventions for obese patients with BED has been the need to address both somatic problems (i.e. obesity) and behavioral/psychological issues, and clinical researchers have drawn from both eating disorder and obesity treatments in designing interventions. A recent study (Pendleton *et al.* 2002) examined the utility of adding a component of exercise, typically thought of as an intervention for obesity, to cognitive–behavioral therapy, often viewed as an eating disorder-based specialized intervention. In this study, 114 obese patients with BED were all treated with four months of weekly group CBT and were randomly assigned to two additional interventions in a two-by-two design as follows: (1) maintenance treatment consisting of 12 biweekly sessions over six months; (2) exercise instruction with provision of exercise-center membership and staff monitoring; (3) both maintenance treatment and exercise; (4) neither additional intervention. Patients were assessed prior to treatment and at 4, 10 and 16 months. Although all of the groups showed improvement, there was a significant main effect of exercise but not of maintenance treatment on binge reduction. However, the greatest difference in reported number of binge days over the course of the study was between patients receiving both exercise and maintenance and patients receiving neither. There were main effects of both exercise and maintenance treatment on reduction in BMI (i.e. each yielded an additional benefit compared with CBT alone), but there was no significant interaction between the two. At the end of treatment, 58% of patients who received both exercise and maintenance treatment achieved binge abstinence, and the combined treatment was associated with a mean weight loss of around 6.4 kg.

Several additional augmentation strategies offered in the context of standard treatment approaches have begun to be explored. In most cases only preliminary data are available, so a detailed discussion of these approaches is premature. However, experiential approaches, including food exposure and body image exposure using virtual reality (Riva *et al.* 2003) or video techniques (Hilbert and Tuschen-Caffier 2002), have been reported to lead to a reduction in binge eating and an improvement in psychological features. An appetite-focused CBT approach (Elder *et al.* 2003) emphasizing the recognition of satiety signals in order to regulate eating patterns has shown promise in overweight and mildly obese young women with BED. In view of the failure of even the most effective treatments to bring about a lasting remission of binge eating in a significant minority of patients, the development of alternative and augmentative treatment approaches such as these is much needed.

Combined treatment studies

Two large-scale studies of combined psychotherapy and medication for obese patients with BED have been presented but not published. Grilo *et al.* (2002) randomly assigned 108 subjects with BED to a 16-week trial of two treatments using a two-by-two design. Patients received individual CBT plus placebo, fluoxetine (60 mg daily), both fluoxetine and CBT, or placebo only. Both CBT conditions were found to be superior to the other two treatments, with 73% of patients who received CBT plus placebo and 55% of those who received CBT plus fluoxetine achieving full remission. Fluoxetine treatment was not found to have any advantage compared with placebo. Overall weight loss was minimal and did not differ between treatment conditions. A preliminary study of potential predictors failed to detect associations of outcome with a variety of psychological and eating disorder-related factors at baseline, but suggested that a rapid initial response to treatment may predict binge cessation at the end of treatment (Grilo *et al.* 2003).

Devlin *et al.* (2002) conducted a somewhat similar study with a more complex protocol, designed to answer the question of whether individual CBT, fluoxetine, or both CBT and fluoxetine would confer significant additional benefit in patients receiving standard group eating and weight management treatment. A total of 116 obese patients with BED participated in a 20-week treatment program. All patients received a 16-session group behavioral treatment adapted for BED. In addition, subjects were randomly assigned, using a two-by-two design, to two additional treatments, namely a 20-session course of individual CBT and fluoxetine at a dosage of 60 mg daily. Individual CBT, but not fluoxetine, was found to significantly augment binge reduction, with nearly two-thirds of patients assigned to group treatment plus individual CBT compared with just over a third of patients receiving group treatment without individual CBT achieving binge cessation. There were suggestions that fluoxetine compared with placebo had a beneficial effect on depressive symptoms. Overall weight loss was minimal and did not differ among treatment groups. However, the nearly 50% of patients who achieved binge abstinence lost an average of approximately 6 kg, while non-abstainers gained approximately 0.9 kg on average. The overall findings were therefore for the most part consistent with those of the study by Grilo *et al.* (2002), although there was a suggestion that fluoxetine may have a useful role in treating the associated symptoms of BED in some patients.

Summary of important findings

Overall, the period under review has been a particularly productive one for pharmacotherapeutic approaches to BED. Well-designed studies have affirmed that SSRIs are effective in the short-term treatment of BED, yielding relatively high rates of binge cessation and, in several cases, clinically significant weight loss. With the exit of dexfenfluramine from the market, sibutramine has been established as an appetite suppressant that promises to be a useful treatment option for patients with BED, with beneficial effects on binge eating and weight, and possibly on depressive symptoms. Most recently, studies of topiramate and zonisamide have established the utility of certain anticonvulsants for patients with BED. Although only preliminary data are available, the open-label extension of the topiramate trial is particularly promising in view of its report of continuing weight loss over a period of one year. This is in marked contrast to the weight trajectory seen in earlier studies of obese patients treated with fluoxetine, in whom weight loss peaked at about five months, with significant weight regain by 12 months of treatment (Goldstein *et al.* 1994).

In the realm of psychotherapeutic approaches, the study Wilfley *et al.* (2002) has established a methodological high-water mark with its careful assessment of subjects, rigorous monitoring of treatment fidelity and highly successful subject retention. The high degree of success of both treatments raises important questions about the specificity of the response. Although there have been hints of differential predictors of response, questions regarding non-specific responses to clinical attention or even spontaneous remission of binge eating remain incompletely answered. Large-scale studies of the natural course of BED over time would provide crucial information about the baseline against which the effects of interventions must be measured.

Finally, the question of whether obese patients with BED respond better to specialized eating-disorder-based approaches than to standard obesity treatment, and the related issue of whether BED is a meaningful or clinically useful diagnosis, deserve mention. Although these questions have been actively discussed over the past two years (Devlin *et al.* 2003; Stunkard and Allison 2003), the current review uncovered relatively little new research in this area. However, one recent study highlighted the importance of examining the psychological concomitants of binge eating and binge cessation in obese populations. Marchesini *et al.* (2002) examined changes in health-related quality of life (HRQL) in obese patients with and without BED treated in a CBT program for eating and weight management in which BED patients received eight weekly group sessions targeting binge eating followed by 12 weekly group weight management sessions, while non-BED patients received only the latter 12 sessions. Obese BED patients experienced less weight reduction but a greater improvement in several dimensions of HRQL than obese non-binge eaters. The suggestion that there is a significant impact of binge reduction, apart from weight loss, on subjective satisfaction was further supported by a recent preliminary report (Dobrow *et al.* 2003). These investigators found that, in a multi-component treatment program for obese patients with BED, binge cessation appeared to be more important than weight loss in bringing about improvements in body image and self-esteem. In summary, there is mounting evidence that stabilization of eating behavior, independent of weight loss, has important beneficial effects for BED patients. Long-term studies of standard vs specialized treatments for BED with careful assessment of behavioral, weight and psychological outcomes over time are needed to definitively establish whether specialized approaches are needed to bring about long-term binge cessation and other desired outcomes.

Clinical implications

Given the uncertainty concerning the diagnostic status and natural course of BED, one might question whether this disorder should be treated at all. The alternative would be to view binge eating as a marker (Stunkard and Allison

2003), targeting obesity and/or psychopathology with the expectation that binge eating will improve with treatment of the primary problem. Although there is preliminary evidence that this may at least sometimes prove to be the case, there is also mounting evidence that treatments which target BED as a primary problem are associated with behavioral, psychological and (in some cases) medical improvement. Despite the need for greater clarity concerning the theoretical underpinnings of treatment for BED and its mechanisms of action, we would argue that treatments which emphasize binge cessation are currently well justified, at least on pragmatic grounds.

Although they have not been extensively studied in the last two years, self-help and minimal treatment approaches may be a useful first step, at least for less severely ill patients. We now have a wide variety of medication-based treatments that offer at least short-term beneficial effects on eating and weight, and in the case of topiramate there is a suggestion of longer-term benefit as well. For those with access to specialized treatments, group treatments including CBT, IPT and DBT are likely to be beneficial in terms of binge reduction and psychological improvement. Improvement in binge eating with specialized psychotherapies may be accompanied by weight stabilization if not weight loss. Behavioral weight control treatment, although not yet as definitively studied as CBT and IPT for BED, is more widely available, also leads to improvements in binge eating (at least in the short term), and appears to yield greater weight loss. Finally, the advantages of combining psychotherapy and medication are unclear. It appears that, for most patients, medication does not significantly augment the binge reduction attributable to psychotherapy, but one study suggested that adding antidepressant medication may yield an additional reduction in depressive symptoms.

For the vast majority of patients receiving treatment for BED who are obese, treatments of known efficacy for obesity, including dietary/behavioral approaches, medication or surgery, should be considered at some point in treatment. Although many clinicians favor treating binge eating prior to targeting weight management, it is not clear that the goals of binge cessation and weight loss cannot be addressed simultaneously.

Little information is yet available to guide the clinician in choosing from among the available treatment approaches. Until more definitive data are available with regard to treatment-specific predictors, clinicians must rely on patient preference, treatment availability and clinical judgment to select treatment. Fortunately, the variety of treatments available is sufficient to provide several options for patients who do not respond to the initial treatment approach.

Future directions

Although BED treatment studies to date have established the efficacy of a number of treatment approaches, there are several open questions that must be addressed by the next generation of studies. For medication studies, questions regarding the optimal length of treatment and relapse rates during treatment and especially following discontinuation of medication are of great clinical importance. Direct comparisons between different classes of medication, although appealing, would probably require extremely large samples to establish definitively the presence or absence of overall differences in response. For psychotherapy studies, the question of the relative benefits over time of specialized eating disorder-based vs standard behavioral weight management approaches is perhaps the most clinically pressing issue at this point. The further investigation of alternative treatment approaches and novel additions to standard treatments is certainly to be encouraged. Given the high placebo response rates and uncertain natural course of BED, placebo, waiting-list or non-specific clinical attention control groups continue to provide a useful comparison to active treatment groups in studies in which binge frequency is the primary outcome measure. For studies that primarily target obesity, placebo or no-treatment controls are less well justified, since the natural course of obesity is known to be chronic.

For all forms of treatment we need more long-term outcome data, particularly with regard to change in weight and HRQL over time in patients who are and are not successful in stopping binge eating. In addition, the identification of overall and treatment-specific predictors would facilitate rational treatment selection and sequencing. Underlying all of these questions is the importance of developing a better understanding of the natural history of BED, without which it is very difficult to definitively assess the long-term impact of intervention.

Corresponding author: Michael J Devlin, MD, New York State Psychiatric Institute – Unit 116, 1051 Riverside Drive, New York, NY 10032, USA. Email: mjd5@columbia.edu

References

Appolinario JC, Fontenelle LF, Papelbaum M, Bueno JR and Coutinho W (2002a) Topiramate use in obese patients with binge-eating disorder: an open study. *Can J Psychiatry.* **47**: 271–3.

Appolinario JC, Godoy-Matos A, Fontenelle LF *et al.* (2002b) An open-label trial of sibutramine in obese patients with binge-eating disorder. *J Clin Psychiatry.* **63**: 28–30.

Appolinario JC, Bacaltchuk J, Sichieri R *et al.* (2003) A randomized, double-blind, placebo-controlled study of sibutramine in the treatment of binge-eating disorder. *Arch Gen Psychiatry.* **60**: 1109–16.

This is a well-designed and well-conducted clinical trial of the appetite suppressant sibutramine, demonstrating beneficial effects of treatment on both binge eating and weight and, interestingly, on depression scores as well. With the exit of dexfenfluramine from the market, this study establishes sibutramine as the leading BED treatment option in the appetite suppressant category.

Arnold LM, McElroy SL, Hudson JI, Welge JA, Bennett AJ and Keck PE (2002) A placebo-controlled, randomized trial of fluoxetine in the treatment of binge-eating disorder. *J Clin Psychiatry.* **63**: 1028–33.

Carter WP, Hudson J, Lalonde JK, Pindyck L, McElroy S and Pope H (2003) Pharmacologic treatment of binge-eating disorder. *Int J Eat Disord.* **34**: S74–88.

Devlin MJ, Goldfein JA and Dobrow I (2002) *Optimizing treatment for binge-eating disorders.* Paper presented at the 155th Annual Meeting of the American Psychiatric Association, 18–23 May 2002, Philadelphia, PA.

Devlin MJ, Goldfein JA and Dobrow I (2003) What is this thing called BED? Current status of binge-eating disorder nosology. *Int J Eat Disord.* **34**: S2–18.

Dobrow IJ, Wolk SL, Devlin MJ and Goldfein JA (2003) *Binge cessation and weight loss in patients with BED: what impacts on body image and self-esteem?* Poster session presented at the International Academy for Eating Disorders Annual Meeting, 29–31 May, 2003, Denver, CO.

Elder KA, Buckner A, Craighead LW, Niemeier HM and Pung MA (2003) *Appetite-focused CBT for early intervention of binge-eating disorder.* Paper presented at the International Academy for Eating Disorders Annual Meeting, 29–31 May 2003, Denver, CO.

Fitchet M (2002) *A double-blind placebo-controlled trial of topiramate in obese subjects.* Paper presented at the Eating Disorders Research Society Annual Meeting, 20–23 November 2002, Charleston, SC.

Goldstein DJ, Rampey AH Jr, Enas GG, Potvin JH, Fludzinski LA and Levine LR (1994) Fluoxetine: a randomized clinical trial in the treatment of obesity. *Int J Obes Relat Metab Disord.* **18**: 129–35.

Grilo C, Masheb RM, Heninger G and Wilson GT (2002) *A controlled study of cognitive-behavioral therapy and fluoxetine for binge-eating disorder.* Paper presented at the Eating Disorders Research Society Annual Meeting, 20–23 November, 2002, Charleston, SC.

Grilo C, Masheb RM and Wilson GT (2003) *Outcome predictors for the treatment of binge-eating disorder.* Paper presented at the International Academy for Eating Disorders Annual Meeting, 29–31 May 2003, Denver, CO.

Hilbert A and Tuschen-Caffier B (2002) *Body image exposure within cognitive-behavioral therapy of binge-eating disorder.* Paper presented at the Eating Disorders Research Society Annual Meeting, 20–23 November 2002, Charleston, SC.

Hoopes SP, Reimherr FW, Hedges DW *et al.* (2003) Treatment of bulimia nervosa with topiramate in a randomized, double-blind, placebo-controlled trial. Part 1. Improvement in binge and purge measures. *J Clin Psychiatry.* **64**: 1335–41.

Kotler LA, Boudreau GS and Devlin MJ (2003) Emerging psychotherapies for eating disorders. *J Psychiatr Pract.* **9**: 431–41.

McElroy SL, Arnold LM, Shapira NA *et al.* (2003a) Topiramate in the treatment of binge-eating disorder associated with obesity: a randomized, placebo-controlled trial. *Am J Psychiatry.* **160**: 255–61.
This is the first double-blind, placebo-controlled study of a new medication category, namely the anticonvulsants, in the treatment of BED. It demonstrates an effect on binge eating that is comparable to that of other types of medication that have been studied, and an impressive weight loss effect.

McElroy SL, Arnold LM, Shapira NA *et al.* (2003b) *Long-term use of topiramate in the treatment of binge-eating disorder.* Paper presented at the 156th Annual Meeting of the American Psychiatric Association, 17–22 May 2003, San Francisco, CA.

McElroy SL, Hudson JI, Malhotra S, Welge JA, Nelson EB and Keck PE (2003c) Citalopram in the treatment of binge-eating disorder: a placebo-controlled trial. *J Clin Psychiatry.* **64**: 807–13.

McElroy SL, Kotwal R, Hudson JI, Nelson EB and Keck PE Jr (in press) Zonisamide in the treatment of binge-eating disorder: an open-label, prospective trial. *J Clin Psychiatry.* **65**: 50–6.

Malhotra S, King KH, Welge JA, Brusman-Lovins L and McElroy SL (2002) Venlafaxine treatment of binge-eating disorder associated with obesity: a series of 35 patients. *J Clin Psychiatry.* **63**: 802–6.

Marchesini G, Natale S, Chierici S *et al.* (2002) Effects of cognitive-behavioral therapy on health-related quality of life in obese subjects with and without binge-eating disorder. *Int J Obes Relat Metab Disord.* **26**: 1261–7.

This is an important study that addresses the underlying question of whether binge eating is best viewed as a target of treatment in its own right or as an epiphenomenon that would be expected to improve with treatment of the underlying problem. The demonstration of an impressive improvement in health-related quality of life with treatment of binge eating, even when the degree of weight loss is somewhat disappointing, provides support for the idea that treating binge eating *per se* is clinically sound.

Mitchell JE, Gosnell BA, Roerig JL *et al.* (2003) Effects of sibutramine on binge eating, hunger, and fullness in a laboratory human feeding paradigm. *Obes Res.* **11**: 599–605.

Pearlstein T, Spurell E, Hohlstein LA *et al.* (2003) A double-blind, placebo-controlled trial of fluvoxamine in binge-eating disorder: a high placebo response. *Arch Womens Ment Health.* **6**: 147–51.

Pendleton VR, Goodrick GK, Poston SC, Reeves RS and Foreyt JP (2002) Exercise augments the effects of cognitive-behavioral therapy in the treatment of binge eating. *Int J Eat Disord.* **31**: 172–84.

Riva G, Bacchetta M, Cesa G, Conti S and Molinari E (2003) Six-month follow-up of in-patient experiential cognitive therapy for binge-eating disorders. *Cyberpsychol Behav.* **6**: 251–8.

Saelens BE, Wilfley DE, Stein RI, Mockus DS, Welch RR and Matt GE (2002) *Patterning and prediction of post-treatment and follow-up abstinence following CBT or IPT for binge-eating disorder.* Paper presented at the Eating Disorders Research Society Annual Meeting, 20–23 November 2002, Charleston, SC.

Safer DL, Lively TJ, Telch CF, Agras WS (2002) Predictors of relapse following successful dialectical behavior therapy for binge-eating disorder. *Int J Eat Disord.* **32**: 155–63.

Schmidt do Prado-Lima PA and Bacaltchuck J (2002) Topiramate in treatment-resistant depression and binge-eating disorder. *Bipol Disord.* **4**: 271–3.

Shapira NA, Goldsmith TD and McElroy SL (2000) Treatment of binge-eating disorder with topiramate: a clinical case series. *J Clin Psychiatry.* **61**: 368–72.

Spitzer RJ, Devlin M, Walsh BT *et al.* (1992) Binge-eating disorder: a multi-site field trial of diagnostic criteria. *Int J Eat Disord.* **11**: 191–203.

Spitzer RL, Yanovski S, Wadden T *et al.* (1993) Binge-eating disorder: its further validation in a multi-site study. *Int J Eat Disord.* **13**: 137–53.

Stunkard A and Allison KC (2003) Binge-eating disorder: disorder or marker? *Int J Eat Disord.* **34**: S107–16.

This provocative and important paper from the investigator who originally described binge eating contends that the latter is best viewed as a marker of psychopathology among the obese rather than as a disorder in its own right. The authors present convincing evidence that the presence or absence of BED is not a useful distinction in selecting treatment for obese patients.

Stunkard A, Berkowitz R, Tanrikut C, Reiss E and Young L (1996) D-fenfluramine treatment of binge-eating disorder. *Am J Psychiatry.* **153**: 1455–9.

Tasca G, Bissada H, Gayton J, Conrad G and Lybanon-Daigle V (2002) *A randomized clinical trial of group psychotherapy for binge-eating disorder: who benefits most from which treatment – MID study report.* Paper presented at the International Academy for Eating Disorders Annual Meeting, 25–28 April 2002, Boston, MA.

Telch CF, Agras WS and Linehan MM (2001) Dialectical behavioral therapy for binge-eating disorder. *J Consult Clin Psychol.* **69**: 1061–5.

Wilfley DE, Welch RR, Stein RI *et al.* (2002) A randomized comparison of group cognitive–behavioral therapy and group interpersonal psychotherapy for the treatment of overweight individuals with binge-eating disorder. *Arch Gen Psychiatry.* **59**: 713–21.

This expertly designed and executed clinical trial is notable for its sound methodology, its high rate of subject retention, and the novel use of interpersonal therapy in a group format. Its finding of similar and impressive improvements in binge eating with both group CBT and group IPT raises interesting questions about the specificity of the treatment response.

Wonderlich SA, de Zwaan M, Mitchell J, Peterson C and Crow S (2003) Psychological and dietary treatments of binge-eating disorder: conceptual implications. *Int J Eat Disord.* **34**: S58–73.

4

Psychiatric comorbidity and eating disorders

James I Hudson, Rebecca A Hudson and Harrison G Pope Jr

Abstract

Objectives of review. We reviewed the literature from the period 2002–2003 in order to identify studies of the psychiatric comorbidity of eating disorders.

Summary of recent findings. Recent studies have confirmed and extended previous findings on the association of eating disorders with mood disorders, anxiety disorders, substance use disorders, impulse control disorders and personality disorders within individuals. Recent research has also expanded the previously scant literature on comorbidity of binge-eating disorder. Similarly, longitudinal studies have for the most part reinforced previous findings that individuals with eating disorders are at risk for subsequent development of mood and anxiety disorders. Finally, family studies have confirmed and extended the finding of a familial coaggregation of eating disorders with mood disorders, as well as the finding of a lack of familial coaggregation of eating disorders with substance use disorders.

Future directions. Studies using population-based samples to assess the comorbidity of eating disorders with a wide range of other disorders – both cross-sectionally and longitudinally – will be helpful in furthering our understanding of patterns of comorbidity. Studies that evaluate binge-eating disorder would be particularly valuable. Family, twin and genetic studies will also be useful to explore further whether common familial or genetic factors underlie the striking degree of comorbidity observed in patients with eating disorders.

Introduction

A wide range of psychiatric comorbidity has been reported in patients with the eating disorders anorexia nervosa (AN), bulimia nervosa (BN) and binge-eating disorder (BED). As of 2001, it had been established that AN and BN were strongly associated with an elevated lifetime prevalence of mood disorders, anxiety disorders, substance use disorders, impulse control disorders and personality disorders (Hudson *et al.* 1983, 1987; Walsh *et al.* 1985; Halmi *et al.* 1991; Godart *et al.* 2002; Grilo 2002; O'Brien and Vincent 2003). Similar patterns had been reported for BED (Yanovski *et al.* 1993; Telch and Stice 1998; Grilo 2002), but there had been fewer and less rigorous studies of this condition, due largely to the fact that it was only formally defined in the early 1990s.

Longitudinal studies of patients with eating disorders had also shown that mood and anxiety disorders were frequently present at follow-up, and that other psychiatric symptomatology was also common. The reader is referred to recent reviews of studies of the outcome of AN (Steinhausen 2002) and BN (Quadflieg and Fichter 2003). However, these studies were limited by the almost exclusive use of clinic samples, by the lack of operational criteria in the assessment of comorbid disorders at follow-up, and by the lack of information on the onset and course of comorbid disorders (including the question of whether these disorders had their onset before or after the development of the eating disorder).

Family studies had weighed in favor of a coaggregation of AN and BN with mood disorders, even though the estimates of the magnitude of this coaggregation ranged from slight to strong (Hudson *et al.* 2001; Mangweth *et al.* 2003). However, there was little support for familial coaggregation of AN or BN with substance use disorders (Kaye *et al.* 1996).

This chapter reviews more recent studies of psychiatric comorbidity of eating disorders, reported during the period 2002–2003, and concludes with suggestions for future research directions in this area.

Literature review

This review is organized by the design of studies that have appeared, namely cross-sectional, longitudinal and family studies. Citations of reviews of the literature are interpolated as the corresponding topics arise.

Cross-sectional studies

Methodology

There are many cross-sectional studies that have examined the psychiatric comorbidity of eating disorders. The goal of these studies is usually to assess whether there is an association between a lifetime diagnosis of an eating disorder and a lifetime diagnosis of one or more other psychiatric disorders. Several methodologic considerations are important to consider when evaluating these studies. First, studies that use in-person interviews with reliable diagnostic instruments, such as standard structured diagnostic interviews, are preferable to those that use other methods, such as questionnaires, chart review, or interview methods that have not been shown to be reliable for assessment of the diagnostic entities under consideration. Secondly, studies that use comparison groups of individuals without eating disorders are critical for the assessment of level of comorbidity. Descriptive studies that present only the prevalence of various psychiatric disorders among patients with eating disorders are severely limited, because the absolute prevalence of a comorbid condition can be strongly influenced by factors such as the type of interview, the interviewer, the location of the study and the demographics (age, sex, ethnicity) of the subjects. Thus comparison of the prevalence of disorders across studies or in relation to general population figures is extremely hazardous. Relevant comparison groups make it possible to control for these effects when assessing the level of comorbidity.

A third particularly important consideration is the sampling of individuals under study. Clinic samples are often used. These have the advantage that they are easy to obtain and they provide information about the characteristics of those coming for treatment. However, their major disadvantage is that the measure of association between an eating disorder and another disorder is vulnerable to the effects of selection bias. This bias usually operates to produce an overestimate of the magnitude of association, because individuals with both an eating disorder and another given disorder are more likely to come for treatment than individuals with either disorder alone.

Community-based samples are usually less prone to the effects of selection bias, because they are less likely to over-represent individuals with multiple disorders relative to individuals with a single disorder. Thus they offer a less biased assessment of the magnitude of the association between two disorders. However, it should be noted that the associations between eating disorders and other psychiatric disorders that have been reported in clinical samples have almost invariably been replicated in community samples (to the extent that such community replications are available), albeit with a slightly lower magnitude of effect. A potential limitation of community samples is that they often use less comprehensive methods of assessment of disorders than those given in clinical settings. Also, because eating disorders are uncommon in the general population, many community samples include only a small number of cases of full-scale eating disorders, and many of these studies rely primarily on information from subthreshold cases of disorders. Although subthreshold cases of eating disorders have usually been found to have the same risk factors and the same comorbidity as the corresponding full syndromes, equivalence in the patterns of comorbidity between full and partial syndromes cannot be assumed.

Clinical samples

Studies using patient samples have replicated and to a limited degree extended previous findings with regard to associations between eating disorders and various other forms of psychopathology within individuals.

Jordan *et al.* (2002) found broad similarity between patients with AN and patients with major depressive disorder in the pattern of comorbidity. The only significant difference was that the AN patients had a higher lifetime prevalence of obsessive-compulsive disorder than the patients with major depressive disorder.

Godart *et al.* (2003) confirmed previous findings that patients with AN or BN have an elevated lifetime prevalence of anxiety disorders relative to non-eating-disordered control subjects from the community. However, Jaisoorya *et al.* (2003) did not find a significantly elevated prevalence of eating disorders in patients with obsessive-compulsive disorder in India, probably because of the very low prevalence of eating disorders in that country. Indeed, these authors found only one case of AN and no cases of BN among 231 patients with obsessive-compulsive disorder, and no cases of eating disorders among 200 control subjects. They also cite additional evidence for a low prevalence of eating disorders in India.

Grant and Kim (2002) reported a high prevalence of eating disorders in kleptomania, consistent with other studies of that disorder, and with the known converse finding of a high prevalence of impulsive stealing and kleptomania in eating disorders, particularly BN (Hudson *et al.* 1983; McElroy *et al.* 1991a,b). Grant *et al.* (2002) found a high prevalence of body dysmorphic disorder among patients with AN, consistent with the prominent body image concerns of patients with this condition.

Of all of the anxiety disorders noted to occur comorbidly with eating disorders, obsessive-compulsive disorder has attracted the most interest, perhaps because obsessive thoughts and compulsive behavior regarding food and weight are almost ubiquitous in patients with AN and BN (see the recent analysis in AN patients by Halmi *et al.* 2003). Case reports continue to receive attention (Fisher *et al.* 2002), as do theoretical pieces that attempt to synthesize the literature on this topic (Serpell *et al.* 2002).

Nestadt *et al.* (2003) performed a latent class analysis of obsessive-compulsive disorder, using data from probands and relatives who had been evaluated in a family study of obsessive-compulsive disorder. They found that the majority of cases of this disorder could be classified into a subgroup consisting of three classes that were distributed ordinally on the basis of increasing severity; comorbidity with AN and BN was part of the third and most severe class. The second group was qualitatively distinct and was not related to eating disorders.

Turning to the issue of whether similar patterns of comorbidity are seen in different ethnic groups, Cerezo *et al.* (2003) examined a community sample of women with eating disorders (most of whom had BN and BED), and found that major depressive disorder, anxiety disorders and substance use disorders were as common among Mexican-American women as they were among white women. This study extends the findings of comorbidity to an ethnic group that had not previously been studied systematically.

Nagata *et al.* (2002) undertook a descriptive study of non-alcohol substance use disorders among 185 Japanese women patients with AN or BN. Solvent fumes and benzodiazepines were the most commonly abused drugs, with no abuse of or dependence on opiates or cocaine, and only one case of amphetamine abuse. The lifetime prevalence of substance use disorders was only 9% – lower than that reported in most Western studies. However, the interpretation of this finding is unclear, because it may reflect a lower base rate of substance use disorders in Japanese women, differences in the clinic population relative to other sources of patients with eating disorders, or differences in diagnostic instruments or thresholds.

In a similar descriptive study involving personality disorders, Godt (2002) assessed the prevalence of various personality disorders among outpatients with eating disorders in Denmark. Although the prevalence of personality disorders was lower than that reported in many other studies, these findings should be interpreted with caution for the same reasons as were cited for the study described above.

Examining the question of whether patterns of comorbidity differ among the various eating disorders, Grilo *et al.* (2003b) found a high prevalence of eating disorders among patients with each of several different personality disorders who were enrolled in a large multi-center study of the course of personality disorders. The prevalence of eating disorders did not differ significantly either between individual personality disorders, or between patients with any personality disorder and a comparison group of patients with major depressive disorder who did not have a personality disorder. The investigators also found that the strength of the association between eating disorders and personality disorders did not vary across the eating disorders AN, BN and eating disorder not otherwise specified (EDNOS). The results of a study by de Jonge *et al.* (2003) are at slight variance with this. These investigators compared the prevalence of personality disorder in patients with BN, with BED, and with obesity without BN or BED. They found a tendency for BN to be more strongly associated with personality disorders than BED, but there was an elevated prevalence of personality disorders in patients with BED relative to those with obesity without BN or BED. It is noteworthy that this was one of the few studies that examined personality disorders in patients with BED, but it was limited by its small sample size of only 15 patients with this condition. Furthermore, in an excellent review of the entire literature, Grilo (2002) notes that finer distinctions may exist in the association between personality disorders and eating disorders, concluding that 'anorexia nervosa may be associated with obsessional and perfectionistic forms of personality disturbances, bulimia nervosa with impulsive and unstable personality disturbances, and binge-eating disorder with avoidant and anxious forms of personality disturbance.'

Looking at the extent to which comorbidity influences prognosis, Milos *et al.* (2002) found that eating-disordered patients (i.e. those with AN or BN) with obsessive-compulsive disorder had an earlier onset of eating disorder and a longer course of illness than those without that disorder. However, it is unclear whether this finding represented a specific effect or a general tendency for more severely ill people to have more comorbidity and a more chronic course. The same group (Milos *et al.* 2003) also found that patients with eating disorders who had higher levels of comorbidity required more intensive treatment interventions, consistent with the latter hypothesis.

Goodwin and Fitzgibbon (2002) found that social anxiety was associated with less engagement with treatment, suggesting that social anxiety, and by inference social anxiety disorder (social phobia), may be a barrier to treatment. However, this interpretation is subject to caveats similar to those mentioned above for obsessive-compulsive disorder.

Community samples

Rowe *et al.* (2002) examined the association between bulimic symptoms (modeled as ordered categories based on the number of symptoms) and various disorders (also modeled as ordered categories based on the number of symptoms) in a population-based sample of female twins aged 8–17 years. They found significant associations of bulimic symptoms with depression, anxiety disorder, conduct disorder and attention-deficit/hyperactivity disorder. This study extends to childhood and adolescence the findings of comorbidity of bulimic symptoms with depression and anxiety previously established in adults, and presents new findings of an association with conduct disorder and attention-deficit/hyperactivity disorder. It uses a population-based sample that is much less vulnerable to selection bias than studies using clinical samples.

Bulik *et al.* (2002) investigated the association between binge eating (assessed by the question 'Have you ever in your life had eating binges during which you ate a lot of food in a short period of time?') and psychopathology among obese women in a population-based registry, evaluated both at a mean age of 30 years and five years later. Binge eating was strongly and significantly associated with major depression and anxiety disorders. These findings suggest that the association of binge eating with mood and anxiety disorders in obese individuals is independent of weight. Moreover, if these findings extend from binge eating to BED among obese individuals, it weighs in favor of the validity of BED as a valid entity, as opposed to its being merely a non-specific pattern of overeating associated with obesity.

von Ranson *et al.* (2002) investigated the association between eating disorders and substance use disorders in a population-based study of female adolescent twins and their mothers. Because few individuals met the full criteria for eating disorders, these investigators used clusters of eating-disorder symptoms to define a 'bulimic eating disorder (ED)' and 'restricting ED' group. They found a higher prevalence of types of substance use disorders among the eating-disorder symptom groups in both girls and mothers, the odds ratio measuring the magnitude of association being greater than 1.5 for all but one of the comparisons. Although none of these effects was statistically significant, the confidence intervals for the odds ratios were very wide because of the small number of subjects with bulimic ED or restricting ED, together with the use of conservative 99% confidence intervals to attempt to control for multiple comparisons across the entire study. Therefore the study's failure to find significant effects could easily have been due to a type II error (failure to reject the null hypothesis when the null hypothesis is true). A further limitation of the study is that adolescents would have passed through less of the period of risk for development of substance use disorders than the period of risk for development of an eating disorder, thus potentially leading to underestimation of the association between the two types of conditions.

Dohm *et al.* (2002) found that substance use disorders were equally common among women with BN and BED in a community sample. Because BN has been associated with substance use disorders in most community-based studies, these results tend to confirm an association between BED and substance use disorders. However, these findings should be interpreted with caution, because there was no comparison group without an eating disorder, so it is not possible to establish that the observed prevalence of substance use disorders was higher than that among women without eating disorders.

Longitudinal studies

Methodology

Two types of longitudinal studies have been reported. The first follows individuals with eating disorders, either from a clinical or community sample, over time and notes the outcome at one or more follow-up points. In the previous literature and in almost all of the studies that have appeared in the past two years, these studies report whether certain types of comorbid conditions are present at follow-up observation. These reports are useful for generating hypotheses about a longitudinal association of eating disorders with other conditions. However, they are limited, because comorbidity is rarely assessed either at the initial evaluation or in the intervals between follow-up visits (even by retrospective means). Moreover, such studies have typically not used reliable diagnostic interviews for a wide range of conditions and symptoms. For example, these studies cannot determine whether the presence of an eating disorder is a risk factor for the subsequent development of other disorders, or whether the comorbidity observed at follow-up is simply an extension of the comorbidity at baseline. Most of these studies were not planned in advance, and have used a convenience sample of patients with eating disorders. Little attention has been paid to the effects of missing data for individuals who were unavailable for follow-up.

The second type of longitudinal study addresses these limitations by assessing individuals with and without eating disorders at baseline for a range of diagnoses (including eating disorders), and then performing similar assessments at later time points. In this manner it can be determined whether individuals with an eating disorder who do not initially have a given comorbid condition are at greater risk of developing that comorbid condition than individuals with no eating disorder. Such studies, which adhere more closely to the methodology of a prospective cohort study, offer a much more rigorous and informative method for studying the developmental trajectories of eating disorders in relation to comorbid disorders.

Clinical samples

MacQueen *et al.* (2003) followed patients with bipolar disorder for a year or more. They found that on follow-up assessment, comorbid eating disorder (classified as 'anorexia,' 'bulimia' or 'binge eating') was significantly more prevalent among patients with either full or subsyndromal bipolar disorder than among euthymic patients, with binge eating accounting for most of this difference. This study exemplifies the increasing interest in the connection between eating disorders and bipolar disorder – an issue that has been less well studied than the link with depression and anxiety disorders. Indeed, Perugi and Akiskal (2002) have called attention to the association of binge eating with bipolar II disorder, impulse dyscontrol and features of temperament.

In a longitudinal study of patients with personality disorders, Grilo *et al.* (2003a) assessed patients with comorbid BN and EDNOS at 6, 12 and 24 months. Although the group with BN had a lower rate of remission than the group with EDNOS, the rate of remission in these two groups was not predicted significantly by the presence and severity of co-occurring personality disorders or co-occurring axis I disorders at baseline. These findings are largely consistent with those from a recent review of the literature concerning the influence of psychiatric comorbidity on the prognosis of BN (Bell 2002). That review found no consistent association between prognosis and baseline comorbid axis I or axis II psychopathology, apart from the fact that the presence of borderline personality disorder at baseline tended to predict a poorer prognosis.

Community samples

Johnson *et al.* (2002a) used data from a community-based longitudinal investigation to determine whether adolescents with eating disorders were at higher risk of developing psychiatric comorbidity in early adulthood. The distribution of cases with eating disorders in adolescence was AN = 1, BN = 14, BED = 2 and EDNOS = 12. These adolescents showed a significantly elevated risk of development of mood disorder (either major depressive disorder or dysthymia) and anxiety disorder (obsessive-compulsive disorder, overanxious disorder, panic disorder, separation anxiety disorder or social phobia) compared with those without eating disorders. Looking at the opposite relationship, the same group (Johnson *et al.* 2002b) also found that depressive disorder and anxiety disorder during early adolescence were both associated with an elevated risk of development of eating disorders during middle adolescence or early adulthood (the distribution of all cases of ED on follow-up was AN = 1, BN = 10 and EDNOS

= 41), as well as with an elevated risk of many types of eating and weight problems, including recurrent binge eating.

In broad agreement with the above two reports, Patton *et al.* (2003) found high levels of symptoms of depression and anxiety at six-year follow-up of female adolescents with anorexic or bulimic symptomatology in a community-based sample.

Rastam *et al.* (2003) followed teenage-onset cases of AN, recruited from community screening, for a mean period of 10 years after the onset of AN. They found that obsessive-compulsive disorder, when present at baseline, was often still present at follow-up and predicted poorer prognosis, whereas mood disorder when present at baseline tended to have remitted by the time of follow-up and did not predict prognosis. The finding that obsessive-compulsive disorder was a negative prognostic factor is somewhat at variance with the results of other studies (see discussion with reference to clinical samples above), which have generally found that comorbid disorders at baseline do not predict long-term outcome.

Family studies

Methodology

Family studies can be used to examine the issue of whether eating disorders travel together, or *coaggregate*, with other disorders in families. Familial coaggregation of two disorders implies that the two disorders share common familial factors. Since twin studies have usually shown that the contribution of shared family environmental factors is either negligible or small relative to genetic factors, the finding of familial coaggregation usually suggests that two disorders share genetic factors.

The family study design most commonly used to assess the coaggregation of two disorders (here termed disorder A and disorder B) involves selecting probands with and without one of the disorders, and then assessing their relatives (usually first-degree relatives) for the presence or absence of disorder A and disorder B. Personal interviews with relatives, using an interviewer blinded to proband status, offer the best method of assessment. The analysis for coaggregation attempts to determine whether the presence of disorder A in an individual is associated with the presence of disorder B in that individual's relative, and vice versa. The most commonly employed analytic method is to use logistic regression or a similar approach to determine whether disorder B in a relative is predicted by disorder A in a proband, and whether disorder A in a relative is predicted by disorder B in a relative (proband predictive models).

Although there are several important aspects of this type of analysis, perhaps the most important of all is to control for proband comorbidity. To illustrate this point, consider a study that obtains probands with and without eating disorders and seeks to examine the coaggregation of eating disorders with mood disorders. Suppose that the prevalence of mood disorders among relatives of probands with eating disorders is found to be higher than the prevalence of mood disorders among relatives of probands without eating disorders. However, it might be the case that the prevalence of mood disorders is elevated only among relatives of probands with both an eating disorder and a mood disorder, and not among relatives of probands with an eating disorder alone. In this instance, therefore, the elevation of mood disorders among relatives of probands with eating disorders might be attributable solely to the well-established familial aggregation of mood disorders alone, and not to a coaggregation of eating disorders with mood disorders. Thus the method of analysis in a family study of this type needs to control for proband comorbidity, and ideally for other effects as well. For a review of family study methods to assess coaggregation, and the application of these methods to studies of the coaggregation of eating disorders with mood disorders, see Hudson *et al.* (2001a) and Hudson *et al.* (2001b).

Studies

Two family studies of coaggregation of eating disorders with other disorders have been reported during the period 2002–2003.

First, Mangweth *et al.* (2003) examined the coaggregation of eating disorders with mood disorders in a study conducted in Austria. This study was a part of a larger investigation of the coaggregation of mood disorders with a number of other disorders postulated to be related to mood disorders, termed forms of 'affective spectrum disorder' (Hudson *et al.* 2003). Probands with and without major depressive disorder were recruited. They and their available first-degree relatives were interviewed for psychiatric disorders and certain medical disorders using structured diagnostic interviews. Relatives were interviewed by an investigator who was blinded to proband diagnosis.

In the analysis of the data on eating disorders, the degree of familial coaggregation of eating disorders (AN, BN or BED) with mood disorders (major depressive disorder or bipolar disorder) was statistically significant, in an analysis that controlled for the aggregation of mood disorders and eating disorders alone in families, the co-occurrence of disorders within probands and relatives, and the effects of age, sex and relationship of relative to the proband. The estimated odds ratio for coaggregation (2.2) was also close to the combined estimated odds ratio of 2.0 from a meta-analysis of previous studies of this coaggregation. The study by Mangweth *et al.* (2003) is important because it sampled probands with and without mood disorders, whereas previous studies have sampled probands with and without AN or BN, and because it used novel analytic techniques that are more rigorous than those employed in most previous studies (Hudson *et al.* 2001a, 2001b). The results of this study combined with the findings from previous studies provide strong overall evidence that eating disorders coaggregate with mood disorders in families. Furthermore, it is likely that this coaggregation arises in part from common genetic factors shared by mood and eating disorders.

More broadly, the results of the larger study (Hudson *et al.* 2003) examining the coaggregation of major depressive disorder with other forms of affective spectrum disorders, which includes BN, suggest that BN may share common familial factors not only with mood disorders, but also with a range of related conditions, including anxiety disorders, attention-deficit/hyperactivity disorder and some medical conditions (e.g. irritable bowel syndrome and fibromyalgia). Although AN and BED were not included in the analysis performed for this larger study, it seems likely by extension that these disorders might also share familial factors with the same range of conditions.

Secondly, von Ranson *et al.* (2003) assessed the coaggregation of eating disorders with substance use disorders in a sample of female adolescent twins and their parents. Note that this sample was described above in our discussion of the study by von Ranson *et al.* (2002) under the heading of community cross-sectional studies. It should be recalled that eating disorders were defined as 'bulimic ED' and 'restricting ED', which represented either full or subthreshold cases of BN or restricting AN. Because of the constraints imposed by a design that had been developed for other purposes, these authors were unable to test for coaggregation in a standard manner, and therefore used adaptations to accommodate the structure of their data. They found no evidence for coaggregation of eating disorders with substance use disorders using several analyses. Although these findings are limited by the preponderance of largely subthreshold cases of eating disorders and the use of ad hoc analyses, the investigators' failure to find a coaggregation of eating disorders with substance abuse disorders is consistent with the findings of a previous family study that controlled for the effects of proband comorbidity (Kaye *et al.* 1996).

Finally, in a study using family data, Garcia-Vilches *et al.* (2002) found no differences in the features of illness in subjects with eating disorders with and without parental alcoholism. However, the small sample of only 25 probands, together with lack of control for other parental characteristics, limits the conclusions that can be drawn from this finding.

Summary of important findings

Recent studies have confirmed and extended previous findings on the association of eating disorders with mood disorders, anxiety disorders, substance use disorders, impulse control disorders and personality disorders within individuals. Particularly notable has been the use of cross-sectional and longitudinal community-based samples to confirm the association of eating disorders with mood and anxiety disorders. Although recent work has also expanded somewhat the previously scant literature on comorbidity of BED, much work remains to be done in this area.

Similarly, family studies have confirmed and extended the finding of a familial coaggregation of eating disorders with mood disorders, as well as the finding of a lack of familial coaggregation of eating disorders with substance use disorders.

Clinical implications

The simple message from these studies is that eating disorders are associated with a wide range of psychiatric comorbidity. Therefore, in the evaluation and treatment of patients with eating disorders, the clinician should maintain a high index of suspicion for other forms of psychopathology – in either full or subthreshold form.

The comorbidity of eating disorders with bipolar disorder has particular relevance for pharmacologic treatment. Selective serotonin reuptake inhibitors (SSRIs) and other agents with antidepressant properties are often used to treat eating disorders, but can also induce mania or mixed states in individuals with bipolar disorder. Therefore the clinician should be cautious about using these agents in individuals with comorbid bipolar disorder, and should be alert for the development of mania, hypomania or mixed affective states when treating any patient with an eating disorder, since antidepressants may bring out a latent bipolar condition.

Future directions

A major goal for future research is to clarify the association between eating disorders and other psychiatric disorders in population-based studies, using either cross-sectional or longitudinal designs. Further study of BED is clearly warranted.

Going beyond simple associations between individual disorders and eating disorders, future studies should address the structure underlying the patterns of comorbidity. Studies that have begun this work include those of Nestadt *et al.* (2003) and Hudson *et al.* (2003), discussed above, as well as previous work by Kendler *et al.* (1995) that attempted to classify eating disorders and other conditions based on common genetic factors. Ultimately, much of the observed comorbidity is likely to be explained by the presence of factors that are common to eating disorders and a number of other conditions. Of particular interest is the question of which of these are relatively non-specific factors associated with mental disorders as a whole, and which may be more specific factors that predispose to eating disorders and related conditions, but not to mental disorders in general (Hudson *et al.* 2003).

Future work should address the effects of genes, environment and gene–environment interactions on the development of eating disorders and associated comorbidity. Family, twin and genetic studies will be helpful when investigating these relationships. Understanding the causation of the patterns of comorbidity seen in eating disorders is likely to contribute greatly to the elucidation of the causes of eating disorders themselves.

Corresponding author: James I Hudson, MD, ScD, 115 Mill Street, Belmont, MA 02478, USA. Email: jhudson@mclean.harvard.edu

References

Bell L (2002) Does concurrent psychopathology at presentation influence response to treatment for bulimia nervosa? *Eat Weight Disord.* **7**: 168–81.

Bulik CM, Sullivan PF and Kendler KS (2002) Medical and psychiatric morbidity in obese women with and without binge-eating disorder. *Int J Eat Disord.* **32**: 72–8.

This population-based study of young women found a significant association between lifetime binge eating and various psychiatric disorders, including major depression, among obese women. The importance of this study is that it points to the possibility that BED may be associated with psychiatric and medical comorbidity over and above any relationship with obesity.

Cerezo A, Matus T, Schug R *et al.* (2003). Psychiatric co-morbidity among white and Mexican-American women with eating disorders. *Int J Eat Disord.* **34**: 62.

de Jonge PVH, van Furth EF, Lacey JH and Waller G (2003) The prevalence of DSM-IV personality pathology among individuals with bulimia nervosa, binge eating disorder and obesity. *Psychol Med.* **33**: 1311–17.

Dohm FA, Striegel-Moore RH, Wilfley DE, Pike KM, Hook J and Fairburn CG (2002) Self-harm and substance use in a community sample of black and white women with binge-eating disorder or bulimia nervosa. *Int J Eat Disord.* **32**: 389–400.

Fisher M, Fornari V, Waldbaum R and Gold R (2002) Three case reports on the relationship between anorexia nervosa and obsessive-compulsive disorder. *Int J Adolesc Med Health.* **14**: 329–34.

Garcia-Vilches I, Badia-Casanovas A, Fernandez-Aranda F *et al.* (2002) Characteristics of bulimic patients whose parents do or do not abuse alcohol. *Eat Weight Disord.* **7**: 232–8.

Godart NT, Flament MF, Perdereau F and Jeammet P (2002) Comorbidity between eating disorders and anxiety disorders: a review. *Int J Eat Disord.* **32**: 253–70.

Godart NT, Flament MF, Curt F *et al.* (2003) Anxiety disorders in subjects seeking treatment for eating disorders: a DSM-IV controlled study. *Psychiatry Res.* **117**: 245–58.

Godt K (2002) Personality disorders and eating disorders: the prevalence of personality disorders in 176 female outpatients with eating disorders. *Eur Eat Disord Rev.* **10**: 102–9.

Goodwin RD and Fitzgibbon ML (2002) Social anxiety as a barrier to treatment for eating disorders. *Int J Eat Disord.* **32**: 103–6.

Grilo CM (2002) Recent research on relationships among eating disorders and personality disorders. *Curr Psychiatry Rep.* **4**: 14–18.

Grilo CM, Sanislow CA, Shea MT *et al.* (2003a) The natural course of bulimia nervosa and eating disorder not otherwise specified is not influenced by personality disorders. *Int J Eat Disord.* **34**: 319–30.

Grilo CM, Sanislow CA, Skodol AE *et al.* (2003b) Do eating disorders co-occur with personality disorders? Comparison groups matter. *Int J Eat Disord.* **33**: 155–64.

Grant JE and Kim SW (2002) Clinical characteristics and associated psychopathology of 22 patients with kleptomania. *Compr Psychiatry.* **43**: 378–84.

Grant JE, Kim SW and Eckert ED (2002) Body dysmorphic disorder in patients with anorexia nervosa: prevalence, clinical features, and delusionality of body image. *Int J Eat Disord.* **32**: 291–300.

Halmi KA, Eckert E, Marchi P, Sampugnaro V, Apple R and Cohen J (1991) Comorbidity of psychiatric diagnoses in anorexia nervosa. *Arch Gen Psychiatry.* **48**: 712–18.

Halmi KA, Sunday SR, Klump KL *et al.* (2003) Obsessions and compulsions in anorexia nervosa subtypes. *Int J Eat Disord.* **33**: 308–19.

Hudson JI, Pope HG Jr, Jonas JM and Yurgelun-Todd D (1983) Phenomenologic relationship of eating disorders to major affective disorder. *Psychiatry Res.* **9**: 345–54.

Hudson JI, Pope HG Jr, Yurgelun-Todd D, Jonas JM and Frankenburg FR (1987) A controlled study of lifetime prevalence of affective and other psychiatric disorders in bulimic outpatients. *Am J Psychiatry*. **144**: 1283–7.

Hudson JI, Laird NM and Betensky RA (2001) Multivariate logistic regression for familial aggregation of two disorders. I. Development of models and methods. *Am J Epidemiol*. **153**: 500–5.

Hudson JI, Laird NM, Betensky RA, Keck PE Jr and Pope HG Jr (2001) Multivariate logistic regression for familial aggregation of two disorders. II. Analysis of studies of eating and mood disorders. *Am J Epidemiol*. **153**: 506–14.

Hudson JI, Mangweth B, Pope HG Jr *et al.* (2003) Family study of affective spectrum disorder. *Arch Gen Psychiatry*. **60**: 170–7.

Jaisoorya TS, Reddy YC and Srinath S (2003) The relationship of obsessive-compulsive disorder to putative spectrum disorders: results from an Indian study. *Compr Psychiatry*. **44**: 317–23.

Johnson JG, Cohen P, Kasen S and Brook JS (2002a) Eating disorders during adolescence and the risk for physical and mental disorders during early adulthood. *Arch Gen Psychiatry*. **59**: 545–52.

This longitudinal community-based study showed that eating disorders in adolescence are associated with an increased risk of mood and anxiety disorders in early adulthood. This study should be viewed in conjunction with its companion-piece (see next reference), which found that mood and anxiety disorders in early adolescence were associated with an elevated risk of development of eating disorders during mid-adolescence or early adulthood.

Johnson JG, Cohen P, Kotler L, Kasen S and Brook JS (2002b) Psychiatric disorders associated with risk for the development of eating disorders during adolescence and early adulthood. *J Consult Clin Psychol*. **70**: 1119–28.

See commentary under previous reference.

Jordan J, Joyce PR, Carter FA *et al.* (2002) Anxiety and psychoactive substance use disorder comorbidity in anorexia nervosa or depression. *Int J Eat Disord*. **34**: 211–19.

Kaye WH, Lilenfeld LR, Plotnicov K *et al.* (1996) Bulimia nervosa and substance dependence: association and family transmission. *Alcohol Clin Exp Res*. **20**: 878–81.

Kendler KS, Walters EE, Neale MC, Kessler RC, Heath AC and Eaves LJ (1995) The structure of the genetic and environmental risk factors for six major psychiatric disorders in women: phobia, generalized anxiety disorder, panic disorder, bulimia, major depression, and alcoholism. *Arch Gen Psychiatry*. **52**: 374–83.

McElroy SL, Hudson JI, Pope HG Jr and Keck PE Jr (1991a) Kleptomania: clinical characteristics and associated psychopathology. *Psychol Med*. **21**: 93–108.

McElroy SL, Pope HG Jr, Hudson JI, Keck PE Jr and White KL (1991b) Kleptomania: a report of 20 cases. *Am J Psychiatry*. **148**: 652–7.

MacQueen GM, Marriott M, Begin H, Robb J, Joffe RT and Young LT (2003) Subsyndromal symptoms assessed in longitudinal, prospective follow-up of a cohort of patients with bipolar disorder. *Bipol Disord*. **5**: 349–55.

Mangweth B, Hudson JI, Pope HG Jr *et al.* (2003) Family study of the aggregation of eating disorders and mood disorders. *Psychol Med*. **33**: 1319–23.

This study replicates and extends previous work suggesting that eating disorders coaggregate with mood disorders in families (see discussion of this issue in the introduction). Previous studies have all been performed using probands with and without eating disorders. This study is the first to use probands with and without mood disorders. Taken together with the results of the larger investigation (Hudson *et al.* 2003) from which this report arose, this study suggests that eating disorders may share common genetic factors with a range of other conditions.

Milos G, Spindler A, Ruggiero G, Klaghofer R and Schnyder U (2002) Comorbidity of obsessive-compulsive disorders and duration of eating disorders. *Int J Eat Disord.* **31**: 284–9.

Milos G, Spindler A, Buddenberg C and Crameri A (2003) Axes I and II comorbidity and treatment experiences in eating disorder subjects. *Psychother Psychosom.* **72**: 276–85.

Nagata T, Kawarada Y, Ohshima J, Iketani T and Kiriike N (2002) Drug use disorders in Japanese eating disorder patients. *Psychiatry Res.* **109**: 181–91.

Nestadt G, Addington A, Samuels J *et al.* (2003) The identification of OCD-related sub-groups based on comorbidity. *Biol Psychiatry.* **53**: 914–20.

O'Brien KM and Vincent NK (2003) Psychiatric comorbidity in anorexia and bulimia nervosa: nature, prevalence, and causal relationship. *Clin Psychol Rev.* **23**: 57–74.

Patton GC, Coffey C and Sawyer SM (2003) The outcome of adolescent eating disorders: findings from the Victorian Adolescent Health Cohort Study. *Eur Child Adolesc Psychiatry.* **12(Suppl.1)**: I24–9.

Perugi G and Akiskal HS (2002) The soft bipolar spectrum redefined: focus on the cyclothymic, anxious-sensitive, impulse-dyscontrol and binge-eating connection in bipolar II and related conditions. *Psychiatr Clin North Am.* **25**: 713–37.

Quadflieg N and Fichter MM (2003) The course and outcome of bulimia nervosa. *Eur Child Adolesc Psychiatry.* **12(Suppl.1)**: I99–109.

Rastam M, Gillberg C and Wentz E (2003) Outcome of teenage-onset anorexia nervosa in a Swedish community-based sample. *Eur Child Adolesc Psychiatry.* **12(Suppl.1)**: I78–90.

Rowe R, Pickles A, Simonoff E, Bulik CM and Silberg JL (2002) Bulimic symptoms in the Virginia Twin Study of adolescent behavioral development: correlates, comorbidity and genetics. *Biol Psychiatry.* **51**: 172–82.

In a population-based sample of female twins aged 8–17 years, this study found a significant association of bulimic symptoms with depression, anxiety disorders, conduct disorder and attention-deficit/hyperactivity disorder. This study extends the findings of comorbidity of bulimic symptoms with depression and anxiety to childhood and adolescence, and is the first to find an association with conduct disorder and attention-deficit/hyperactivity disorder.

Serpell L, Livingston A, Neiderman M and Lask B (2002) Anorexia nervosa: obsessive-compulsive disorder, obsessive-compulsive personality disorder, or neither? *Clin Psychol Rev.* **22**: 647–69.

Steinhausen HC (2002) The outcome of anorexia nervosa in the twentieth century. *Am J Psychiatry.* **159**: 1284–93.

Telch CF and Stice E (1998) Psychiatric comorbidity in women with binge-eating disorder: prevalence rates from a non-treatment-seeking sample. *J Consult Clin Psychol.* **66**: 768–76.

von Ranson KM, Iacono WG and McGue M (2002) Disordered eating and substance use in an epidemiological sample. I. Associations within individuals. *Int J Eat Disord.* **31**: 389–403.

von Ranson KM, McGue M and Iacono WG (2003) Disordered eating and substance use in an epidemiological sample. II. Associations within families. *Psychol Addict Behav.* **17**: 193–202.

Walsh BT, Roose SP, Glassman AH, Gladis M and Sadik C (1985) Bulimia and depression. *Psychosom Med.* **47**: 123–31.

Yanovski SZ, Nelson JE, Dubbert BK and Spitzer RL (1993) Association of binge-eating disorder and psychiatric comorbidity in obese subjects. *Am J Psychiatry.* **150**: 1472–9.

5

Psychosocial risk factors for eating disorders

Corinna Jacobi

Abstract

Objective of review. The objective of this review is to provide an overview of risk factors for eating disorders. Risk factors identified in longitudinal studies and fixed and variable markers from cross-sectional studies are presented for the eating disorder syndromes anorexia nervosa (AN) bulimia nervosa (BN), and binge-eating disorder in accordance with the risk factor taxonomy by Kraemer *et al.* (1997). Additional factor characteristics (e.g. specificity, need for replication) are pointed out.

Summary of recent findings. The results of recent studies are integrated with the results of an earlier review. Common risk factors that have emerged from longitudinal and cross-sectional studies are pregnancy complications, gender, ethnicity, early childhood eating, feeding and gastro-intestinal problems, concerns about weight and shape, negative self-evaluation, sexual abuse and other adverse experiences, and general psychiatric morbidity. Longitudinal evidence of risk factors is much stronger for BN and binge-related syndromes, whereas our knowledge of risk factors for AN and binge-eating disorder is still very limited.

Future directions. Suggestions are made for the conceptualization of future risk factor studies.

Introduction

In the past, risk and etiologic factors for eating disorders have either been proposed from a specific theoretical perspective (e.g. biologic, cognitive–behavioral, psychodynamic model) or from an integrative perspective (e.g. biopsychosocial model). The empirical foundation of these models can vary from very strong to very weak, and can comprise a wide range of methods and definitions for risk and etiology factors. The inconsistent use of the term 'risk factor' as well as the lack of precise definitions led Kraemer and colleagues to set out a conceptual basis for a typology of risk factors (Kazdin *et al.* 1997; Kraemer *et al.* 1997). Because the methods and definitions of this theoretical framework are applied to the present review, we shall briefly summarize them here.

If, according to their criteria, a statistically significant association between the potential risk factor and an outcome (e.g. onset of anorexia nervosa (AN)) can be shown in a defined population, the factor is called a *correlate*. Only if a correlate can be demonstrated to *precede* the outcome is the term 'risk factor' justified. To establish a factor's status as a risk factor, precedence is a crucial criterion. A risk factor that can be shown to change spontaneously within a subject (e.g. age, weight) or to be changed by intervention (e.g. by medication or psychotherapy) is called a *variable risk factor*. A risk factor that cannot change or be changed (e.g. race, gender, year of birth) is called a *fixed marker*. A variable risk factor for which it can be shown that manipulation changes the risk of the outcome (e.g. onset of disorder) is called a *causal risk factor*. If this cannot be shown, it is called a *variable marker*.

Because precedence is a crucial criterion for risk factors, the majority of risk factors can only be assessed in longitudinal studies. Exceptions are fixed markers documented before the onset of the eating disorder in medical records or birth registers. Cross-sectional studies (e.g. epidemiological studies, case–control studies, family studies), on the other hand, only lend themselves to the assessment of correlates. Again the exceptions are some fixed markers, such as race or gender. The status of variable markers and causal risk factors can only be established in randomized clinical trials (prevention or intervention studies) which confirm that the modification of the factors leads to a change in the risk of the outcome (e.g. onset of the disorder).

In a recent paper (Jacobi *et al.* 2004), these risk factor definitions and this methodology were applied to potential risk factors for eating disorders (AN, bulimia nervosa (BN) and binge-eating disorder). The present review is largely based on the methodology and findings reported there, but in addition it integrates studies published between April 2002 and December 2003.

Method

Inclusion/exclusion criteria for studies

After a detailed computerized and manual literature search of potential risk factor studies, the following criteria were established for the present review. With few exceptions (regarding epidemiological studies), only studies with a control group (healthy or unaffected group) were included. Studies comparing different eating disorder groups alone were excluded. To establish specificity an additional clinical group was required. Sample size in the studies had to include a minimum of 10 subjects per cell. The follow-up interval for longitudinal studies had to be at least one year in length to allow enough time for symptoms of eating disturbances or disorders to change or emerge. Because the focus of our overview was on risk factors for eating disorder *syndromes*, longitudinal studies solely addressing (dimensional) disturbances or symptoms assessed via questionnaires (e.g. Eating Disorder Inventory (EDI)) were not included.

Factors from the included studies were first classified according to the typology of Kraemer *et al.* (1997) as outlined above. Factors were also classified with regard to outcome status – that is, they were categorized according to whether they were associated with or predicted (1) *full* syndrome AN, BN or binge-eating disorder, or (2) *partial* syndrome eating disorders, otherwise defined 'eating disturbances', or mixed outcomes of syndromes and symptoms. Finally, factors were classified according to additional risk factor characteristics (e.g. specificity, potency, need of replication) (for further details see Jacobi *et al.* 2004).

In our previous risk factor review, the terminology of Kraemer *et al.* (1997) was expanded to include a separate category for factors which were assessed retrospectively in cross-sectional studies (retrospective correlates). Although these cross-sectional studies try to address the precedence of the potential risk factor to the onset of the disorder, retrospective assessment of risk factor information is problematic because of retrospective recall or memory biases. In contrast to the previous risk factor review, retrospective correlates will only be mentioned briefly here, and the respective studies will not be described in detail.

Research on biologic risk factors for eating disorders, especially genetic factors and neurobiologic disturbances, will be presented in separate chapters. Research on factors related to pubertal development and pre- and perinatal complications will be reviewed in this chapter.

Results

Characteristics of longitudinal risk factor studies for eating disorders

Because longitudinal studies represent the 'gold standard' of risk factor research, the main characteristics of the included studies will be described here first in more detail. In the following sections I shall summarize the results of longitudinal risk factor research for the diagnostic syndromes AN, BN and binge-eating disorder (*see also* Tables 5.1, 5.2 and 5.3).

A total of 28 longitudinal studies were found. Of these, 13 studies were excluded from our overview due to there being too few cases, insufficient information on risk factors and reported methodology, lack of control for initial eating disorder symptoms, too broad outcome measures, or too short follow-up intervals.

Despite the large sample sizes, the majority of longitudinal studies have only been able to identify risk factors for a *mixture of full DSM syndromes* of AN and BN and/or *partial syndromes* or eating disorders not otherwise specified (ED-NOS); (Marchi and Cohen 1990; Patton *et al.* 1990, 1999; Vollrath *et al.* 1992; Killen *et al.* 1994, 1996; Ghaderi and Scott 2001; Kotler *et al.* 2001; Johnson *et al.* 2002). In six studies, the outcome samples were high-risk samples usually defined as scoring above the Eating Attitudes Test (EAT-26) cut-off value (Attie and Brooks-Gunn 1989; Graber *et al*. 1994; Leon *et al*. 1995, 1999; Button *et al*. 1996; Calam and Waller 1998). A closer examination of the outcomes in longitudinal studies reveals that the focus is on bulimic and binge-eating syndromes, while reports of anorexic syndromes as outcomes were very rare. Taken together, only 27 cases of AN (in contrast to 65 BN cases and 198 EDNOS/partial cases) out of a total of 12 776 subjects in the 15 studies emerged during the follow-up periods.

Samples in the studies consist mostly of adolescents between 12 and 15 years of age. Three studies assessed infants or younger children (Marchi and Cohen 1990; Kotler *et al*. 2001; Johnson *et al*. 2002), and two studies assessed young adults (Vollrath *et al*. 1992; Ghaderi and Scott 2001). In eight studies the samples included female subjects only, and in seven studies the samples consisted of both male and female subjects. The duration of follow-ups ranged from one to 18 years. The number and broadness of included potential risk factors, and the definitions and assessment of risk status or caseness (symptomatic/asymptomatic, cases/non-cases, high/moderate/low risk) varied significantly. Seven studies assessed eating disorder symptoms and syndromes with structured diagnostic interviews, and eight studies relied solely on questionnaire cut-off points or score combinations.

In addition to the above-mentioned longitudinal studies, three more longitudinal studies that met our inclusion criteria were found during the past two years. The McKnight Investigators (2003) conducted one of the most comprehensive risk factor studies for eating disorders. A large number of potential risk factors was examined in 1103 girls in grades 7–9 over a follow-up-period of four years. Emerging cases (*n* = 32) were mostly partial (BN) syndromes, and no cases of AN were detected. Cevera *et al*. (2003) assessed two potential risk factors (neuroticism and low self-esteem) in the largest sample to date (*n* = 2743) of young girls in Spain. During the follow-up period of 18 months, 90 incident cases of eating disorders were identified, most of which were partial syndromes (EDNOS). Finally, Moorhead *et al*. (2003) investigated early childhood and adolescent predictors of eating disorders in young adulthood in 21 women with a lifetime diagnosis of full or partial syndrome eating disorders compared with women with no eating disorder. Of the eating disorder sample, nine women met the lifetime criteria for anorexia or bulimia nervosa and 12 met the criteria for partial-syndrome disorders. The original sample consisted of female participants (*n* = 763) in the Simmons longitudinal study interviewed between the ages of 5 and 26 years at seven time points. Because the precedence of some of the factors assessed in adolescence to the eating disorders is not quite clear, only childhood factors are included here. Due to the small number of cases of anorexia nervosa emerging in these recent studies, the results with regard to potential risk factors are reported in the respective sections on risk factors for bulimia nervosa and binge-eating disorder below.

Risk factors for anorexia nervosa

Pregnancy and perinatal complications

Associations between pregnancy and perinatal complications and eating disorders have recently received increasing attention. Two studies examining these factors on the basis of hospital or case registers allow for a risk factor classification according to the typology of Kraemer et al. (1997).

Cnattingius et al. (1999) reported a (prospectively assessed) more than threefold increased risk of very preterm birth in a large case-register sample of anorexic patients. Furthermore, the risk (odds ratio) of severe birth trauma (cephalhematoma) was two- to threefold higher in anorectic patients. An elevation of these obstetrical complications was not found in a related study of patients with schizophrenia, affective psychosis or reactive psychosis (Hultman et al. 1999).

Utilizing a Swedish hospital register, Lindberg and Hjern (2003) addressed a number of sociodemographic, perinatal and psychosocial variables as potential risk factors for anorexia nervosa in a large sample of anorexic inpatients ($n = 1122$). The role of perinatal variables could be confirmed in this study. Premature children with a gestational age of 23–32 and 33–36 weeks showed a higher risk of developing anorexia nervosa. In addition, cephalhematoma and premature rupture of membrane were associated with a higher risk of developing anorexia nervosa. Early gestational age, preterm birth, birth trauma, cephalhematoma, and premature rupture of the membrane are therefore classified as specific *fixed markers* for AN.

Pattern of birth

Watkins et al. (2002) compared the distributions of births across the year between a group of children and adolescents with diagnoses of AN or other eating disorders relative to standard population norms. There was a significant preponderance of births among those with AN between April and June compared with the other months of the year and with the other eating disorders. AN was also associated with a higher environmental temperature at the assumed time of conception. On the basis of this study, season of birth and (although less reliably assessed) temperature at time of conception are classified as fixed markers for AN, but these findings are in need of replication.

Gender

In both clinical and non-clinical samples, anorexia and bulimia nervosa have been observed to occur predominantly in females (Schotte and Stunkard 1987; Nielsen 1990; Whitaker et al. 1990; Vollrath et al. 1992; Lewinsohn et al. 1993; Patton et al. 1999). Population-based studies estimate a female:male ratio of 10:1 (American Psychiatric Association 1994; Hsu 1996). Since gender is an immutable characteristic, and asymmetric gender distributions have been found for other mental disorders (e.g. Blazer *et al.* 1994), female status is classifiable as a non-specific fixed marker for both anorexia and bulimia nervosa.

Ethnicity

Although eating disorders have traditionally been regarded as a predominantly Caucasian issue (see review by Striegel-Moore and Smolak 1996), a literature survey by Crago *et al.* (1996) revealed a more complex ethnic distribution pattern. Native Americans were noted to have higher rates of eating disorders than Caucasians, while equal rates were reported for Hispanics and lower rates for Asians and blacks. The results of two further studies also point to lower rates of anorexia and bulimia nervosa among Asians (Ohzeki *et al.* 1990; Chen *et al.* 1993). Therefore non-Asian ethnicity can be classified as a fixed marker of currently unknown specificity.

Age

In both clinical and population-based surveys, the peak incidence of eating disorders has been found in the age range from adolescence to early adulthood (Woodside and Garfinkel 1992). The magnitude of the age-associated increase in risk depends on which age groups are compared. As yet, direct comparisons of eating disorder rates in younger vs older adolescent samples have not been made. In the Kraemer typology, age is classified as a variable risk factor, and because it is related to other psychiatric disorders age is categorized as non-specific.

Early childhood eating and digestive problems

Two longitudinal studies have addressed the role of early feeding, eating, and digestive problems with regard to the emergence of AN in adolescence. The first study, which included a sample of younger children, found digestive problems and picky eating to be prospectively related to subsequent anorexic symptoms, and anorexic symptoms to be related to later full diagnoses of AN (Marchi and Cohen 1990).

The second study also found a range of early childhood eating problems, assessed between the ages of 1 and 10 years, to predict eating disorder diagnoses in early and late adolescence and young adulthood. Eating conflicts, struggles concerning meals, and unpleasant meals in childhood predicted later diagnosis of AN (Kotler *et al.* 2001). On the basis of these studies, picky eating, anorexic symptoms in childhood, digestive and other early eating-related problems as well as eating conflicts, struggles concerning meals, and unpleasant meals are classified as variable risk factors for AN or anorexic symptoms. The specificity of these eating and digestive problems has not yet been tested. Given the small number of studies involved, replication is needed.

Pubertal timing

Based on cross-sectional evidence from the studies by Hayward *et al.* (1997) and Graber *et al.* (1997), early pubertal timing can be regarded as a non-specific fixed marker of AN and BN. Indicators of pubertal timing were also assessed in six longitudinal studies, in which neither an association with subsequent eating disturbances (Attie and Brooks-Gunn 1989; Graber *et al.* 1994; Killen *et al.* 1994; Leon *et al.* 1995; McKnight Investigators 2003) nor predictive status in a structural model (Leon *et al.* 1999) could be found. In the study by Graber *et al.* (1994), timing of pubertal maturation was related to eating disturbances present at study onset, with the girls in the 'chronic' group evidencing the earliest age of menarche. Taken together, there is no longitudinal basis for the classification of pubertal timing as a risk factor.

Weight concerns/dieting/negative body image

The association between dieting and eating disorders is probably one of the most often quoted in theories of the etiology of eating disorders. The (cross-sectional) relationship between dieting and eating disorders seems to be particularly strong for patients who binge (i.e. patients with AN binge-eating/purging subtype, BN and binge-eating disorder). Longitudinal evidence for a relationship between weight concerns or dieting and AN is scarce because most of the cases emerging in longitudinal studies were bulimic or partial bulimic cases, sometimes mixed with a few anorexic cases. Only one study (Marchi and Cohen 1990) found that elevations on a measure of anorexic symptoms during childhood predicted adolescent AN or symptoms of anorexia. Accordingly, weight concerns, negative body image and dieting are tentatively considered as (variable) risk factors for AN, but replication is needed. The specificity of these factors has not yet been addressed.

General psychiatric disturbance/negative emotionality

Although both etiologic theories of eating disorders and research on comorbidity have stressed the role of other psychiatric disorders (e.g. affective disorders, substance abuse disorders, anxiety disorders, personality disorders) as underlying and/or associated conditions in clinical samples of anorexic and bulimic patients (for reviews, *see* Mitchell *et al.* 1991; Wonderlich and Mitchell 1997), to date longitudinal evidence does not support the role of any of these disorders as risk factors for AN. Although eight longitudinal studies included general psychiatric morbidity, psychopathology or, more specifically, negative emotionality as potential predictors of eating disorders (Attie and Brooks-Gunn

1989; Patton *et al.* 1990, 1999; Graber *et al.* 1994; Leon *et al.* 1995, 1999; Killen *et al.* 1996; McKnight Investigators 2003; Moorhead *et al.* 2003), one of these studies (Leon *et al.* 1999) was only able to detect one case of AN and the second study (Moorhead *et al.* 2003) identified nine cases of AN or BN.

Sexual abuse

Sexual abuse in childhood, adolescence or adulthood has been discussed as a risk factor for eating disorders (anorexia and bulimia nervosa) in many cross-sectional studies as well as in early (Pope and Hudson 1992) and more recent reviews (Wonderlich and Mitchell 1997). To date, only one longitudinal study has addressed the role of sexual abuse as a risk factor for eating disorders (Johnson *et al.* 2002). Because only one patient developed AN at follow-up, the results will be reported in the respective section on risk factors for bulimia.

Family interaction/family functioning/attachment styles

Historically, the role of dysfunctional family interaction styles was put forward in theories on the development of eating disorders (Bruch 1973; Minuchin *et al.* 1978). Characteristics of the family relationships of eating-disordered patients include problematic family structures, interaction, communication styles (e.g. overprotection, enmeshment) and attachment styles.

In the majority of studies (e.g. Garfinkel *et al.* 1983; Strober and Humphrey 1987; Waller *et al.* 1989; McNamara and Loveman 1990; Shisslak *et al.* 1990; Friedman *et al.* 1997), both anorexic and bulimic patients describe different aspects of their family structure (interaction, communication, cohesion, affective expression, attachment disturbances, etc.) as more disturbed, conflictual, pathological or dysfunctional than normal controls across different family assessment measures. However, the issue of precedence to the eating disorders was not addressed in any of these studies. Furthermore, similar patterns of family interaction or family functioning have been found in connection with other disorders, indicating that these disturbances possibly have a non-specific nature.

As AN was not included as an outcome in any of the longitudinal studies assessing variables of family interaction, no evidence for these variables as risk factors for AN exists.

Family history/family psychopathology

To date, a large body of cross-sectional research has examined the role of familial psychiatric disorders as a risk factor for eating disorders utilizing both the family history and family study method (for details, *see* Jacobi *et al.* 2004). The majority of these studies suggest that there are elevated rates of psychiatric disorders in first-degree relatives of anorexic patients. The evidence is particularly strong for rates of eating disorders (AN and BN), affective disorders and some anxiety disorders, including panic disorder, generalized anxiety disorder, obsessive-compulsive disorder (OCD) and obsessive-compulsive personality disorder (OCPD), and rather weak for rates of substance abuse disorders. However, the chronology of the onset of AN in relation to the respective psychiatric disorders in the families was not addressed in any of these studies. No longitudinal evidence exists for the role of family psychopathology as a risk factor for AN.

Low self-esteem/negative self-concept/ineffectiveness

Low self-esteem, a negative self-concept or 'ineffectiveness' has assumed a central role in many clinically derived theories of eating disorders (e.g. Bruch 1962). Constructs related to low self-esteem, especially ineffectiveness (operationalized by the EDI ineffectiveness subscale), have been examined in many cross-sectional studies. In such studies, anorexic patients have consistently been found to exhibit lower self-esteem, a more negative self-concept, or higher levels of ineffectiveness compared with normal controls (Jacobi et al. 2004a, 2004b). On the other hand, longitudinal evidence for the role of low self-esteem or negative self-evaluation is for the most part based on studies with BN or binge-related syndromes as outcome. Thus it cannot be classified as a risk factor for AN.

Perfectionism

From a clinical point of view it is well recognized that anorexic patients often display rigid, stereotypic, ritualistic or perfectionistic behaviors. Most recently, these characteristics have been examined in a psychobiological light, connecting perfectionistic traits with alterations in serotonin activity in a number of cross-sectional studies. These (cross-sectional) studies found elevated scores for perfectionism in remitted anorexic (and bulimic) patients, confirming the role of perfectionism as a correlate (e.g. Bastiani et al. 1995; Srinivasagam et al. 1995; Kaye et al. 1998). The basis of longitudinal studies including cases of AN as outcome is currently too weak for perfectionism to be classified as a risk factor for AN.

Athletic competition/participation in weight-related subculture/ exercise

Members of professions that overemphasize a certain (low) weight or shape and athletes from certain sports disciplines (ballet dancers, gymnasts, wrestlers, swimmers, jockeys, etc.) were originally proposed more than 20 years ago as high-risk groups for the development of eating disorders (Garner and Garfinkel 1978). In the past few years interest has focused primarily on the examination of eating disorder symptoms in elite athletes. Although elite athletes often show higher levels of eating disorder-related symptoms and behaviors (Braistedt *et al.* 1985; Kurtzman *et al.* 1989; Abraham 1996a, 1996b), rates for the full syndromes of eating disorders (anorexia and bulimia nervosa) are, when assessed, usually not higher than in the control groups (e.g. Sundgot-Borgen 1994; Johnson *et al.* 1999). Another major focus has been on the role of physical activity or high-level exercise in the development and maintenance of eating disorders (Davis *et al.* 1990, 1997). As all of these studies are cross-sectional in nature, it is as yet impossible to draw conclusions about the status of these factors as risk factors.

Inter-country adoption and foster care

The role of inter-country adoption and foster care was examined for the first time in the Swedish hospital register study (Lindberg and Hjern 2003), in which they could be confirmed as variable risk factors for AN. Precedence of these variables to the onset of the disorder was not fully addressed in this study. However, since the addressed time-frame for both variables was before the age of 13 years, it seems likely that their influence pre-dated the onset of the disorder.

Risk factors for bulimia nervosa

Gender, ethnicity, age and pubertal timing

The cross-sectional evidence for these factors has been presented in full in the section on AN above. According to the taxonomy of Kraemer *et al.* (1997), female status and early pubertal timing are classifiable as non-specific fixed markers, non-Asian ethnicity can be classified as a fixed marker of currently unknown specificity, and adolescent age is classifiable as a non-specific variable risk factor.

Early childhood eating and health problems

Three longitudinal studies have addressed the association between early childhood eating or health problems and BN. Marchi and Cohen (1990) found pica, early digestive problems and weight reduction efforts to be related to later bulimic symptoms. The risk of BN was found to be almost seven times higher in individuals with a history of pica in early childhood. Eating problems typically occurring between the ages of 1 and 10 years were assessed in a second longitudinal study (Kotler *et al.* 2001) in order to predict eating disorder diagnoses in the time span from early adolescence to young adulthood. Only eating too little was predictive of future BN. Pica, digestive problems, not eating, not being interested in food, picky eating, and eating too slowly were not predictive of the disorder. In the third longitudinal study, mothers of girls who later developed eating disorders were significantly more likely to report that their daughters had health problems as infants and toddlers than mothers whose children did not develop an eating disorder (Moorhead *et al.* 2003). In addition, mothers of eating-disordered girls were twice as likely to report having had complications during their pregnancy with the affected daughter.

On the basis of the latter study, early childhood health problems are classified as variable risk factors for BN and, since a few cases of anorexia were included, probably also for AN. With regard to early childhood eating and digestive problems, the results of the longitudinal studies are inconclusive and the studies are too few in number, so further research is necessary.

Weight concerns/dieting/negative body image

Dieting has long been considered an important precursor if not cause of eating disorders. Clinical studies addressing the chronology of dieting and bingeing are few in number, and the majority date back almost 20 years. In these studies, the onset of bulimia (i.e. onset of binge eating) has been observed to occur for the vast majority of afflicted cases (73–91%) either during a period of voluntary dieting (Pyle *et al.* 1981; Mitchell *et al.* 1986) or following weight loss (Russell 1979; Garfinkel *et al.* 1980). Although the studies by Mitchell *et al.* (1986) and Pyle *et al.* (1981) remain rather vague in their description of the temporal sequence of the two behaviors, recent studies have corroborated the temporal precedence of dieting in bulimic subjects (Mussell *et al.* 1987; Haiman and Devlin 1999; Brewerton *et al.* 2000). Taken together, the cross-sectional research provides strong evidence of the temporal sequence of dieting followed by binge eating. On the basis of longitudinal studies, a factor best labeled as 'weight concerns', consisting of fear of weight gain, dieting behavior, negative body image and specific eating disorder symptoms or attitudes (e.g. bulimic behavior) has been assessed quite often in eating disorder research (in 13 of the total of 18 longitudinal studies). It predicted the development of eating disturbances and caseness (mixed bulimic and partial syndromes) in 10 of the 11 studies controlling for initial eating symptomatology (Attie and Brooks-Gunn 1989; Patton *et al.* 1990, 1999; Vollrath *et al.* 1992; Graber *et al.* 1994; Killen *et al.* 1994, 1996; Leon *et al.* 1995, 1999; Ghaderi and Scott 2001; McKnight Investigators 2003). In the study by Patton *et al.* (1999), subjects initially classified as 'dieters' were found to have an almost eighteenfold higher risk of becoming 'cases' than those initially classified as non-dieters.

Weight concerns, negative body image and dieting can be classified as variable risk factors on the basis of the longitudinal studies. However, the specificity of weight concerns remains unclear, as none of the longitudinal studies included other psychiatric outcomes.

General psychiatric disturbance/negative emotionality

As mentioned before, several psychiatric disorders (affective disorders, anxiety disorders, eating disorders and substance abuse disorders) have been postulated to play a role as 'primary underlying conditions' in the development of eating disorders in general (*see* AN section). For the most part, these studies are cross-sectional in nature.

General psychiatric morbidity, psychopathology and, more specifically, negative emotionality have been investigated as potential predictors of eating disturbances and disorders in nine longitudinal studies (Attie and Brooks-Gunn 1989; Patton *et al.* 1990, 1999; Graber *et al.* 1994; Leon *et al.* 1995, 1999; Killen *et al.* 1996; McKnight Investigators 2003; Moorhead *et al.* 2003).

The change in score for general psychiatric morbidity turned out to be the only predictor of BN caseness in the study by Patton *et al.* (1990). Psychiatric morbidity was also found to predict the onset of eating disorders (including partial syndromes) independently of dieting status in a further study by Patton *et al.* (1999). Subjects in the highest psychiatric morbidity category exhibited an almost sevenfold risk of developing an eating disorder. Leon *et al.* (1999) found negative affectivity to be the only significant (although moderate) predictor of eating disorder risk measured 3–4 years later. Mothers of women with lifetime eating disorders in the longitudinal study by Moorhead *et al.* (2003) reported that their children at the age of nine years experienced more problems with anxiety–depression measured by the Simmons Behavior Checklist (SBC) than did their non-eating-disordered peers. In five other studies (Attie and Brooks-Gunn 1989; Graber *et al.* 1994; Leon *et al.* 1995; Killen *et al.* 1996; McKnight Investigators 2003), negative emotionality or psychopathology did not predict the outcome at all or did not predict it independently. However, two of the temperament scales (distress and fear) used in the study by Killen *et al.* (1996) discriminated between asymptomatic and symptomatic girls. In the McKnight Longitudinal Risk Factor Study (McKnight Investigators 2003), general psychological influences (including depressed mood) turned out to be a potential risk factor in the Cox's proportional hazards model only in the Arizona sample, not in the Stanford sample. However, subsequent pairwise analysis suggested that general psychological influences were a proxy for thin body preoccupation and social pressure, and were therefore dropped as an independent risk factor.

On the basis of the above studies, including the two recent longitudinal studies, prior psychiatric morbidity is classifiable as a variable risk factor for BN, but the ratio of studies supporting to studies not supporting this factor is currently rather small. Longitudinal studies in other fields indicate that premorbid anxiety disorders and negative affectivity are risk factors for the development of other psychiatric conditions, including affective disorders and substance abuse (Pine *et al.* 1998; Hayward *et al.* 2000; Ingram and Price 2000). Therefore they should be considered to be non-specific risk factors.

Sexual abuse

Sexual abuse, especially during childhood, has been discussed as a risk factor for BN in many studies and reviews (e.g. Pope and Hudson 1992; Wonderlich *et al.* 1997). In cross-sectional studies using both clinical and community samples, elevated rates of sexual abuse are consistently found in bulimic patients compared with non-morbid controls (Steiger and Zanko 1990; Garfinkel *et al.* 1995; Vize and Cooper 1995; Dansky *et al.* 1997). The results are less consistent if restricted to sexual abuse before the age of 16 years or during childhood (Garfinkel *et al.* 1995; Casper and Lubomirsky 1997; Webster and Palmer 2000). The few studies comparing bulimic patients with psychiatric controls could not find any differences in the rates of sexual abuse (Folsom *et al.* 1993; Welch and Fairburn 1994).

As yet the association between childhood adversities, including sexual abuse, and later eating- or weight-related problems has only been investigated in one longitudinal study (Johnson *et al.* 2002). In the large community-based sample of mothers and their offspring, individuals who had experienced sexual abuse or physical neglect during childhood were at increased risk for later eating disorders and eating problems. Information on sexual abuse and physical neglect was obtained from a central registry and (for a subgroup of the sample) from maternal interviews. Sexual abuse and physical neglect are classified as non-specific, variable risk factors on the basis of this study. However, further prospective replication studies are needed.

Body mass index (BMI) and other weight-related variables

The results of longitudinal studies investigating body mass index (BMI) are inconsistent. In three studies, higher BMI or body fat was found to be predictive of eating problems (Killen *et al.* 1994), weight control, caseness (Patton *et al.* 1990), or a partial diagnosis of 'binge eating' (Vollrath *et al.* 1992). In four studies, BMI or percentage body fat at time 1 was not related to subsequent eating disturbances, caseness or partial syndromes (Graber *et al.* 1994; Killen *et al.* 1996; Patton *et al.* 1999; McKnight Investigators 2003). Accordingly, higher BMI cannot be classified as a risk factor. However, as the number of studies supporting and the number not supporting BMI as a risk factor are almost equal, replication studies are needed. The specificity of BMI has not been addressed in longitudinal studies.

Family interaction/family functioning/attachment styles

In the majority of the cross-sectional studies of family interaction, functioning or attachment style, bulimic (and anorexic) patients describe different aspects of their family structure as being more disturbed or dysfunctional than normal controls (*see* anorexia section for more details). However, none of the longitudinal studies assessing variables of family interaction included BN as an outcome. Accordingly, as yet there is no evidence for these variables as risk factors for the disorder.

Family history/family psychopathology

The majority of cross-sectional studies suggest that there are elevated rates of certain psychiatric disorders in first-degree relatives of bulimic patients. Eating disorders, affective disorders, anxiety disorders, substance use disorders and cluster B personality disorders are found more frequently among the relatives of bulimics compared with the relatives of control probands. Unfortunately, the temporal relationship of the psychiatric disorders of bulimics' family members to the onset of BN in the patient was not addressed in any of these studies (Jacobi et al. 2004). Because no longitudinal evidence exists for the role of family psychopathology as a risk factor for BN, it cannot be classified as a risk factor.

Low self-esteem/negative self-concept/ineffectiveness

Measures of self-concept have been included in six longitudinal studies (Leon et al. 1995; Button et al. 1996; Calam and Waller 1998; Ghaderi and Scott 2001; Cevera et al. 2003; McKnight Investigators 2003). In the studies by Leon et al. (1995) and Calam and Waller (1998), such measures did not prove to be important in risk prediction or disordered eating. On the other hand, low self-esteem predicted elevated EAT scores four years later in the study by Button et al. (1996). Girls in the lowest self-esteem range had an eightfold increased risk of high EAT scores (≥ 20) compared with those with high self-esteem. Similarly, Ghaderi and Scott (2001) reported significantly lower self-esteem at time 1 for the incidence group that developed an eating disorder two years later. The confidence variable (part of the general psychological influences domain) turned out to be a potential risk factor in the McKnight longitudinal study in the Arizona sample, but was identified as a proxy for thin body preoccupation and social pressure in subsequent pairwise analysis. At the California site, this variable just approached the level of significance in the univariate analysis. Significantly lower self-esteem was also found among girls who subsequently developed eating disorders (mostly partial syndromes) in the study by Cevera et al. (2003).

The EDI ineffectiveness subscale was included in four of the studies at baseline (Killen et al. 1994, 1996; Leon et al. 1995, 1999), but turned out to be predictive of disturbed eating patterns or caseness in only one of the multivariate analyses as part of the latent variable negative affectivity (Leon et al. 1999). However, significant differences, were found in the univariate comparisons of the subsequent symptomatic and asymptomatic groups (Killen et al. 1994, 1996).

Based on longitudinal assessment, there is a superiority of studies confirming the presence of a negative self-concept, low self-esteem or higher ineffectiveness prior to the onset of an eating disorder. Low self-esteem and ineffectiveness are therefore classified as variable risk factors. Based on existing studies, their specificity is unclear, although it seems reasonable to assume that they are not highly specific for eating disorders.

Perfectionism

Perfectionism has been assessed using the corresponding EDI subscale in four longitudinal studies (Killen *et al.* 1994, 1996; Leon *et al.* 1995, 1999). In the studies by Killen *et al.* (1994, 1996), perfectionism at time 1 was not found to be related to subsequent eating disturbances in multivariate analyses, but it differentiated between symptomatic and asymptomatic girls at baseline in univariate comparisons (Killen *et al.* 1994). In both studies by Leon *et al.* (1995, 1999), perfectionism did not turn out to be predictive in multivariate comparisons. No other measures of perfectionism have been employed in any of the longitudinal studies. On the basis of these results, perfectionism is classified as a correlate for BN.

Low interoception

Low interoception or low interoceptive awareness is, in line with ineffectiveness and body image disturbances, one of the three core psychopathological features of eating-disordered patients as originally suggested by Bruch (1962). The construct of low interoception addresses difficulties in the interpretation of internal (emotional and gastrointestinal) stimuli. Its correlate status has been confirmed in numerous cross-sectional studies using the corresponding EDI subscale. In contrast, longitudinal evidence for the role of interoception is much more scarce. Low interoceptive awareness was predictive of year 3 disordered eating in one longitudinal study (Leon *et al.* 1995). In three other studies in which it was assessed, it was not found to be predictive when considered in a multivariate model (Killen *et al.* 1994, 1996; Leon *et al.* 1999). However, differences were found in univariate comparisons between the group that turned out to be symptomatic, and the asymptomatic group (Killen *et al.* 1994, 1996). Low interoceptive awareness is therefore classified as a variable risk factor of unclear specificity.

Athletic competition/participation in a weight-related subculture/exercise

A longitudinal investigation of the role of athletic competition, participation in a weight-related subculture or exercise in BN has not yet been undertaken.

Other factors

Girls who later turned out to be symptomatic in the study by Killen *et al.* (1994) showed elevated scores on the Aggressive and Unpopular subscales of the Youth Self-Report (YSR) Inventory when compared with asymptomatic girls. Girls who developed a partial syndrome in the study by Killen *et al.* (1996) had a higher 30-day prevalence of alcohol consumption. High use of escape–avoidance coping as well as low perceived social support were found to be prospective risk factors for subsequent eating disorders (primarily BN and binge-eating disorder) in the study by Ghaderi and Scott (2001). Cevera *et al.* (2003) found that girls with higher levels of neuroticism (as measured by the Eysenck Personality Inventory, EPI) were more likely to develop a clinically defined eating disorder than girls with low levels of neuroticism. Finally, at the Arizona site, an increase in negative life events was found to be an independent (although weak) risk factor for onset of partial syndromes in the McKnight risk factor study (McKnight Investigators 2003). All of these factors are classified as variable risk factors. Because no outcomes other than eating disorders had been included in these studies, their specificity is unclear.

Risk factors for binge-eating disorder

Binge-eating disorder (BED) is not a distinct diagnostic category like anorexia and BN, but is part of the eating disorders not otherwise specified (EDNOS). Because the research criteria have only been put forward in the latest revision of the *Diagnostic and Statistical Manual of Mental Disorders* (DSM) (DSM-IV), the number of risk factor studies that explicitly include the proposed BED criteria is very small. As the outcome of the longitudinal studies is often a mixture of bulimic or binge-eating syndromes, it can be assumed that some of the risk factors listed in the bulimia section are also relevant to binge-eating disorder. Unfortunately, however, the majority of the longitudinal studies do not permit a strict differentiation between bulimic and binge-eating-related syndromes. Therefore only longitudinal and cross-sectional studies that explicitly rely on the research criteria for BED will be covered in this section.

BED has been observed to occur predominantly in females, as is also the case for anorexia and BN. However, the gender distribution is not quite so asymmetrical for BED. Preliminary estimates suggest a female:male ratio of 2.5 (Spitzer *et al.* 1992). Accordingly, gender is classified as a non-specific fixed marker for BED.

Eating disorders have generally been seen as afflictions of Caucasian females (*see* Striegel-Moore and Smolak 1996 and the AN section of this book). However, although lower rates of body dissatisfaction and weight concerns have been found among African-Americans, the rates of bingeing behavior are equal to or higher than those in Caucasians (Striegel-Moore *et al.* 2000). African-American and Caucasian ethnicity can therefore be classified as a fixed marker for BED of currently unknown specificity.

Three longitudinal studies were able to identify BED cases based on the *DSM-IV* research criteria. Johnson *et al.* (2002), in a large community-based sample of mothers and offspring, found that individuals who had experienced sexual abuse or physical neglect during childhood were at increased risk of developing eating disorders (primarily BN and BED) and some eating problems during adolescence or early adulthood. Information on sexual abuse and physical neglect had been obtained from a central registry and, for a subgroup of the sample, from maternal interviews. In this study, sexual abuse and physical neglect are classified as non-specific, variable risk factors for BED.

Low self-esteem, high levels of body concern, high use of escape–avoidance coping as well as low levels of perceived social support were found to be prospective risk factors for subsequent eating disorders in the study by Ghaderi and Scott (2001). Of the 28 subjects who developed an eating disorder during follow-up, 13 were BED cases. Therefore these factors are classified as variable risk factors.

In the McKnight longitudinal study (McKnight Investigators 2003), higher scores on a factor (thin body preoccupation and social pressure) measuring concerns about weight, shape and eating (including media modeling, social eating, dieting and testing about weight) significantly predicted the onset of eating disorders at both sites (Stanford and Arizona). An increase in negative life events was also an independent risk factor for onset of illness in Arizona. Because the outcome in this study included partial BN syndromes as well as cases of BED, thin body preoccupation, social pressure and negative life events are classified as variable risk factors for BED.

Probable risk factors

In addition to risk factors from longitudinal studies and fixed markers from cross-sectional studies, a number of cross-sectional studies have addressed potential risk factors by retrospectively assessing whether these factors occurred prior to the onset of the eating disorder. In our previous review (Jacobi *et al.* 2004), these factors have been classified as 'retrospective correlates'. The relevant studies have been presented in detail in that paper, and will only be summarized briefly here in temporal order from childhood to adolescence (*see* Tables 5.1, 5.2 and 5.3).

For AN, pregnancy complications and shorter gestational age were confirmed as specific retrospective correlates. Furthermore, feeding and gastrointestinal problems, infant sleep difficulties and a high-concern parenting style are retrospective correlates during early childhood, followed by obsessive-compulsive personality disorders and childhood anxiety disorders, both starting in childhood. Retrospective correlates during early adolescence include a high level of exercise, dieting behavior, body dysmorphic disorder, obsessive-compulsive disorder and acculturation. Increased exposure to sexual abuse and other adverse life events are retrospective correlates occurring before the age of 12–19 years, depending on the study. Finally, a higher level of perfectionism, negative self-evaluation and premorbid obsessive-compulsive disorder represent retrospective correlates specific for AN that could have occurred at any time before onset (Fairburn *et al.* 1999). Factors that have been found only once include early feeding and gastrointestinal problems, a high-concern parenting style, infant sleep difficulties, childhood overanxious disorders, a high level of exercise, body dysmorphic disorder and negative self-evaluation. For factors such as obsessive-compulsive personality disorder, obsessive-compulsive disorder and perfectionism, although these are separate syndromes, we assume that they overlap considerably.

Two recent studies have confirmed and extended the cross-sectional findings of these previous studies. Anderluh *et al.* (2003) found that women with eating disorders (AN: *n* = 44; BN: *n* = 28) showed higher levels of obsessive-compulsive personality traits in childhood than control subjects. There was a strong relationship between the number of retrospectively reported childhood traits of obsessive-compulsive personality (e.g. perfectionism, inflexibility, rule-bound trait) and the odds of developing an eating disorder. Troop and Bifulco (2002) interviewed women with a history of eating disorders (*n* = 43; AN = 31, BN = 12) retrospectively about social influences, especially about their feelings and experiences of loneliness, shyness and inferiority during childhood and adolescence. Women with a history of AN reported higher levels of all of these potential risk factors in adolescence, while women with a history of BN reported only higher levels of shyness in adolescence than women without a history of eating disorders.

For BN, retrospective correlates reported to emerge at birth or in childhood are pregnancy complications, childhood obesity and childhood overanxious disorder. As was the case for AN, a number of adverse life events, including sexual abuse, some parental problems (alcoholism, depression, drug abuse, obesity), a number of family environmental factors (e.g. critical comments on weight and shape, low levels of contact), other adverse family experiences and negative self-evaluation could have occurred at any time before the onset of the disorder (Fairburn *et al.* 1997). For sexual abuse and adverse life events, occurrence before the age of 12 to 18 years has been reported. Other retrospective correlates reported for early adolescence are social phobia, dieting and acculturation. Finally, mood- and anxiety-related prodromal symptoms including severe dieting, were found during late adolescence (for details, *see* Jacobi *et al.* 2004). Pregnancy complications, childhood obesity, parental alcoholism, family environmental factors and negative self-evaluation are specific retrospective correlates for BN. The majority of these factors have been reported only once, and there is therefore a need for replication. No additional recent studies with retrospectively assessed potential risk factors were found.

For BED, three cross-sectional studies (Fairburn *et al.* 1998; Dominy *et al.* 2000; Striegel-Moore *et al.* 2002) retrospectively assessed potential risk factors in BED patients compared with healthy controls. In the first study (Fairburn *et al.* 1998), the following non-specific retrospective correlates were found: negative self-evaluation, major depression, marked conduct problems, deliberate self-harm, greater levels of exposure to parental criticism, high expectations, minimal affection, parental underinvolvement, and maternal low care and high overprotection. In addition, women with BED reported higher rates of sexual abuse, repeated severe physical abuse, bullying, critical comments by family members about their shape, weight or eating, and teasing about their shape, weight, eating or appearance. The following factors turned out to be specific retrospective correlates in comparison with the psychiatric controls: low parental contact, critical comments about shape, weight or eating, and childhood obesity.

In the second study (Dominy *et al.* 2000), women with BED were compared with obese and non-obese women without eating disorders with regard to perception of their parents. Women with BED reported greater paternal (not maternal) neglect and rejection than did non-obese women, while the obese women without BED did not differ significantly from the other two groups. Perceived paternal neglect and rejection are therefore classified as retrospective correlates. Because no clinical control groups were included, the specificity of these correlates is not known.

The third study (Striegel-Moore *et al.* 2002) compared exposure to sexual and physical abuse, bullying and ethnicity-based discrimination in a community sample of women with BED vs healthy and psychiatric comparison subjects retrospectively. White women with BED reported significantly higher rates of sexual and physical abuse, bullying by peers and discrimination than healthy subjects, but only rates of discrimination were significantly higher in white women with BED than in psychiatric comparison subjects. Although discrimination can be considered a specific retrospective correlate in white women with BED, the remaining factors represent non-specific retrospective correlates. In black women with BED, rates of sexual and physical abuse, bullying by peers, but not discrimination were significantly higher than in healthy comparison subjects. In addition, rates of sexual abuse were significantly higher in black women with BED than in psychiatric comparison subjects. Sexual abuse can be considered a specific retrospective correlate for black women with BED, while physical abuse and bullying represent non-specific retrospective correlates for this ethnic group. With the exception of sexual and physical abuse and bullying, the majority of the above-mentioned retrospective correlates are in need of replication.

Summary and conclusions

Although many potential risk factor studies of eating disorders have been conducted, the application of rigorous risk factor methodology makes evident a number of limitations of previous research. First, the majority of so-called risk factor studies are cross-sectional, thus only allowing for the identification of correlates. Secondly, although the majority of longitudinal studies included sample sizes of several hundred subjects, the samples are still too small for consistent and meaningful risk factor detection of full syndromes of eating disorders. Given the low prevalence of eating disorders, especially of AN, this is not surprising. Thirdly, longitudinal evidence of risk factors is much stronger for BN and binge-related syndromes, whereas our knowledge of risk factors for AN is still very limited. When attrition rates of longitudinal studies are taken into account, one may question whether risk factor identification for full syndromes of AN is possible at all. Fourthly, because of the overlap of the different full and partial syndromes in longitudinal studies, current research does not permit a valid differentiation of risk factors for BN vs BED vs partial syndromes.

Table 5.1   Risk factors and retrospective correlates for anorexia nervosa

Time	Risk factors and retrospective correlates* for anorexia nervosa
Birth	• Genetic factors • Gender • Ethnicity • Pregnancy complications, gestational age • Preterm birth, birth trauma • Season of birth
Childhood	• Early childhood health problems • Digestive problems, picky eating, anorexic symptoms • Eating conflicts, struggles around meals, unpleasant meals • Intercountry adoption and foster care • *Feeding and gastrointestinal problems* • *Infant sleep difficulties* • *High-concern parenting* • *Childhood anxiety disorders* • *Acculturation* • *Obsessive-compulsive personality disorder and traits* • *Sexual abuse, adverse life events* • *Higher levels of loneliness, shyness and inferiority*
Adolescence	• Adolescent age • Early pubertal timing • Weight concerns/dieting (binge-eating subtype) • *High level of exercise* • *Obsessive-compulsive disorders* • *Body dysmorphic disorder* • *Greater level of exposure to personal, environmental and dieting risk domains (e.g. negative self-evaluation, perfectionism)*

* Retrospective correlates are shown in italic.

To summarize, the following factors have consistently been reported as risk factors for eating disorders and partial syndromes in longitudinal studies and as fixed markers and retrospective correlates in cross-sectional studies. Genetic factors, female gender, ethnicity (not Asian) and pregnancy complications represent fixed markers for eating disorders. In addition, early childhood health, feeding, eating and gastrointestinal problems are precursors of later adolescent syndromes. Furthermore, childhood and adolescent adversity, including both sexual and physical adverse experiences, have to be considered as early precursors of AN, BN and BED.

Although childhood anxiety disorders in general are retrospective correlates with a high probability of increasing the risk for both anorexia and bulimia nervosa, retrospectively assessed obsessive-compulsive personality traits and perfectionism were found specifically in AN. In adolescence, which itself constitutes a risk period, eating disorders seem to be foreshadowed by negative

Table 5.2   Risk factors and retrospective correlates for bulimia nervosa

Time	Risk factors and retrospective correlates* for bulimia nervosa
Birth	• Genetic factors • Gender • Ethnicity • *Pregnancy complications*
Childhood	• Early childhood health problems • Anxiety–depression • Sexual abuse/physical neglect • *Childhood overanxious disorder* • *Childhood obesity* • *Acculturation*
Adolescence	• Adolescent age • Early pubertal timing • Weight and shape concerns/dieting/negative body image • Low self-esteem/ineffectiveness • Psychiatric morbidity/negative affectivity • 30-day alcohol consumption • Unpopular and Aggressive subscales of the Youth Self-Report (YSR) Inventory • Higher levels of neuroticism • Negative life events • Low interoception • Escape-avoidance coping • Low social support • *Sexual abuse/adverse life events* • *Greater level of exposure to personal, environmental and dieting risk domains (e.g. adverse family experiences, parental alcoholism, depression, drug abuse; parental obesity, parental critical comments on weight and shape, low contact, high expectations)* • *Social phobia* • *Prodromal symptoms* • *Higher levels of shyness*

*Retrospective correlates are shown in italic.

self-evaluation or low self-esteem, an increased risk of psychiatric morbidity, including mood- and anxiety-related syndromes (especially for BN and BED), and (probably most strongly of all) by heightened weight and shape concerns, body dissatisfaction and dieting behavior.

To date, the best-supported factors are ethnicity, gender, weight concerns and negative self-evaluation. The best-supported high-potency factors are gender and weight concerns. However, the current state of research does not support other putative factors (e.g. variables of family interaction, perfectionism, higher BMI) which have frequently been designated as risk factors in previous reviews. On the other hand, because many of the risk factors are based on a relatively

Table 5.3   Risk factors and retrospective correlates for binge-eating disorder

Time	Risk factors and retrospective correlates* for binge-eating disorder
Birth	• Genetic factors • Gender • Ethnicity
Childhood	• Sexual abuse/physical neglect • *Perceived paternal neglect and rejection* • *Childhood obesity*
Adolescence	• Dieting • Low self-esteem • High body concern, thin body preoccupation and social pressure • Negative life events • High use of escape-avoidance coping • Low perceived social support • *Greater level of exposure to personal, environmental and dieting risk domains (e.g. negative self-evaluation, major depression, marked conduct problems, deliberate self-harm; greater levels of exposure to parental criticism, high expectations, minimal affection, parental underinvolvement, and maternal low care and high overprotection)* • *Any sexual abuse/repeated severe physical abuse* • *Bullying, discrimination, critical comments by family about shape, weight or eating, and teasing about shape, weight, eating or appearance*

*Retrospective correlates are shown in italic.

small number of studies, they may be population-specific and their classification status may change with newly emerging studies. Accordingly, for most of the factors classified as risk factors, replication studies are needed. Finally, the specificity of factors has only been addressed for a few retrospective correlates of anorexia and bulimia nervosa, but not for risk factors from longitudinal studies.

Clinical implications and future directions

The majority of risk factors for eating disorders are variable factors, theoretically amenable to modification. As yet no causal factors have been confirmed (i.e. factors preceding the onset of eating disorders which change the probability of the risk of the outcome). For some of the factors found, experimental manipulation is impossible or unethical. However, for other factors (e.g. weight concerns, low self-esteem), testing the causal role is feasible. The most realistic way in which to manipulate a potential causal factor would be to target the most potent variable risk factors in a high-risk group within a preventive approach, and to show that by reducing exposure to the factor the risk of developing the disorder can be decreased compared with a low-risk group. Preliminary studies (Taylor and Altman 1997; Winzelberg *et al.* 2000) indicate that such targeted approaches may result in stronger effects than those found in previous, more universal (e.g. school-based) preventive approaches. Large-scale studies testing the causal status of variable risk factors in high-risk samples are currently under way, and these will help to clarify further the status of specific factors.

Finally, as was pointed out above, some of the risk factors and retrospective correlates (e.g. some parental factors, early feeding, eating and gastrointestinal problems) are already present at birth or during the first years of a child's life. To manipulate these, preventive interventions would have to target parental attitudes and behaviors. To our knowledge, none of the prevention programs to date have focused on or included parents in order to reduce the risk for their children. Alternatively, preventive interventions may have to be tailored for children of younger ages in order to address early childhood factors. As a consequence of the improved knowledge of risk factors during different developmental periods, current preventive interventions may have to be adapted. These differential recommendations may then result in improved effectiveness of preventive interventions in the future.

Corresponding author: Corinna Jacobi, Dipl. Psych., Clinical Psychology and Psychotherapy Technical University, Chemnitzer Str. 46, D-01187 Dresden, Germany. E-mail: cjacobi@psychologie.tu-dresden.de

References

Abraham S (1996a) Eating and weight-controlling behaviors of young ballet dancers. *Psychopathology.* **29**: 218–22.

Abraham S (1996b) Characteristics of eating disorders among young ballet dancers. *Psychopathology.* **29**: 223–9.

American Psychiatric Association (1994) *Diagnostic and Statistical Manual of Mental Disorders* (4e). American Psychiatric Association, Washington, DC.

Anderluh MB, Tchanturia K, Rabe-Hesketh S and Treasure J (2003) Childhood obsessive-compulsive personality traits in adult women with eating disorders: defining a broader eating disorder phenotype. *Am J Psychiatry.* **160**: 242–7.

Attie I and Brooks-Gunn J (1989) Development of eating problems in adolescent girls: a longitudinal study. *Dev Psychol.* **25**: 70–79.

Bastiani AM, Rao R, Weltzin T and Kaye WH (1995) Perfectionism in anorexia nervosa. *Int J Eat Disord.* **17**: 147–52.

Blazer DG, Kessler RC, McGonagle KA and Swartz MS (1994) The prevalence and distribution of major depression in a national community sample: the National Comorbidity Survey. *Am J Psychiatry.* **151**: 979–86.

Braistedt JR, Mellin L, Gong EJ and Irwin CE Jr (1985) The adolescent ballet dancer. Nutritional practices and characteristics associated with anorexia nervosa. *J Adolesc Health Care.* **6**: 365–71.

Brewerton TD, Dansky BS, Kilpatrick DG and O'Neil PM (2000) Which comes first in the pathogenensis of bulimia nervosa – dieting or bingeing? *Int J Eat Disord.* **28**: 259–64.

Bruch H (1962) Perceptual and conceptual disturbances in anorexia nervosa. *Psychosom Med.* **14**: 187–94.

Bruch H (1973) *Eating Disorders: obesity, anorexia nervosa, and the person within*. Basic Books, New York.

Button EJ, Sonuga-Barke EJS, Davies J and Thompson M (1996) A prospective study of self-esteem in the prediction of eating problems in adolescent schoolgirls: questionnaire findings. *Br J Clin Psychol*. **35**: 193–203.

Calam R and Waller G (1998) Are eating and psychosocial characteristics in early teenage years useful predictors of eating characteristics in early adulthood? A 7-year longitudinal study. *Int J Eat Disord*. **24**: 351–62.

Casper RC and Lubomirsky S (1997) Individual psychopathology relative to reports of unwanted sexual experiences as predictor of a bulimic eating pattern. *Int J Eat Disord*. **21**: 229–36.

Cevera S, Lahortiga F, Martinez-Gonzáles MA, Gual P, Irala-Estévez J de and Alonso Y (2003) Neuroticism and low self-esteem as risk factors for incident eating disorders in a prospective cohort study. *Int J Eat Disord*. **33**: 271–80.

Chen CN, Wong J, Lee N, Chan-Ho MW, Lau JT and Fung M (1993) The Shatin Community mental health survey in Hong Kong. II. Major findings. *Arch Gen Psychiatry*. **50**: 125–33.

Cnattingius S, Hultman CM, Dahl M and Sparén P (1999) Very preterm birth, birth trauma, and the risk of anorexia nervosa among girls. *Arch Gen Psychiatry*. **56**: 634–8.

Crago M, Shisslak CM and Estes LS (1996) Eating disturbances among American minority groups: a review. *Int J Eat Disord*. **19**: 239–48.

Dansky BS, Brewerton TD, Kilpatrick DG and O'Neal PM (1997) The National Women's Study: relationship of victimization and post-traumatic stress disorder to bulimia nervosa. *Int J Eat Disord*. **21**: 213–28.

Davis C, Fox J, Cowles M, Hastings P and Schwass K (1990) The functional role of exercise in the development of weight and diet concerns in women. *J Psychosom Res*. **34**: 563–74.

Davis C, Katzman DK, Kaptein S *et al*. (1997) The prevalence of high-level exercise in the eating disorders: etiological implications. *Compr Psychiatry*. **38**: 321–6.

Dominy NL, Johnson WB and Koch C (2000) Perception of parental acceptance in women with binge-eating disorder. *J Psychol*. **134**: 23–36.

Fairburn CG, Welch SL, Doll HA, Davies BA and O'Connor ME (1997) Risk factors for bulimia nervosa. A community-based case–control study. *Arch Gen Psychiatry*. 54: 509–17.

Fairburn CG, Doll HA, Welch SL, Hay PJ, Davies BA and O'Connor ME (1998) Risk factors for binge-eating disorder: a community-based case–control study. *Arch Gen Psychiatry*. **55**: 425–32.

Fairburn CG, Cooper Z, Doll HA and Welch SL (1999) Risk factors for anorexia nervosa. Three integrated case–control comparisons. *Arch Gen Psychiatry*. **56**: 468–76.

Folsom V, Krahn D, Nairn K, Gold L, Demitrack MA and Silk KR (1993) The impact of sexual and physical abuse on eating-disordered and psychiatric symptoms: a comparison of eating-disordered and psychiatric inpatients. *Int J Eat Disord*. **13**: 249–57.

Friedmann MA, Wilfley DE, Welch RR and Kunce JT (1997) Self-directed hostility and family functioning in normal-weight bulimics and overweight binge eaters. *Addict Behav*. **22**: 367–75.

Garfinkel PE, Modolfsky H and Garner DM (1980) The heterogeneity of anorexia nervosa: bulimia as a distinct subgroup. *Arch Gen Psychiatry*. **37**: 1036–40.

Garfinkel PE, Garner DM, Rose J *et al*. (1983) A comparison of characteristics in the families of patients with anorexia nervosa and normal controls. *Psychol Med*. **13**: 821–8.

Garfinkel PE, Lin E, Goering P *et al*. (1995) Bulimia nervosa in a Canadian community sample: prevalence and comparison of subgroups. *Am J Psychiatry*. **152**: 1052–8.

Garner DM and Garfinkel PE (1978) Sociocultural factors in anorexia nervosa. *Lancet*. **2**: 674.

Ghaderi A and Scott B (2001) Prevalence, incidence and prospective risk factors for eating disorders. *Acta Psychiatr Scand*. **104**: 122–30.

Graber JA, Brooks-Gunn J, Paikoff RL and Warren MP (1994) Prediction of eating problems: an 8-year study of adolescent girls. *Dev Psychol*. **30**: 823–34.

Graber JA, Lewinsohn PM, Seeley JR and Brooks-Gunn J (1997) Is psychopathology associated with the timing of pubertal development? *J Am Acad Child Adolesc Psychiatry*. **36**: 1768–76.

Haiman C and Devlin MJ (1999) Binge eating before the onset of dieting: a distinct subgroup of bulimia nervosa? *Int J Eat Disord*. **25**: 151–7.

Hayward C, Killen JD, Wilson DM *et al.* (1997) Psychiatric risk associated with early puberty in adolescent girls. *J Am Acad Child Adolesc Psychiatry*. **36**: 255–62.

Hayward C, Killen JD, Kraemer HC and Taylor CB (2000) Predictors of panic attacks in adolescents. *J Am Acad Child Adolesc Psychiatry*. **39**: 207–14.

Hsu LKG (1996) Epidemiology of the eating disorders. *Psychiatr Clin North Am*. **19**: 681–700.

Hultman CM, Sparén P, Takei N, Murray RM and Cnattingius S (1999) Prenatal and perinatal risk factors for schizophrenia, affective psychosis and reactive psychosis of an early onset: case–control study. *BMJ*. **318**: 421–6.

Ingram RE and Price JM (eds) (2000) *Vulnerability to Psychopathology*. Guilford Press, New York.

Jacobi C, Hayward C, de Zwaan M, Kraemer H and Agras WS (2004a) Coming to terms with risk factors for eating disorders: application of risk terminology and suggestions for a general taxonomy. *Psychol Bull*. **130**: 19–65.

Jacobi C, Paul Th, de Zwaan M, Nutzinger DO and Dahme B (2004b) The specificity of self-concept disturbances in eating disorders. *Int J Eat Disord*. **35**: 1–7.

Johnson C, Powers PS and Dick R (1999) Athletes and eating disorders: the National Collegiate Athletic Association Study. *Int J Eat Disord*. **26**: 179–88.

Johnson JG, Cohen P, Kasen S and Brook JS (2002) Childhood adversities associated with risk for eating disorders or weight problems during adolescence or early adulthood. *Am J Psychiatry*. **159**: 394–400.

Kaye WH, Greeno CG, Moss H *et al.* (1998) Alterations in serotonin activity and psychiatric symptoms after recovery from bulimia nervosa. *Arch Gen Psychiatry*. **55**: 927–35.

Kazdin AE, Kraemer HC, Kessler RC, Kupfer DJ and Offord DR (1997) Contributions of risk factor research to developmental psychopathology. *Clin Psychol Rev*. **17**: 375–406.

Killen JD, Taylor CB, Hayward C *et al.* (1994) Pursuit of thinness and onset of eating disorder symptoms in a community sample of adolescent girls: a three-year prospective analysis. *Int J Eat Disord*. **16**: 227–38.

Killen JD, Taylor CB, Hayward C *et al.* (1996) Weight concerns influence the development of eating disorders: a 4-year prospective study. *J Consult Clin Psychol*. **64**: 936–40.

Kotler LA, Cohen P, Davies M, Pine DS and Walsh BT (2001) Longitudinal relationships between childhood, adolescent and adult eating disorders. *J Am Acad Child Adolesc Psychiatry*. **40**: 1424–40.

Kraemer HC, Kazdin AE, Offord DR, Kessler RC, Jensen PS and Kupfer DJ (1997) Coming to terms with the terms of risk. *Arch Gen Psychiatry*. **54**: 337–43.

Kurtzman FD, Yager J, Landsverk J, Wiesmeier E and Bodurka DC (1989) Eating disorders among selected female student populations at UCLA. *J Am Diet Assoc*. **89**: 45–53.

Leon GR, Fulkerson JA, Perry CL and Early-Zald MB (1995) Prospective analysis of personality and behavioral influences in the later development of disordered eating. *J Abnorm Psychol*. **104**: 140–9.

Leon GR, Fulkerson JA, Perry CL, Keel PK and Klump KL (1999) Three- to four-year prospective evaluation of personality and behavioral risk factors for later disordered eating in adolescent girls and boys. *J Youth Adolesc*. **28**: 181–96.

Lewinsohn PM, Hops H, Roberts RE, Seeley JR and Andrews JA (1993) Adolescent psychopathology. I. Prevalence and incidence of depression and other DSM-III-R disorders in high-school students. *J Abnorm Psychol.* **102**: 133–44.

Lindberg L and Hjern A (2003) Risk factors for anorexia nervosa: a national cohort study. *Int J Eat Disord.* **34**: 397–408.

McKnight Investigators (2003) Risk factors for the onset of eating disorders in adolescent girls: results of the McKnight longitudinal risk factor study. *Am J Psychiatry.* **160**: 248–54.

McNamara K and Loveman C (1990) Differences in family functioning among bulimics, repeat dieters and nondieters. *J Clin Psychol.* **46**: 518–23.

Marchi M and Cohen P (1990) Early childhood eating behaviors and adolescent eating disorders. *J Am Acad Child Adolesc Psychiatry.* **29**: 112–17.

Minuchin S, Rosman BL and Baker L (1978) *Psychosomatic Families: anorexia nervosa in context.* Harvard University Press, Cambridge, MA.

Mitchell JE, Hatsukami D, Pyle RL and Eckert ED (1986) The bulimia syndrome: course of the illness and associated problems. *Compr Psychiatry.* **27**: 165–70.

Mitchell JE, Specker SM and de Zwaan M (1991) Comorbidity and medical complications of bulimia nervosa. *J Clin Psychiatry.* **52 (Suppl. 10)**: 13–20.

Moorhead DJ, Stashwick CK, Reinherz HZ, Giaconia RM, Striegel-Moore RM and Paradis AD (2003) Child and adolescent predictors for eating disorders in a community population of young adult women. *Int J Eat Disord.* **33**: 1–9.

Mussell MP, Mitchell JE, Fenna CJ, Crosby RD, Miller JP and Hoberman HM (1997) A comparison of onset of binge eating versus dieting in the development of bulimia nervosa. *Int J Eat Disord.* **21**: 353–60.

Nielsen S (1990) The epidemiology of anorexia nervosa in Denmark from 1973 to 1987: a nationwide register study of psychiatric admission. *Acta Psychiatr Scand.* **81**: 507–14.

Ohzeki T, Hanaki K, Motozumi H *et al.* (1990) Prevalence of obesity, leanness and anorexia nervosa in Japanese boys and girls aged 12–14 years. *Ann Nutr Metab.* **34**: 208–12.

Patton GC, Johnson-Sabine E, Wood K, Mann AH and Wakeling A (1990) Abnormal eating attitudes in London schoolgirls: A prospective epidemiological study. Outcome at twelve month follow-up. *Psychol Med.* **20**: 383–94.

Patton GC, Selzer R, Coffey C, Carlin JB and Wolfe R (1999) Onset of adolescent eating disorders: population-based cohort study over 3 years. *BMJ.* **318**: 765–8.

Pine DS, Cohen P, Gurley D, Brook J and Ma Y (1998) The risk for early adulthood anxiety and depressive disorders in adolescents with anxiety and depressive disorders. *Arch Gen Psychiatry.* **55**: 56–64.

Pope HG and Hudson JI (1992) Is childhood sexual abuse a risk factor for bulimia nervosa? *Am J Psychiatry.* **149**: 455–63.

Pyle RL, Mitchell MD and Eckert ED (1981) Bulimia: a report of 34 cases. *J Clin Psychiatry.* **42**: 60–64.

Russell GF (1979) Bulimia nervosa: an ominous variant of anorexia nervosa. *Psychol Med.* **9**: 429–48.

Schotte DE and Stunkard AJ (1987) Bulimia vs bulimic behaviors on a college campus. *JAMA.* **258**: 1213–15.

Shisslak CM, McKeon RT and Crago M (1990) Family dysfunction in normal weight bulimic and bulimic anorexic families. *J Clin Psychol.* **46**: 185–9.

Spitzer RL, Devlin M, Walsh BT *et al.* (1992) Binge-eating disorder: a multi-site field trial of the diagnostic criteria. *Int J Eat Disord.* **11**: 191–203.

Srinivasagam NM, Kaye WH, Plotnicov KH, Greeno C, Weltzin TE and Rao R (1995) Persistent perfectionism, symmetry, and exactness after long-term recovery from anorexia nervosa. *Am J Psychiatry.* **152**: 1630–4.

Steiger H and Zanko M (1990) Sexual traumata among eating-disordered, psychiatric and normal female groups. *J Interpers Violence*. **5**: 74–86.

Striegel-Moore R and Smolak L (1996) The role of race in the development of eating disorders. In: L Smolak, MP Levine and R Striegel-Moore (eds) *The Developmental Psychopathology of Eating Disorders*. Lawrence Erlbaum Associates, Mahwah, NJ, pp. 259–84.

Striegel-Moore RH, Schreiber GB, Lo A, Crawford P, Obarzanek E and Roding J (2000) Eating disorder symptoms in a cohort of 11- to 16-year-old black and white girls: the NHLBI growth and health study. *Int J Eat Disord*. **27**: 49–66.

Striegel-Moore RH, Dohm F-A, Pike KM, Wilfley DE and Fairburn CG (2002) Abuse, bullying, and discrimination as risk factors for binge-eating disorder. *Am J Psychiatry*. **159**: 1902–7.

Strober M and Humphrey LL (1987) Familial contributions to the etiology and course of anorexia nervosa and bulimia. *J Consult Clin Psychol*. **55**: 654–9.

Sundgot-Borgen J (1994) Risk and trigger factors for the development of eating disorders in female elite athletes. *Med Sci Sports Exerc*. **26**: 414–19.

Taylor CB and Altman T (1997) Priorities in prevention research for eating disorders. *Psychopharmacol Bull*. **33**: 413–17.

Troop NA and Bifulco A (2002) Childhood social arena and cognitive sets in eating disorders. *Br J Clin Psychol*. **41**: 205–11.

Vize CM and Cooper PJ (1995) Sexual abuse in patients with eating disorder, patients with depression and normal controls. A comparative study. *Br J Psychiatry*. **167**: 80–85.

Vollrath M, Koch R and Angst J (1992) Binge eating and weight concerns among young adults. Results from the Zurich Cohort Study. *Br J Psychiatry*. **160**: 498–503.

Waller G, Calam R and Slade P (1989) Eating disorders and family interaction. *Br J Clin Psychol*. **28**: 285–6.

Watkins B, Willoughby K, Waller G, Serpell L and Lask B (2002) Pattern of birth in anorexia nervosa: early-onset cases in the United Kingdom. *Int J Eat Disord*. **32**: 11–17.

Webster JJ and Palmer RL (2000) The childhood and family background of women with clinical eating disorders: a comparison with women with major depression and women without psychiatric disorder. *Psychol Med*. **30**: 53–60.

Welch SL and Fairburn CG (1994) Sexual abuse and bulimia nervosa: three integrated case–control comparisons. *Am J Psychiatry*. **151**: 402–7.

Whitaker AH, Johnson J, Shaffer D *et al.* (1990) Uncommon troubles in young people: prevalence estimates of selected psychiatric disorders in a non-referred adolescent population. *Arch Gen Psychiatry*. **47**: 487–96.

Winzelberg AJ, Eppstein D, Eldredge KL *et al.* (2000) Effectiveness of an Internet-based program for reducing risk factors for eating disorders. *J Consult Clin Psychol*. **68**: 346–50.

Wonderlich SA and Mitchell JE (1997) Eating disorders and comorbidity: empirical, conceptual and clinical implications. *Psychopharmacol Bull*. **33**: 381–90.

Wonderlich SA, Brewerton TD, Jocic Z, Dansky B and Abbott DW (1997) Relationship of childhood sexual abuse and eating disorders. *J Am Acad Child Adolesc Psychiatry*. **36**: 1107–15.

Woodside DB and Garfinkel P (1992) Age of onset in eating disorders. *Int J Eat Disord*. **12**: 31–6.

6

Self-help for eating disorders

Sarah Perkins and Ulrike Schmidt

Abstract

Objectives of review. The aim is to review studies published during the period 2002–2003 that have evaluated the acceptability, efficacy, effectiveness and cost-effectiveness of self-help treatments with or without guidance by a professional against no treatment or against other types of self-help (symptom-specific vs non-specific), medication or specialist psychological treatments in child and adult patients with eating disorders.

Summary of recent findings. We identified three systematic reviews, seven randomized controlled trials and four other studies that evaluated the use of self-help interventions in eating disorders during the index period 2002–2003. Self-help with some guidance from a professional is superior to waiting list in patients with bulimia nervosa and related disorders, whereas the efficacy of unguided self-help compared with waiting list, at least in patients presenting to specialist settings, is uncertain. Guided self-help seems to be as effective as some forms of specialist care in some settings. There is insufficient evidence to determine the relative efficacy of medication and self-help alone or in combination.

Future directions. Future research will need to concentrate on the effectiveness and cost-effectiveness of self-help methods in different (non-specialist) settings. Interactive computerized methods of self-help may be a fruitful area for development. Self-help for anorexia nervosa is currently under-researched.

Introduction

Go into any major bookshop and you will be sure to find a large section on 'self-help' – that is, books and other materials (audio- and videotapes) written for the lay public giving information and advice on an often motley range of topics, from physical to psychological disorders and various life crises and problems. Books on diet and weight-related issues abound, together with a good smattering of those on eating disorders. The content and quality of these books vary widely, but the many yards of shelf-space occupied attest to the growing popularity of self-help approaches, with at least one survey suggesting that self-help approaches for some psychological disorders are more popular with the general public than medication or psychotherapy (Jorm *et al.* 1997).

Clinicians and researchers use more specific definitions of self-help (SH, or self-management, self-care, self-instruction or bibliotherapy as it is sometimes called) (*see*, for example, Marrs 1995; Cuijpers 1997). One researcher defined self-help as 'the use of written materials or computer programs or the listening to/viewing of audio/video tapes for the purpose of gaining understanding or solving problems relevant to a person's developmental or therapeutic needs' (Marrs 1995). SH treatment goes beyond providing people with one-off information (Cuijpers 1997) or mere support, in that it implies a more structured approach, translating a psychological treatment based on a clear model into a program which people can follow over time. SH treatments are thus program led, contain a longitudinal element and require the participant to follow the advice provided by the self-help material, carry out tasks and then evaluate what has been achieved. SH aims to improve clinical outcome by teaching users relevant skills to overcome and manage their health problem. SH treatments can be provided independently from (pure or unguided SH) or in addition to (guided SH) sessions with a healthcare practitioner or lay person (Williams 2003). If guidance is provided, the aim is for the SH material to do some of the work of treatment and thereby reduce the number and/or length of sessions that patients require with a therapist. Guidance can fulfill a number of functions:

> Guidance may encompass clarifying material, answering questions, helping the participant to remain on task, and modifying the program to fit the individual's needs, all of which may make the didactic materials more readily accessible to users with diverse levels of literacy or educational backgrounds. In addition, guidance allows initial screening, ongoing risk assessment, and referral for additional or alternative treatments, as needed.
>
> (Wells *et al.* 1997, p. 342)

Thus there is a continuum between pure and guided self-help and brief structured (typically cognitive–behavioral) therapies, which are therapist led.

Self-help for eating disorders before 2002

In parallel to the general rise in interest in self-help, during the early 1990s there was a dramatic rise in the number of individuals presenting for treatment of bulimia nervosa (BN) (Turnbull *et al.* 1996). By then cognitive–behavioral therapy (CBT) had become established as the gold-standard treatment for this condition, initially with very optimistic estimates of the rates of recovery that this treatment would produce. However, many sufferers were unable to access CBT or only accessed it after long delays. There was also a growing recognition that not everyone might need a full course of CBT (typically 16 to 20 sessions), and that some patients might be treated perfectly adequately with briefer interventions. This led to the notion of stepped care for BN with the recommendation that more minimal, less costly interventions should be offered routinely as a first step, with more intensive, costly interventions reserved for more complex cases. Manual-based SH treatments involving CBT for BN and related conditions were developed and evaluated by a number of investigators in order to bridge these gaps. Evidence from early cohort studies and randomized controlled trials suggested that the use of both pure and guided self-help seemed acceptable and feasible in patients with BN, and that the therapeutic gains made were maintained over time. It was thought that these approaches might be as effective as full CBT in many patients and could be used in stepped-care models of delivery of treatment (for reviews, see Birchall and Palmer 2002; Carter 2003). Gradually, manualized CBT self-help applications also began to be used in the treatment of binge-eating disorder (BED) and, similar to the findings in BN, were shown to have promise in terms of a successful and sustained reduction in/cessation of binge eating in many sufferers.

Thus, in summary, the literature up to and including 2001 demonstrated the feasibility and preliminary efficacy of pure and guided manual-based SH in both BN and BED. There was no evidence available with regard to the efficacy of SH for anorexia nervosa (AN), and no evidence on the use of other SH modalities (e.g. audio- or videotapes, computerized applications).

Aims and methodology of the present review

The aims of the present paper were to review studies (randomized controlled trials (RCTs) and cohort studies) published during 2002–2003 evaluating the acceptability, efficacy, effectiveness and cost-effectiveness of SH treatments with or without guidance against no treatment, other types of SH (symptom-specific or non-specific), medication or specialist psychological treatments in child and adult patients with eating disorders.

Studies of people at risk of developing eating disorders were not included. SH was defined as the translation of a psychological treatment based on a clear model into materials that employ a media-based format for treatment, such as a book, computer or videotape, with the aim of improving clinical outcome by teaching users relevant skills to overcome and manage their health problem (Williams 2003). We excluded research on supportive SH groups, which were not program led. The literature search conducted for the present piece was part of the search for trials for a systematic review on 'Self-help and guided self-help treatments in eating disorders' for the Depression, Anxiety and Neurosis Group of the Cochrane Collaboration with a review date of 31 December 2003. Relevant trials were identified by searching a number of electronic databases, hand searching relevant journals, examining the grey literature, reference searching and personal contact. Details of the full search strategy are published in the abstract for the Cochrane Review (Schmidt et al. 2003). Cohort studies and systematic reviews were identified using the similar search terms for the period 2002–2003 (hereafter referred to as the index period).

Recent research on the efficacy and effectiveness of self-help in eating disorders

We found three systematic reviews, seven RCTs and four other studies published during the index period containing information relevant to the questions addressed in this chapter. Two of the systematic reviews were conducted by Hay and Bacaltchuk (2003a, 2003b), and the third was conducted by the Guidelines Development Group of the National Guideline for Eating Disorders for England and Wales (National Collaborating Centre for Mental Health (NCCMH) 2004). This latter systematic review took the review by Hay and Bacaltchuk (2003a) produced for the Cochrane Collaboration as its starting point, but conducted a new systematic review of the evidence of psychologic and pharmacologic treatments of BN and BED. The review covered studies up to and including July 2003 (i.e. well into the index period). In the following account, we summarize the evidence, firstly in relation to the meta-analytical findings of this most up-to-date systematic review, and secondly describing all of the RCTs contributing to the evidence over the last two years, whether or not they were included in the systematic review. The findings of all seven RCTs published on the topic of self-help during the index period can also be found in Table 6.1. All RCTs, whether published during the index period or before it, concerned the delivery of SH through books rather than any other form of delivery. Studies published prior to the index period on the whole evaluated the efficacy of SH in pure samples of BN patients or BED patients, studies published during the index period either covered BN patients only or contained a mixture of BN, partial BN and BED patients.

Evidence from the NCCMH systematic review

Separate literature reviews for BN and BED were conducted as part of this systematic review. Based on limited evidence from a meta-analysis of two randomized controlled trials in BN patients (Treasure et al. 1994; Carter et al. 2003) (also see Table 6.1), the NCCMH review concluded that it was unlikely that pure SH compared with waiting list improves remission from binge eating/ purging by the end of treatment ($n = 139$; bingeing: RR (relative risk) = 0.96; 95% CI = 0.85–1.09; purging: RR = 0.97; 95% CI = 0.87–1.07).

For all other comparisons addressed by the systematic review and relating to the use of guided or unguided self-help (e.g. pure SH vs guided SH for BED, pure or guided SH vs specialist treatment in BN and SH vs antidepressants in BN), the conclusion was that there was insufficient evidence to determine whether SH differed from these other interventions in terms of key outcomes, such as remission rates of bingeing and vomiting.

Table 6.1 Randomized controlled trials published/in press during the index period (2002–2003)

Author	Comparison groups	Guider of SH	Therapist contact time	Duration and follow-up	Patients & setting	Eating disorder-related outcomes	Quality criteria	Comment
Bailer et al. (2004)	GSH[a] (n = 40) vs CBT (n = 41)	Psychiatry residents with no prior experience of eating disorders or formal psychotherapy training	GSH: 18 weekly visits of up to 20 minutes each CBT: 18 weekly sessions of 90 minutes each	Follow-up 1 year after end of treatment	DSM-IV diagnosis for BN; Outpatient clinic for eating disorders	1: Frequency of bingeing and vomiting episodes in month preceding treatment and follow-up assessed by self-report Eating Disorder Questionnaire (Mitchell et al. 1985) Patient classified as fully 'recovered' if they were abstinent from bingeing or purging during preceding month; 'remitted' if bingeing or purging episodes more than twice a week	1: Individuals were assigned to groups upon enrollment which were subsequently randomized to each condition. Concealment of randomization not specified. 2: GSH: 25 subjects (62.5%) participated in 1-year follow-up (including 2 treatment dropouts) CBT: 30 subjects (73.1%) participated in follow-up (including 5 dropouts) 3: Primary outcomes specified. No mention of power calculation	30 subjects (75%) in GSH and 26 (63.4%) in CBT completed treatment. Dropouts: 10/40 subjects (25%) in GSH and 15/41 subjects (36.6%) in CBT At end of treatment: no differences between groups in proportion recovered and remitted (based on intent to treat): 3 subjects (7.5%) in GSH and 5 subjects (12.2%) in CBT recovered; 16 subjects (40%) in GSH and 12 subjects (29.3%) in CBT remitted. At follow-up: 9 subjects (22.5%) in GSH and 6 subjects (14.6%) in CBT recovered; 20 subjects (50%) in GSH and 15 subjects (36.6%) in CBT remitted. Completer analysis: in GSH significantly more 'recovered' subjects. Significant difference in number of subjects who binged less than twice a week: GSC (73.9%) vs CBT (44%)

continued

Table 6.1 (Continued)

Author	Comparison groups	Guider of SH	Therapist contact time	Duration and follow-up	Patients & setting	Eating disorder-related outcomes	Quality criteria	Comment
Banasiak et al. (2001)	GSH[b] (n = 54) vs delayed treatment control (DTC) group (n = 55)	GP guider	10 sessions, each 20–30 minutes in duration	3, 6 and 12-month follow-up	DSM-IV BN: primary care setting	1: Eating-related pathology measured by EDE	1: Blind randomization 2: 3-month follow-up of 30 subjects (55.6%) from GSH 3: Primary outcome not specified. Power calculation not available	Completed treatment: 36/54 subjects (66.7%) completed treatment in GSH group and 39/55 subjects (70.9%) in DTC group completed end of DTC analyses GSH: post-test: 46% and 33% remitted in bingeing and purging behaviors DTC: post-test: 13% and 12% remitted from bingeing and purging GSH: 3-month follow-up: 58% and 39% remitted from bingeing and purging. 6-month follow-up: 60% and 50% remitted from bingeing and purging
Carter et al. (2003)	PSH with BN-specific self-help book[b] (n = 28) vs SH with non-specific manual[c] (n = 28) vs waiting list (n = 29)	No guider	Not applicable	Treatment phase lasted 2 months. No follow-up	DSM-IV BN; specialist clinic setting	1: Frequency of objective binge eating, compensatory behaviors and eating-related pathology assessed by EDE interview	1: Restricted randomization procedure employing random permuted blocks of three people used. Randomization concealment by envelope. Blind assessments took place before and after treatment.	23.5% dropped out: 5 subjects (17.9%) from CBT SH; 7 subjects (25%) from non-specific SH; 8 subjects (27.6%) from WL Intention-to-treat analysis: 53.6% in CBT SH, 50% in non-specific SH and 31% on waiting list had a 50% reduction in bingeing or purging post-treatment. No significant difference

					2: Not applicable 3: Primary outcome specified a priori. No mention of power calculation	between SH conditions. Primary outcome results unchanged in completer analysis
Durand and King (2003)	GSH[b] (n = 34) vs specialist clinic treatment (e.g. IPT, CBT) (n = 34) GP Time allowed with GP not specified. Participants asked to work through manual and keep in regular contact with GP	6- and 9-month follow-up (from baseline)	DSM-IV BN; primary care vs specialist clinic setting	1: Self-report score on Bulimic Investigatory Test, Edinburgh (Henderson and Freeman 1987)	1: Stratified block randomization used. Randomization concealment by envelope. First author who interviewed participants was not blind to treatment allocation. Unblind assessment at follow-up. 2: GSH: 64.7% and 76.5% followed up at 6 and 9 months. Specialist care: 82.4% followed up at 6 and 9 months. 3: Primary outcome specified. No mention of power calculation	GSH: 34 subjects received allocated intervention Specialist treatment: 26 subjects received allocated intervention Intention-to-treat analysis: significant main effect for time but not for intervention by group Both groups improved significantly over time, with no difference between them. Analysing only patients with full data led to the same results

continued

Table 6.1 (Continued)

Author	Comparison groups	Guider of SH	Therapist contact time	Duration and follow-up	Patients & setting	Eating disorder-related outcomes	Quality criteria	Comment
Ghaderi and Scott (2003)	PSH[b] (n = 15) vs GSH[b] (n = 16)	Specially trained undergraduate psychology students	6–8 sessions (25 minutes each)	6 months	DSM-IV BN, BED or EDNOS with binge eating as principal problem. Treatment setting not specified	1: Reduction in behavioral symptoms on EDE scales	1: Concealment of randomization 2: 18 subjects (58%) followed up 3: Primary outcomes not specified. No mention of power calculation	Dropouts: 6 subjects from PSH and 7 subjects from GSH. In intent-to-treat analysis, participants reduced binge-eating episodes by 33% over course of treatment. This was 58% for treatment completers (n = 18). No significant differences between pure and guided SH. Mean percentage reduction in bingeing and purging for GSH was 33% and 25%, respectively. Corresponding figures for PSH were 33% and 28%, respectively. No further significant improvements or deterioration at follow-up
Palmer et al. (2002)	SH book[b] plus minimal one-off guidance (n = 32) vs SH book[b] plus telephone guidance (n = 28) vs SH book[b] plus	Nurse therapists experienced in treatment of eating disorders	SH and phone guidance: 4 × 30 minutes SH and face-to-face guidance: 4 × 30 minutes	Treatment took place over 4 months 8-month follow-up (follow-up 8 and 12 months after baseline)	DSM-IV full or partial BN or BED; specialist eating disorders service	1: Percentage change in key behavioral symptoms on EDE scales (objective binge episodes, self-induced vomiting and global score).	1: Randomization concealment by envelope. Research assessor not masked to treatment assignment	SH with minimal guidance not superior to waiting list. SH with guidance, in particular GSF-F was superior to waiting list. Initial guided SH was associated with a lower final dropout than being on a waiting list

Study	Intervention	Therapist	Self-help format	Diagnosis/setting	Follow-up	Outcomes	Quality criteria / Results
	face-to-face guidance (n = 30) vs WL (n = 121)					No improvement: <25% reduction in key symptoms; some improvement; 25–75% improvement; significant improvement: 75%	2: At 12-month reassessment, 77 subjects (64%) seen 3: Primary outcome specified. No mention of power calculation
Walsh et al. (2004)	Placebo only (n = 22) Fluoxetine only (n = 20) vs placebo and GSH[b] (n = 25) vs fluoxetine and GSH[b] (n = 24)	Nurses with no specialized training or experience in treatment of eating disorders	GSH: 6–8 sessions, 30 minutes long (in addition to the 4 monthly sessions with physicians lasting 15 minutes received by all patients)	DSM-IV criteria for BN. Primary care setting	No follow-up	1: Frequencies of binge eating and vomiting assessed via abbreviated EDE and EDE-Q	1: Randomization process and concealment not specified 2: Not applicable 3: Primary outcomes specified. No mention of power calculation	High dropout rate: only 28 (30.8%) of 91 patients completed full course of treatment. Proportions completing full study similar for those in SH and on pills only. No significant difference in numbers of patients remitted in GSH (6/49) or pills only (4/42) conditions, for patients receiving fluoxetine (7/44) or placebo (3/47). GSH had no effect on retention or symptomatic improvement. Fluoxetine was clearly of benefit

Quality criteria: 1, concealment; 2, follow-up rate (after the end of treatment, minimum of 3–6 months) > 80%; 3, primary outcome stated with a priori power calculation. Self-help materials used: [a]German version of Schmidt U and Treasure J (1993) *Getting Better Bite by Bite*. Psychology Press, Hove, East Sussex. [b]Fairburn CG (1995) *Overcoming Binge Eating*. Guilford Press, New York. [c]Butler PE (1992) *Self-Assertion for Women*. HarperCollins, New York.

Evidence from RCTs published during the index period

Pure self-help (PSH) or guided self-help (GSH) vs waiting list

Three RCTs compared SH with no guidance, or with different intensities or types of guidance, against waiting list in patients with BN or related disorders (Banasiak *et al.* 2001; Palmer *et al.* 2002; Carter *et al.* 2003). Banasiak *et al.* (2001) compared cognitive behavioral GSH vs a delayed treatment control in 109 patients with BN in a primary care setting. Guidance for SH was provided by general practitioners. Preliminary findings suggest that at the end of treatment GSH was clearly superior to delayed treatment, and these gains were well maintained at the six-month follow-up.

Palmer *et al.* (2002) compared SH with minimal guidance, face-to-face or telephone guidance (four 30-minute sessions) and a waiting-list control in 121 patients with BN, partial BN or BED. Patients were treated in a specialist eating disorders service for adults, and the guides were nurse therapists experienced in the treatment of eating disorders. An interesting design feature of the study was that at the end of the initial SH or waiting phase, the dose of further treatment was carefully titrated depending on the treatment response. In the short term, patients who received GSH (either face to face or over the telephone) did better than those on the waiting list. However, at 12-month follow-up remission rates and overall service consumption in terms of number of sessions attended were comparable in all four groups, suggesting that SH did not save clinical input in the long term.

Carter *et al.* (2003) compared two forms of unguided SH with a waiting list in 85 patients with BN referred to a specialist eating disorder service. One of the self-help interventions used a CBT manual that specifically addressed the symptoms of BN, and the other was a non-specific SH program focused on self-assertion skills. In total, 53.6% of people who received the BN-specific self-help intervention and 50% of those who received the self-assertion intervention showed a 50% reduction in bingeing or purging post-treatment, compared with 31% of those on a waiting list. However, abstinence rates from bingeing and vomiting were low and did not differ between the three groups.

Pure self-help vs guided self-help

Two RCTs compared PSH and GSH in samples consisting of patients with BN, subthreshold BN and BED. In a very small study ($n = 31$) by Ghaderi and Scott (2003), undergraduate psychology students were trained to provide guidance. The setting of the sessions was not given, but some were conducted by telephone. Both groups improved, with no differences between them, and gains were maintained at follow-up. The study by Palmer *et al.* (2002) (*see above*) found GSH, especially if delivered face to face, to be superior to PSH in the short term. However, at 12 months these differences had disappeared. The service utilization of patients who had initially been allocated to different types of SH was similar at one year.

Pure or guided SH vs specialist treatment

Two RCTs addressed this question. One of them (Bailer *et al.* 2004) compared CBT with GSH. Both groups improved. An intention-to-treat analysis found no differences between groups in terms of remission or recovery from bulimic symptoms at the end of treatment.

The second RCT (Durand and King 2003) compared general practitioner-supported SH with specialist treatment consisting of either CBT or interpersonal therapy (IPT) in 68 BN patients. Both groups improved, with no difference in outcome.

SH vs antidepressant medication

One study (Walsh *et al.* 2004), conducted on 91 patients with BN in a primary care setting, used a four-group comparison of placebo alone, fluoxetine alone, placebo plus GSH and fluoxetine plus GSH. The dropout rate from the study was very high, with just under one-third (30.8%) of patients completing the full course of treatment, making it difficult to interpret the results. Remission rates were low, with no difference between groups in the number of patients in remission. Patients assigned to fluoxetine showed a greater reduction in binge eating and vomiting and also showed a greater improvement in psychological symptoms than those assigned to placebo, whereas GSH had no effect on retention or symptomatic improvement.

Are the gains made with SH treatment maintained in the long term?

We found one study, published during the index period, which addressed this question (Thiels *et al.* 2003). It followed up 62 patients who had previously been treated with either 16 sessions of weekly CBT or eight sessions of manual assisted GSH. In total, 45% of the original cohort were followed up, and most of the remainder could not be traced. There was no difference between those patients who did and did not complete the follow-up on either pre- or post-treatment variables. At follow-up, on average 54.2 months (SD 5.8 months) after the end of therapy, significant improvements were achieved or maintained in both groups. There were no differences between the groups in terms of the number of patients who had received additional treatment.

Other studies

Three other studies which are not RCTs deserve to be mentioned. All three address very different but important questions.

Guided SH for BN patients with comorbid impulsivity

Bell and Newns (2002) addressed the question of whether patients with comorbid multi-impulsivity can benefit from guided manual-based self-help. A cohort of 46 patients with BN, BED or EDNOS was studied. In total, 11 out of 46 patients participating in the study were assessed as multi-impulsive on a questionnaire measure. At pre-treatment both groups had similar levels of bulimic behaviors, but the multi-impulsive patients reported higher levels of depression as assessed by self-report questionnaire. Both groups showed significant improvements in symptoms of depression and bulimic behaviors. However, the multi-impulsive group remained moderately to severely depressed, and their post-treatment eating disorder symptom scores remained at sub-clinical level. This study provides preliminary evidence to suggest that patients with comorbidity may benefit from SH treatments with guidance, but may need longer or additional treatment in order to prevent relapse.

Guided SH for AN

In an ongoing controlled study conducted by Fichter *et al.* (2003), 100 patients with binge-purge AN were allocated to either six weeks of telephone-guided self-help using a cognitive–behavioral manual or to a waiting list prior to admission to a specialist inpatient program for AN. Outcomes were assessed prior to the start of inpatient treatment, at the end of inpatient treatment and at six-month follow-up. Preliminary findings suggest that uptake and acceptance of the intervention are excellent. Patients who had received GSH showed somewhat greater improvements in terms of a reduction in eating disorder pathology and depression, and the duration of admission was shorter in the SH group compared with the waiting-list group (72 days vs 60 days).

Computerized SH for BN

One study examined a cognitive–behavioral CD-ROM-based multi-media SH treatment for BN (Williams *et al.* 1998). A cohort of 60 patients with full or partial BN referred to a specialist eating disorder service was offered the CD-ROM-based treatment (Bara-Carril *et al.* 2004). Patients accessed the CD-ROM in the clinic. In total, 47 out of 60 patients (78%) took up the intervention, two further patients were withdrawn and 39 out of 45 patients were followed up at 16 weeks; 19 out of 45 patients (42%) completed all eight sessions. The proportion of patients below the DSM-IV threshold for bingeing increased from 18% at pre-treatment to 36% at follow-up, and for vomiting it increased from 30% to 69%.

A quantitative and qualitative study of the views of individuals who were offered the CD-ROM package was conducted by Murray *et al.* (2003). At pre-treatment, those who did not take up the package reported more frequent bingeing, but there were no other differences in demographics, eating disorder or comorbid symptoms compared with those who did take up the package. In terms of attitudes to SH, those who took up the treatment were more positive about the usefulness of SH for themselves. There were no differences between groups in the proportion with previous experience of using SH, views on previous SH, and views on the usefulness of SH for others. In the qualitative analysis, those who took up the treatment seemed more 'willing to give it a go' and understood that 'self-help is the first step in treatment', whereas those who did not take up the treatment viewed the CD-ROM as a 'cheap replacement' for a human therapist. There were no differences between those who did and did not take up the treatment in terms of their confidence in using computers or their knowledge of the symptoms of BN and strategies to overcome them.

Summary of important findings

Over the last two years seven randomized controlled trials and several further studies have consolidated our knowledge of the use of SH in BN and related disorders (i.e. partial BN and BED). Recent trials are small to medium-sized and of variable quality (*see* Table 6.1). The message that emerges most clearly is that for adults with BN or other bulimic disorders, guided CBT SH is superior to remaining on a waiting list, and may be as effective as specialist treatments such as CBT or interpersonal therapy. It is noteworthy that the guidance in these studies varies considerably in intensity, ranging from three or four brief telephone sessions to up to 18 face-to-face sessions. Guiders on the whole were highly sophisticated healthcare professionals, such as nurses experienced in the treatment of eating disorders (Palmer *et al.* 2002) or general practitioners (Banasiak *et al.* 2001; Durand and King 2003). Importantly, three of the studies were conducted in primary care settings supporting the use of GSH in non-specialist settings. Studies were conducted in a range of cultures and healthcare settings (Austria, Australia, Canada, Sweden, the UK and the USA), often with very different expectations and opportunities with regard to accessing psychological treatment (also *see* Bailer *et al.* 2004). This lends considerable validity to the findings.

   In contrast, PSH, at least when given to patients who have been referred to a specialist eating disorder service, may have little advantage over remaining on a waiting list. However, it could be argued that the difficulties experienced by the kind of patients who are referred to specialist tertiary care centers for eating disorders may be too complex to respond to PSH. Moreover, in this context, patients' expectations may also go against their being 'willing to give self-help a go', as in order to access care from a tertiary center, they often have to face a number of 'hurdles', including multiple assessments and delays, with the expectation that eventually they will see a 'super-specialist' rather than be asked to help themselves.

Clinical implications

Given that the existing literature on SH in eating disorders emphasizes treatment of adults with BN or BED, we shall focus on the treatment of these disorders in this section.

Implications for assessment and treatment

If SH interventions for BN and BED are to be used routinely in clinical settings, this will require careful assessment of the suitability of the client, taking into account their preferences for SH or therapist-guided approaches. In this context, healthcare professionals should routinely ask their patients about their previous use of any SH materials. Patients' reservations about the use of SH need to be explored carefully, making sure that they do not feel that they are being 'short-changed' by being offered SH. Patients also need to be made aware of what to do if a crisis occurs, or who to contact if they 'get stuck' or have questions, or if the SH approach does not work. In our view PSH should only be offered to highly motivated, resourceful patients with milder disorders. For most patients with BN who agree to work with an SH manual, it would be advisable to schedule some guidance sessions. This is likely both to increase compliance and to help the patients get the most out of the SH material they are working with. With these provisos, harm due to SH treatment should be minimal. Multi-impulsive comorbidity is not a contraindication to the use of GSH, but expectations of treatment success need to be lowered, and these patients should be given very regular support.

Implications for services

It could be argued that SH approaches should be mainly situated in primary care settings. One interesting model developed in the UK is a primary care-based CBT SH clinic (Marks *et al.* 2003) to which patients can self-refer or be referred by their general practitioner with a nurse therapist giving some support.

Alternatively, in specialist settings, interested and suitable patients may be fast-tracked into receiving SH or GSH interventions as a first step, with regular reviews by the assessing clinician to monitor their progress and decide on the need for further treatment.

Implications for training of healthcare professionals

Healthcare professionals who are giving guidance for SH need to familiarize themselves with the intervention that they are guiding or building on in later treatment. Thus healthcare professionals need to be provided with brief training in the use of SH materials in order to translate an 'off-the-peg' treatment into an individually tailored treatment for a specific patient. The duration and nature of the education should depend on the needs of the professional group.

What SH materials to choose

Several different SH texts have been evaluated, some of which are available commercially. We do not know whether any of these texts are linked to greater acceptability or better outcomes. Recommendation of SH materials should be based on the best evidence available and a set of objective criteria, including the content, presentation of materials and readability. A recent expert review on SH for mental disorders in the UK (Lewis *et al.* 2003) identified a number of such criteria. Applying the latter would enable new materials to be included in any recommendation so long as they fit these criteria.

Future directions

A number of gaps remain in our knowledge. In their review, Lewis *et al.* (2003) made a number of research recommendations, most of which are relevant to the area of SH in eating disorders.

1 There remains an urgent need to investigate the relative effectiveness of PSH and GSH compared with the gold standard of CBT and compared with medication for BN and related disorders within pragmatic trials in primary care and other non-specialist settings. Any such trial should be large (i.e. adequately powered) and should include a formal economic analysis (something that to date has been completely missing from studies of this kind).
2 At present most research into SH in eating disorders has concerned manual-based treatments. Other media need to be explored, too. In particular, approaches using new technologies such as the Internet, text messaging or CD-ROMs need to be researched further, as they are likely to be more interactive and thus more attractive to patients than manual-based approaches (Bauer *et al.* 2003; Norton *et al.* 2003; Schmidt, 2003; Zabinski *et al.* 2003).
3 With the exception of the study by Fichter *et al.*, the investigation of SH treatments of AN is as yet poorly charted territory, and remains an important area for future research and development. Given that family-based approaches for the treatment of AN have been successfully manualized (Lock *et al.* 2001), the development of SH interventions for parents/families of young people with AN may also be fruitful. Such work is in progress in our unit.
4 None of the existing interventions have been developed for or studied in children and adolescents with eating disorders. Adolescents with BN may well benefit from GSH, delivered either by manual or by computer. However, it is likely that existing interventions could be improved to meet the specific developmental needs of young people.

5 Very little is currently known about the characteristics of individuals who are willing and able to follow and complete a course of SH treatment. Different people might prefer different SH media. Such information might enable clinicians to best predict which patients might have a better outcome with SH treatment.

6 More research needs to be done into the extent and nature of guidance and the settings that might be needed and/or best suited to ensure that SH materials are effective.

7 In addition to quantitative research, there is a real need to conduct qualitative research into the best way of providing SH treatments (including type of materials, intensity of guidance and setting).

8 Research also needs to address the question of what the 'active' ingredients in SH treatments are and whether SH based on other models apart from CBT might be effective. In this context, the study by Carter *et al.* (2003) is of interest. This compared two forms of pure SH, namely a CBT manual which addressed the symptoms of BN, and a non-symptom-specific SH program which focused on self-assertion skills. Both treatments were superior to waiting list, with no difference between them. This suggests that non-specific factors such as receiving an SH manual, hearing a plausible rationale and expecting improvement may be at work.

9 As far as we know, existing SH materials used in the treatment of eating disorders have been developed by experts. Revision of these and new materials should be developed in collaboration with patients and their carers to meet their needs in the most appropriate fashion. Such developments would be consistent with the 'expert patient model' that has been found to be beneficial in a number of chronic disorders (Department of Health 2001).

Corresponding author: Ulrike Schmidt, MD, PhD, Section of Eating Disorders, PO Box 59, Institute of Psychiatry, De Crespigny Park, London SE5 8AF, UK. E-mail: u.schmidt@iop.kcl.ac.uk

References

Bailer U, de Zwaan M, Leisch F *et al.* (2004) Guided self-help versus cognitive behavioural group therapy in the treatment of bulimia nervosa. *Int J Eat Disord.* **35**: 522–37.

Banasiak SJ, Paxton SJ and Hay PJ (2001) *Cognitive behavioural guided self-help for bulimia nervosa in primary care. Preliminary results.* Academy for Eating Disorders Ninth International Conference on Eating Disorders, May 2000, New York Hilton & Towers, NY.

Bara-Carril N, Williams CJ, Pombo-Carril MG *et al.* (2004) A preliminary investigation into the feasibility and efficacy of a CD-ROM-based cognitive–behavioural self-help intervention for bulimia nervosa. *Int J Eat Disord.* **35**: 538–48.
This cohort study is the first to address the use of computer-based treatment in bulimia nervosa patients attending a specialist eating disorders clinic.

Bauer S, Percevic R, Okon E, Meermann R and Kordy H (2003) Use of text messaging in the aftercare of patients with bulimia nervosa. *Eur Eat Disord Rev.* **11**: 279–90.

Bell L and Newns K (2002) What is multi-impulsive bulimia and can multi-impulsive patients benefit from supervised self-help? *Eur Eat Disord Rev.* **10**: 413–27.

Birchall H and Palmer B (2002) Doing it by the book: what place for guided self-help for bulimic disorders? *Eur Eat Disord Rev.* **10**: 379–85.

Carter J (2003) Self-help books in the treatment of eating disorders. In: CG Fairburn and KD Brownell (eds) *Eating Disorders and Obesity. A comprehensive handbook* (2e). Guilford Press, New York, pp. 358–61.

Carter JC, Olmsted MP, Kaplan AS *et al.* (2003) Self-help for bulimia nervosa: a randomized controlled trial. *Am J Psychiatry.* **160**: 973–8.

This RCT of pure self-help vs waiting list has an interesting feature as it includes the use of an assertiveness manual as a control condition.

Cuijpers P (1997) Bibliotherapy in unipolar depression: a meta-analysis. *J Behav Ther Exp Psychiatry.* **28**: 139–47.

Department of Health (2001) *The Expert Patient: a new approach towards chronic disease management for the twenty-first century.* Department of Health, London.

Durand MA and King M (2003) Specialist treatment versus self-help for bulimia nervosa: a randomised controlled trial in general practice. *Br J Gen Pract.* **53**: 371–7.

This is the first ever randomized controlled trial to study the use of a self-help treatment for BN in a primary care setting.

Fichter M, Cebulla M, Kranzlin N *et al.* (in press) Prästationäre manualisierte therapie und darauffolgende stationäre behandlung bei Anorexia Nervosa: eine kontrollierte studie. *Der Nervenarzt.* **74, Supplement 2**: 599.

Ghaderi A and Scott B (2003) Pure and guided self-help for full and sub-threshold bulimia nervosa and binge-eating disorders. *Br J Clin Psychol.* **42**: 257–69.

Hay PJ and Bacaltchuk J (2003a) Psychotherapy for bulimia nervosa and bingeing. *Cochrane Database Syst Rev.* CD000562.

Hay PJ and Bacaltchuk J (2003b) Bulimia nervosa. *Clin Evidence.* **9**: 997–1009.

Jorm AF, Korten AE, Jacomb PA *et al.* (1997) Helpfulness of interventions for mental disorders: beliefs of health professionals compared with the general public. *Br J Psychiatry.* **171**: 233–7.

Lewis G, Anderson L, Araya R *et al.* (2003) *Self-help interventions for mental health problems.* Unpublished Expert Report for Department of Health, London.

Lock J, Le Grange D, Agras WS and Dare C (2001) *Treatment Manual for Anorexia Nervosa. A family-based approach.* Guilford Press, London.

Marks IM, Mataix-Cols D, Kenwright M, Cameron R, Hirsch S and Gega L (2003) Pragmatic evaluation of computer-aided self-help for anxiety and depression. *Br J Psychiatry.* **183**: 57–65.

Marrs R (1995) A meta-analysis of bibliotherapy studies. *Am J Commun Psychol.* **23**: 843–70.

Murray K, Pombo-Carril MG, Bara-Carril N *et al.* (2003) Factors determining uptake of a CD-ROM-based CBT self-help treatment for bulimia: patient characteristics and subjective appraisals of self-help treatment. *Eur Eat Disord Rev.* **11**: 243–60.

National Collaborating Centre for Mental Health (2004) *Eating Disorders. Core interventions in the treatment and management of anorexia nervosa, bulimia nervosa and related eating disorders.* British Psychological Society and Royal College of Psychiatrists, London.

Norton M, Wonderlich SA, Myers T, Mitchell JE and Crosby RD (2003) The use of palmtop computers in the treatment of bulimia nervosa. *Eur Eat Disord Rev.* **11**: 231–42.

Palmer RL, Birchall H, McGrain L and Sullivan V (2002) Self-help for bulimic disorders: a randomised controlled trial comparing minimal guidance with face-to-face or telephone guidance. *Br J Psychiatry.* **181**: 230–5.

This RCT is unique in that it studies different types of guidance added to self-help. The design of the study is interesting in that a stepped-care approach was taken to decision making about further treatment.

Schmidt U (2003) Getting technical (editorial). *Eur Eat Disord Rev.* **11**: 147–54.

Schmidt U, Perkins S, Winn S, Murphy R and Williams C (2003) *Self-Help and Guided Self-Help for Eating Disorders. Protocol for a systematic review;* www.nelh.nhs.uk/cochrane.asp

Thiels C, Schmidt U, Troop N, Treasure J and Garthe R (2001) Compliance with a self-care manual in guided self-change for bulimia nervosa. *Eur Eat Disord Rev.* **9**: 115–22.

Thiels C, Schmidt U, Treasure J and Garthe R (2003) Four-year follow-up of guided self-change for bulimia nervosa. *Eat Weight Disord.* **8**: 212–17.

Treasure J, Schmidt U, Troop N et al. (1994). First step in the management of bulimia nervosa: controlled trial of a therapeutic manual. *BMJ.* **308**: 686–9.

Turnbull S, Ward A, Treasure J et al. (1996) The demand for eating disorder care. An epidemiological study using the general practice research database. *Br J Psychiatry.* **169**: 705–12.

Walsh BT, Fairburn CG, Mickley D, Sysko R and Parisdes MK (2004) Treatment of bulimia nervosa in a primary care setting. *Am J Psychiatry.* **161**: 556–61.
   This study is of importance as it attempts to evaluate the efficacy of antidepressant medication vs self-help, a neglected area of investigation of great practical significance.

Wells AM, Garvin V, Dohm FA and Striegel-Moore RH (1997) Telephone-based guided self-help for binge-eating disorder: a feasibility study. *Int J Eat Disord.* **21**: 341–6.

Williams C (2003) New technologies in self-help: another effective way to get better? *Eur Eat Disord Rev.* **11**: 170–82.

Williams CJ, Aubin SD, Cottrell D and Harkin PJR (1998) *Overcoming Bulimia: a self-help package.* University of Leeds, Leeds.

Zabinski MF, Celio AA, Jacobs MJ, Manwaring J and Wilfley DE (2003) Internet-based prevention of eating disorders. *Eur Eat Disord Rev.* **11**: 183–97.

7

Assessment of eating disorders

Carol B Peterson and Kathryn B Miller

Abstract

Objectives of review. The purpose of this review is to summarize research that has been published or presented on the topic of assessment of eating disorders during the period 2002–2003. This research has included new data on previously established instruments as well as the development of new questionnaires and interviews. In addition, several innovative approaches have been developed or applied to eating disorders.

Summary of recent findings. Studies conducted during the past two years that have focused on the agreement between interview and questionnaire data have yielded inconsistent findings. A number of new instruments have been developed to assess eating disorder symptoms and associated features that upon further validation are likely to be valuable contributions to the field. Ecological momentary assessment is a promising technique that reduces potential biases and error in self-report data.

Future directions. Further attention needs to be focused on the ongoing issue of establishing the reliability and validity of assessment techniques, and evaluating the psychometric properties of instruments with samples that vary in age and ethnic status. Future research should focus on improving the accuracy of assessment of the most complex features of eating disorders, including binge eating, dietary restraint, and the influence of shape and weight on self-evaluation. Research is also needed to develop measurement tools for the assessment of eating disorder diagnoses that have received less empirical attention, including non-purging bulimia nervosa (BN) and eating disorder not otherwise specified (EDNOS).

Introduction

The accurate assessment of eating disorder symptoms serves as the cornerstone of empirical investigations. Because the integrity of research results relies on the use of reliable and valid instruments, assessment measures must be empirically evaluated. Consistent with previous investigations, research on the assessment of eating disorder symptoms during the past two years has continued to focus on establishing the reliability and validity of various interviews and questionnaires. In addition, studies have investigated the use of new assessment measures and methods.

Assessment instruments are evaluated on the basis of their psychometric properties, specifically their reliability and validity. Establishing the reliability and validity of evolving instruments remains a difficult but critical task in psychopathology research. Reliability refers to a measure's consistency, including test–retest, internal and inter-rater consistency (Anastasi 1988). Validity refers to the extent to which an instrument accurately measures what it is intended to assess. Criterion validity is supported by the instrument's ability to correlate with another variable (concurrent validity) or predict another variable (predictive validity). Construct validity is the extent to which the instrument measures the attribute that is it is supposed to measure, including high correlations with measures of the same construct (convergent validity) and low correlations with measures of different constructs (discriminant validity) (Anastasi 1988; Anderson and Paulosky 2004).

There are several reasons why eating disorders can be difficult to assess. Firstly, participants may deny or minimize symptoms, or may lack the self-awareness to answer certain questions (Vitousek *et al.* 1991; Anderson and Paulosky 2004). Secondly, eating disorders affect children, adolescents and adults as well as women and men, resulting in problems designing instruments that are appropriate for all of these different populations. Thirdly, diagnostic criteria have evolved and changed, making it difficult to compare the results of assessment studies conducted over time that utilized different criteria.

The constructs associated with eating disorders are also difficult to define and measure. Binge eating is challenging to assess because a patient's opinion of what constitutes an objectively large amount of food is often quite different from that of a clinical interviewer (Beglin and Fairburn 1992; Fairburn and Beglin 1994). The extent to which self-evaluation is unduly influenced by shape and weight, included in DSM-IV (American Psychiatric Association 1994) criteria for both anorexia nervosa (AN) and bulimia nervosa (BN), is also difficult to measure because it is an abstract concept that requires an awareness of self-definition. Although perception of body size and attitudes towards shape and weight are critical aspects of eating disorders, measuring these variables accurately has been problematic, in part because of the multidimensional nature of the body image construct (Smeets 1997; Thompson 2004). Dieting, dietary restriction and dietary restraint are recognized as important aspects of eating disorders, but have also been difficult both to define and to assess (Anderson and Paulosky 2004). In summary, given the significant challenges associated with eating disorder assessment, it is critical to develop the most accurate and effective measurement instruments and techniques possible.

This review includes articles published on the topic of the assessment of eating disorders during the period 2002–2003 identified by PsychInfo and MEDLINE searches, as well as selected presentations from professional conferences. These studies are summarized in four sections: (1) comparisons of interviews with self-report questionnaires; (2) psychometric data on previously developed instruments; (3) new interviews and questionnaires; (4) innovative approaches to assessment.

Comparisons of questionnaire vs interview methods

A number of studies conducted recently have compared questionnaire and interview methods of assessing eating disorder symptoms. The implications of these types of studies are significant. Although questionnaires are easier to administer, less expensive, free of potential interview bias and usually less time-consuming (Garner 2002), they may not provide reliable data for constructs that are more abstract and difficult to define (Wilson 1993).

The EDE compared with the EDE-Q

One of the measures that is receiving most attention in this area of research is the Eating Disorder Examination (EDE) (Fairburn and Cooper 1993), a clinician-administered interview that is widely used in clinical studies. The authors have also developed a questionnaire version known as the EDE-Q (Fairburn and Beglin 1994). Earlier studies that have evaluated the agreement between the EDE and the EDE-Q yielded inconsistent findings, particularly with regard to whether the interview method (e.g. Wilfley *et al.* 1997; Carter *et al.* 2001) or the questionnaire method (e.g. Fairburn and Beglin 1994; Black and Wilson 1996) yields more pathologic responses. Inconsistencies may be due in part to diagnostic differences between the samples.

More recent studies have found better agreement between the two methods for those who binge eat, especially when the EDE-Q directions are augmented. Sysko *et al.* (2002) examined the differences between the two measures in assessing change in patients with BN, and found that reports of binge eating and vomiting were highly correlated at baseline and at the end of treatment. Celio *et al.* (2003) administered items from the EDE and EDE-Q to 157 women and men who were seeking treatment for binge-eating disorder (BED). The investigators found that modifying the EDE-Q to include more detailed instructions improved the agreement between the two measures. Similarly, Goldfein *et al.* (2002) found that the binge-eating section of the EDE-Q that included detailed instructions and definitions of binge eating correlated significantly with the EDE, while the EDE-Q administered without instructions did not correlate significantly with the interview version. These studies suggest that the accuracy of the EDE-Q is enhanced by providing the participant with detailed instructions and definitions of binge eating.

An exception to the conclusion that the EDE and modified EDE-Q can produce similar binge-eating data was found in a sample of post-gastric-bypass patients. de Zwaan *et al.* (2003) found poor agreement for binge eating between the EDE and the EDE-Q, as well as differences on the Restraint subscale, in a sample of post-gastric-bypass patients. Their findings suggest that it is appropriate to administer the EDE to post-gastric-bypass samples, but that the EDE-Q may have limited utility.

Two studies compared the EDE with the EDE-Q in AN samples. Wolk and Walsh (2002) administered the instruments to 60 women with AN and found that, in the majority of cases, the two measures were within one point of each other. Kappa coefficients were 0.56 for AN diagnosis and 0.79 for diagnostic subtype. Correlations ranged from modest to good (0.49–0.92) for the subscales and eating disorder behaviors, and EDE-Q scores tended to be higher than the EDE scores. Passi *et al.* (2002), the first investigators to compare the EDE with the EDE-Q in a sample of adolescents with AN, administered the questionnaire both before and after the EDE interview. Although they observed high correlations between the two methods when the questionnaire was given prior to the interview, the authors found significant differences for all of the subscales except Dietary Restraint, with higher ratings on the questionnaire than in the interview. Agreement between the EDE and the EDE-Q improved for the second administration of the questionnaire. Consistent with the conclusions of other investigators (Goldfein *et al.* 2002; Celio *et al.* 2003), these authors suggest that providing definitions of concepts before administering the EDE-Q may increase the reliability and validity of this instrument. Overall, however, these two studies suggest that in AN populations, EDE-Q scores tend to be higher than EDE scores.

Comparisons of other interview and questionnaire measures

Fichter and Quadflieg (2000) compared the Structured Interview for Anorexic and Bulimic Syndromes (SIAB-EX) (Fichter *et al.* 1998; Fichter and Quadflieg 2001), a widely used semi-structured interview, with a questionnaire version, and found good correspondence between the two versions and a similar factor structure using principal-component analyses. The questionnaire version resulted in higher ratings for measures of general psychopathology and atypical eating patterns and lower ratings for reports of binge eating, compensatory behavior, attitudes toward eating, and social interactions compared with the interview.

Tanofsky-Kraff *et al.* (2003) compared the EDE adapted for Children (ChEDE) (Bryant-Waugh *et al.* 1996) with two self-report measures, namely the adolescent version of the Questionnaire on Eating and Weight Patterns (QEWP-A) (Johnson *et al.* 1999) and the Children's Eating Attitude Test (ChEAT) (Maloney *et al.* 1988), in a community sample of normal and overweight children. They found significant correlations between the ChEDE and the ChEAT, but poor agreement between the ChEDE and the QEWP-A. In particular, higher rates of binge eating were reported on the QEWP-A. The investigators conclude that interviews are more accurate measures of eating pathology in non-treatment-seeking samples of children.

Keel *et al.* (2002) compared the diagnostic agreement between the SCID (First *et al.* 1995) and the Eating Disorder Questionnaire (EDQ) (Mitchell *et al.* 1985) in a long-term follow-up study of BN. Interviews were administered in person (57%) or by telephone (43%), allowing a direct comparison between face-to-face and more anonymous interviews. Diagnostic agreement was poor for BN (kappa = 0.49) and adequate for eating disorders (kappa = 0.64). The investigators found that the EDQ yielded higher rates of eating disorders, consistent with previous findings, suggesting that these types of questionnaires have high sensitivity but may have lower specificity, leading to false-positive diagnoses (Fairburn and Beglin 1994; French et al. 1998; Leon et al. 1999). A further comparison was made between EDQ data and SCID information obtained either by telephone or by face-to-face interviews. Interestingly, agreement was better between the questionnaires and telephone interviews than between the questionnaires and face-to-face interviews. Keel et al. (2002) raise the possibility that elevated rates of eating pathology on questionnaires may reflect accurate reporting that is obtained because the method is more anonymous.

Perry et al. (2002) compared the oral delivery of the SCOFF (Morgan et al. 1999), a brief five-item screening instrument for detecting eating disorders, with the written version of the instrument. Kappa coefficients (0.75–0.86) and excellent agreement indicated that the measure is suitable for administration in the written format. Consistent with previous studies, more pathologic responses were reported on the written form compared with the interview, which the authors, similar to Keel et al. (2002), interpret as evidence of greater self-disclosure.

In summary, a number of investigations published or presented during the period 2002–2003 raise questions about whether studies of eating disorders should rely on questionnaire or interview methods of assessment. These studies suggest that both formats have advantages and disadvantages, and that investigators need to consider these issues when selecting measures. Self-report questionnaires are less expensive, easier to administer, less time-consuming, potentially enhance self-disclosure, and eliminate interview bias. However, they may also be less specific and lead to false-positive diagnoses. Interviews have the advantage of allowing the clinician to explain potentially confusing constructs to the participant (e.g. binge eating, overvaluation of shape and weight), thus minimizing the likelihood of false-positive diagnoses. One promising method for decreasing false-positive diagnoses with self-reported binge eating on questionnaires is to provide participants with detailed instructions that include definitions and examples of what constitutes a binge-eating episode.

New data for previously developed instruments

In the past two years, a number of studies have examined previously developed questionnaires and instruments. These investigations have included data from measures that have not been previously studied with eating disorder samples, screening instruments, assessment tools that have been widely used, and questionnaires that have been developed more recently.

Eating Disorders Inventory

The Eating Disorders Inventory (EDI-2) (Garner 1990) is a widely used questionnaire that is currently under revision (Garner 2003). Tasca *et al.* (2003) evaluated the EDI-2 in clinical samples with BN and BED. They found that the EDI-2 scales had acceptable internal consistency for both groups of patients, as well as test–retest reliability for the BED sample. Factor analysis also supported the use of the original EDI scales with BED. However, Rofey *et al.* (2002) found that the psychometric properties of the EDI-2 were more limited with an older sample of female outpatients (average age 42.6 years). Specifically, the average subscale internal consistency coefficient was 0.31, and body dissatisfaction, ineffectiveness, interpersonal distrust and maturity fears subscales all yielded coefficients below 0.30. Only the bulimia subscale had good internal consistency (0.83). Franko *et al.* (2002) and Striegel-Moore *et al.* (2002) administered the EDI to a large, ethnically diverse sample of adolescent girls ($n = 2228$). A principal-components analysis found that black and white participants differed on eight factors, suggesting that EDI data from ethnic minority samples may need to be interpreted with caution. These data suggest that the EDI remains psychometrically sound in BN samples, but may not generalize as well to older BED or ethnically diverse samples.

Eating Attitudes Test

Pung *et al.* (2003) conducted a confirmatory factor analysis on the Eating Attitudes Test (EAT) (Garner and Garfinkel 1979) using a sample of 487 college students. The investigators found that 27% scored above the clinical cut-off value. Although tests for three-factor and four-factor models yielded significant Chi-square statistics, the fit indices for both models were poor.

Survey of Eating Disorders

Ghaderi and Scott (2002) evaluated the psychometric properties of the Survey for Eating Disorders (SEDs) (Gotestam and Agras 1995), a questionnaire designed to assess DSM-IV eating disorder criteria. Compared with the EDE, the SEDs yielded only two cases of false positives in a clinical sample of 45 patients. The SEDs demonstrated good test–retest reliability in a student sample, as well as evidence of discriminant and concurrent validity in its correlations with the EDI-2.

Minnesota Eating Disorders Inventory

Cassin *et al.* (2003) administered the Minnesota Eating Disorders Inventory (M-EDI) (Klump *et al.* 2000), a briefer version of the EDI that can be used with both adult and youth samples, to 423 undergraduates, along with the EDI and the Eating Disorder Diagnostic Scale (EDDS) (Stice *et al*. 2000). The investigators found high internal consistency for both the total score (0.89) and most of the subscales (0.78–0.83), except for compensatory behaviors (0.56). Correlations with the other measures indicated both convergent and discriminant validity.

SCOFF questionnaire

Luck *et al*. (2002) evaluated the accuracy of the SCOFF questionnaire (Morgan *et al*. 1999) in a primary care setting by comparing it with a clinical interview based on the DSM-IV criteria. The investigators found that the SCOFF questionnaire had a sensitivity of 84.6% and a specificity of 89.6%, and that generally it was an effective tool for identifying patients with eating disorders.

Impact of Weight on Quality of Life

Kolotkin and Crosby (2002) evaluated the shorter version of the Impact of Weight on Quality of Life (IWQOL) (Kolotkin *et al*. 1995) in a community sample and found that the IWQOL-Lite (Kolotkin *et al*. 2001) demonstrated excellent levels of internal consistency (0.82–0.96) and test–retest reliability (0.81–0.88), as well as evidence of convergent and discriminant validity.

Anorexia Nervosa Stages of Change Questionnaire

Rieger *et al*. (2002) administered the Anorexia Nervosa Stages of Change Questionnaire (ANSCQ) (Rieger *et al*. 2000) to 44 inpatient participants and found that it correlated significantly with measures of decisional balance, self-efficacy and concerns about change.

Preoccupation with Eating, Weight and Shape Scale

Hill and Craighead (2003) examined gender differences in the factor structure of the Preoccupation with Eating, Weight and Shape Scale (PEWSS). They found only one factor for women, suggesting that women did not distinguish between thoughts about their body and thoughts about eating. However, two factors were found for men, indicating that thoughts about food were separate from distress about food, which was linked to thoughts about weight and shape.

Personality Assessment Inventory

Tasca *et al*. (2002) observed acceptable levels of reliability and validity on the Personality Assessment Inventory (PAI) (Morey 1991) with a sample of patients with eating disorders, and a principal-components analyses revealed a factor structure similar to that obtained by Morey (1991).

Measures used in adolescent samples

Four studies investigated the use of eating disorder measures with adolescent samples. Serpell *et al.* (2003) administered the recently developed Pros and Cons of Anorexia Nervosa (P-CAN) scale to children and adolescents and found that the subscales were generally independent, correlated significantly with the EDE, and demonstrated moderate to high levels of internal consistency (0.73–0.97). Campbell *et al.* (2002) compared the Stirling Eating Disorder Scales (SEDS) (Williams *et al.* 1994) with the EDE in a sample of adolescent patients and found that the EDE and SEDS scales correlated significantly. The SEDS also demonstrated good internal consistency and showed evidence of criterion and discriminant validity. McCarthy *et al.* (2002) evaluated the psychometric properties of the EDI-2 and the Bulimia Test-Revised (BULIT-R) (Thelen *et al.* 1991) in a school-based sample of 12–18-year-old females by administering it longitudinally. Their results support the reliability and stability of these measures over a three-year time period. Canals *et al.* (2002) administered the EAT and a clinical interview to a sample of 304 Spanish 18-year-olds and found that a cut-off value of 25 was more sensitive (87.5%) than a cut-off value of 30 (75%) in detecting eating disorders, with minimal difference in specificity between the two cut-off points. In general, these studies support the use of these eating disorder measures with adolescent populations.

Eating Inventory (modified)

An interesting study was conducted by Mazzeo *et al.* (2003), who used confirmatory factor analytic methods to assess the structure of the widely used Three Factor Inventory, now known as the Eating Inventory (EI) (Stunkard and Messick 1985). The sample included 1510 twins who were administered a shortened version of the scale. The findings did not support the three factors described by Stunkard and Messick (1985), the three factors proposed by Hyland *et al.* (1989) or the four factors proposed by Ganley (1988). Because this study utilized a modified version of the EI, these findings require replication using the full version. In addition, confirmatory factor analytic methods should be replicated using a clinical sample.

New instruments

A number of new self-administered written questionnaires and one interview have been published or presented during the period 2002–2003 to assess eating and weight problems. Table 7.1 summarizes these studies in detail, including reliability and validity data when these are available.

Jackson *et al.* (2003) developed the Motivations to Eat scale, which includes four types of motivation, namely negative affect, social, compliance and pleasure. The authors first conducted unstructured interviews to generate an item pool, which was then administered to 812 college students. Factor analysis

Table 7.1 Overview of new measurement instruments published during the period 2002–2003

Title	Authors	Year	Purpose	Number of items	Format	Sample tested	Internal consistency	Test–retest reliability	Selected validity indicators
Body Checking Questionnaire	Reas et al.	2002	Measure the frequency of body checking behaviors	23	5-point Likert scale	149 female college students and 16 females with an ED	0.88 OA 0.92 SBP 0.83 IC	0.94 OA 0.91 SBP 0.90 IC 0.94 total	Content with experts in field. Concurrent with BSQ ($r = 0.86$), EAT-26 ($r = 0.70$), BIAQ ($r = 0.66$). Discriminant with Shipley ($r = -0.104$)
Body Image Quality of Life Inventory	Cash and Fleming	2002	'Quantifies the effects of one's body image on various self-experiences and life contexts'	19	7-point bipolar scale	116 female college students	0.95	0.79	Convergent: with BASS, ASI, SATAQ. Correlated with BMI ($r = -0.52$)
Carers' Needs Assessment Measure (CaNAM)	Haigh and Treasure	2003	'Assesses the needs of carers of people with AN'	7 areas assessed	Open-ended plus yes/doesn't apply/no	28 people caring for someone with a history of AN			Proxy validation with the ECI, three ECI scales correlated with one CaNAM scale
Decisional Balance	Cockell et al.	2002	Measures 'motivation and readiness for change in AN'	60	5-point Likert scale; and 30 pro and con items	246 women with AN	0.88 BUR 0.88 BEN 0.88 FA	0.64 BUR 0.71 BEN 0.70 FA	
Dieting Peer Competitiveness Scale (DPS)	Huon et al.	2002	Assesses 'dieting-related competitiveness among adolescent girls'	9	5-point Likert scale	319 high-school girls, 3 samples (S1, S2, S3)	S1 = 0.77 S2 = 0.76 S3 = 0.76	S1 = 0.71 S2 = 0.75 S3 = 0.71	Convergent: EDI BD = 0.71 EDI DT = 0.69 Divergent: Frequency of exercise = 0.11 Discriminant: As dieting increases DPC score increases

continued

Table 7.1 (Continued)

Title	Authors	Year	Purpose	Number of items	Format	Sample tested	Internal consistency	Test–retest reliability	Selected validity indicators
Motivations to Eat	Jackson et al.	2003	'Assesses psychological motivations to eat based on a 4-category model'	39	5-point Likert scale	812 college students	CP = 0.88 S = 0.88 CM = 0.84 P = 0.82		Convergent and discriminant with EES and DEBQ subscales Concurrent with eating-related behaviors
Rating of Anorexia and Bulimia Interview– Revised	Nevonen et al.	2003	Assesses 'a wide range of eating disorder and concomitant psychopathology'	70	Semi-structured interview: 3–5 point scales plus open-ended	71 women with an ED and 31 female controls	AEB = 0.42 BSWP = 0.85 BS = 0.71 PR = 0.77 PRTR = 0.86 PRR = 0.63 AI = 0.83	AEB = 0.39 BSWP = 0.95 BS = 0.76 PR = 0.70 PRTR = 0.89 PRR = 0.17	Criterion: significant differences between ED and controls Concurrent: correlates with the EDI-2
Verbal Commentary on Physical Appearance Scale	Herbozo et al.	2003	'To measure three types of appearance-related commentary: negative, neutral and positive'	24	5-point Likert scale	50 college students	0.81	0.80	

ED, eating disorder; OA, overall appearance; SBP, specific body parts; IC, idiosyncratic checking; BSQ, Body Shape Questionnaire; EAT, Eating Attitudes Test; BIAQ, Body Image Avoidance Questionnaire; BASS, Body Areas Satisfaction Scale; ASI, Appearance Schemas Inventory; SATAQ, Sociocultural Attitudes Towards Appearance Questionnaire; BMI, body mass index; AN, anorexia nervosa; ECI, Experience of Caregiving Inventory; BUR, burdens; BEN, benefits; FA, functional avoidance; S1, sample 1; S2, sample 2; S3, sample 3; EDI BD, Eating Disorder Inventory Body Dissatisfaction subscale; EDI DT, Eating Disorder Inventory Drive for Thinness subscale; CP, coping; S, social; CM, compliance; P, pleasure motivations; EES, Emotional Eating Scale; DEBQ, Dutch Eating Behavior Questionnaire; AEB, anorexic eating behavior; BSWP, body shape and weight preoccupations; BS, bulimic symptoms; PR, partner relationships; PRTR, parental relationships; PRR, peer relationships; AI, anorexia index.

supported the four types of motivation, which were found to be predictive of eating disorder symptoms in a multiple regression analysis.

Cockell *et al.* (2002) constructed the Decisional Balance measure to assess readiness for change in AN. The investigators administered the questionnaire to 246 patients and obtained a three-factor solution, namely burdens, benefits and functional avoidance (i.e. ways in which the AN helps to avoid distress, responsibilities and challenges). Alpha coefficients were 0.88 for each of the subscales, and test–retest reliability ranged from 0.64 to 0.71.

Huon *et al.* (2002) developed the Dieting Peer Competitiveness (DPC) scale to assess dieting-related competition among adolescent girls, and administered it to 319 subjects. Factor analysis yielded two factors. The first factor included items related to comparing appearance to others. The second consisted of items that focus on public aspects of eating behavior. Internal consistency, split-half reliability and test–retest reliability yielded coefficients ranging from 0.70 to 0.80. The investigators also found support for convergent and divergent validity based on correlations with other questionnaires, as well as discriminant validity in distinguishing serious from non-serious dieters.

Herbozo *et al.* (2003) developed the Verbal Commentary on Physical Appearance Scale (VCPAS) to evaluate positive and neutral as well as negative feedback from others. The one-week test–retest reliability was 0.80 and the internal consistency was 0.81.

Two questionnaires have been developed to assess different aspects of body image. The Body Checking Questionnaire (BCQ) (Reas *et al.* 2002) provides an overall measure of body checking as well as checking pertaining to specific body parts, overall appearance and idiosyncratic behaviors. The instrument demonstrated good internal consistency (0.88–0.92) and test–retest reliability (0.94), as well as concurrent validity as demonstrated by significant correlations with body dissatisfaction and body image avoidance behaviors. The BCQ also discriminated between clinical and non-clinical samples and between non-clinical participants. Cash and Fleming (2002) developed the Body Image Quality of Life Inventory (BIQOLI) to measure the impact of body image on psychosocial functioning. The investigators observed good levels of internal consistency (0.95), test–retest reliability (0.79) and convergent validity when they administered the questionnaire to 116 college women. In addition, they found that body mass index was associated with greater negative impact of body image on quality of life.

Two articles described preliminary scale development that did not include reliability and validity data. Haigh and Treasure (2003) constructed the Carers' Needs Assessment Measure (CaNAM) to assess the needs of individuals who take care of people with eating disorders (usually family members or partners). After interviewing care providers to generate items, the instrument was administered to a sample of 28 individuals who cared for patients with AN. The results indicated high levels of unmet needs for support and information. Niero *et al.* (2002) developed two questionnaires to assess quality of life among individuals who are overweight or obese, namely the Obesity and Weight Loss Quality of Life Questionnaire (OBWLQOLQ) and the Weight-Related Symptom Measure (WRSM). The authors sought to develop measures that would pertain to the full spectrum of obesity and would include multicultural items for cross-cultural studies. Items developed from qualitative interviews were then translated. Items that were not accepted by multiple cultures were excluded.

Finally, Nevonen *et al.* (2003) developed a revised version of the Rating of Anorexia and Bulimia Interview (RABI) (Clinton and Norring 1999), a semi-structured interview designed to assess a range of eating disorder symptoms and associated psychopathology. Most of the internal consistency alpha levels were at least acceptable, although the alpha value for the Anorexic Eating Behavior scale was 0.43. Inter-rater reliability ranged from 0.65 to 0.85, and test–retest coefficients were more variable, ranging from 0.17 to 0.95. Several of the subscales correlated with the EDI-2, and the interview discriminated between patients and controls.

In summary, many new scales reflect growing areas of research into eating disorders. Broadly, they cover the spectrum of motivation, obesity, body image and the importance of social comparison. These new measures suggest that the development of eating disorder assessment instruments is staying abreast with current research findings and striving to define and measure relevant constructs more accurately.

Innovative approaches

Most research in the field of eating disorders has relied on self-report question-naires and semi-structured clinician-administered interviews. Although widely used, these types of measures have a number of limitations, including the extent to which participant responses are influenced by biases. Several innovative strategies have been developed to improve the accuracy of assessment data, including Ecological Momentary Assessment and two new methods of assess-ing body image.

Ecological Momentary Assessment

Ecological Momentary Assessment (EMA) (Stone and Shiffman 1994) has been used to assess various types of symptoms and behaviors, and has recently been used with eating disorders (Smyth *et al.* 2001). This technique attempts to assess the target behavior naturalistically with greater accuracy by asking participants to make multiple recordings each day and/or at the time when the behavior occurs, reducing the interval between the occurrence of the behavior and the time of assessment. One of the main advantages of EMA is that it reduces retrospective recall bias, which significantly limits the accuracy of self-report data (Stone and Shiffman 1994; Schacter 1999).

Stein and Corte (2003) undertook a pilot study to examine the feasibility of conducting EMA using hand-held computers with 16 eating disorder partici-pants for a four-week period. In addition, the investigators sought to evaluate the reactivity of eating disorder symptoms to EMA and the extent to which these behaviors were altered by using this type of measurement procedure. They found that 80% of the participants completed the EMA procedures as instructed, and these participants indicated that they had recorded their symptoms most or all of the time (although 15% reported that they typically completed the measure more than two hours after their eating disorder symptom had occurred). The vast majority (92%) indicated a willingness to participate in an EMA study in the future. Reactivity was examined by comparing the frequency of eating disorder symptoms between the early and later portions of the monitoring period. No significant differences were found between initial and later time periods, although on average symptoms were less frequent in the second half of the month. Comparisons with the EDE indicated that frequencies of self-reported symptoms were lower for EMA than for the EDE, especially binge eating and excessive exercise. The results of this study suggest that EMA is a feasible approach to the measurement of eating disorder symptoms.

The use of EMA has considerable implications for the field of eating disorders research. Because this approach reduces memory biases, EMA may yield more accurate data about the precipitants of eating disorder symptoms. Using EMA with an eating disorder sample, for example, Wegner et al. (2002) examined 27 college students with subclinical binge-eating behavior and found that although mood was worse on binge days than on non-binge days, mood actually worsened after the binge-eating episode had occurred rather than before it. Similarly, Wonderlich et al. (2003b) found that negative mood did not predict eating disorder behavior in women with BN, but mood worsened after the behavior, particularly for women with comorbid borderline personality disorder. The authors conclude that EMA is a useful technique for testing conceptual models related to eating disorders.

Results using EMA with BED samples have yielded somewhat different results. Le Grange et al. (2001) used EMA (with programmable wrist watches) to identify triggers of binge eating and found that negative affect, dietary restraint and desire to binge were antecedents. Interestingly, the investigators found similar levels of binge eating and antecedents to binge eating in women diagnosed with BED to those in women who had denied binge eating during the initial diagnostic interview. Le Grange et al. (2002) added EMA to cognitive–behavioral therapy for BED to improve the identification of binge antecedents, but found that it did not enhance treatment outcome. The authors conclude that EMA is a valuable measurement technique that will provide important data for assessment and diagnosis, but is not clearly useful as an adjunct to cognitive–behavioral therapy for BED.

Body image

Three studies published during the period 2002–2003 have focused on assessing aspects of body image more accurately. The first study describes a new body image assessment tool that uses video distorting techniques to estimate body size. Shibata (2002) designed software (BodyImage) for a personal computer in order to assess body image disturbance. In contrast to traditional video distorting techniques that require a video camera and anamorphic lens, this software allows the participant to adjust the image of a digital picture. Reliability and validity data will be needed to establish the appropriateness of using this software in empirical studies.

Shafran and Fairburn (2002) developed a new method for assessing the perception of body size that uses projected images which are consistent with the experience of viewing oneself in the mirror, thus providing a more eco-logically valid measure of body size estimation and ideal size. The investigators found that participants with eating disorders overestimated their size to a greater degree than the comparison sample, and identified a significantly thinner ideal size. Body size and ideal size were not significantly correlated, although they did correlate with the EDE-Q. Farrell *et al.* (2003) compared the mirror-size body size estimation procedures with a life-size procedure in a community sample of participants without eating disorders. Participants tended to overestimate their size using the new mirror-sized assessment and to under-estimate their size using the life-size method. This difference was not observed with a mannequin or neutral image. The authors conclude that this new technique is an improvement on older body image assessment methods – firstly, because it measures perception of body image rather than memory of it, and secondly, because it is more ecologically valid as it uses a mirror-sized estimation, which is actually half of one's body size, instead of a life-size estimation.

Summary of important findings

Despite numerous comparisons of interview and written self-report measures of eating disorders, findings have been inconsistent. Overall, however, question-naire methods tend to produce more pathologic responses than interview methods. One significant finding is that adding detailed directions (e.g. defin-itions and examples of concepts such as binge eating) to the questionnaire version of the EDE increases its level of agreement with the EDE interview (Goldfein *et al.* 2002; Passi *et al.* 2002; Celio *et al.* 2003). It has also been hypothesized that increased rates of eating pathology on questionnaires may reflect increased candor in reporting compared with face-to-face interviews (Keel *et al.* 2002; Perry *et al.* 2002).

Most of the research studies published and presented during the period 2002–2003 on the validity and reliability of previously established instruments pro-vided further support for their use. However, confirmatory factor analysis of a modified version of the EI (formerly referred to as the TFEQ) raised questions about the extent to which underlying factors were robust (Mazzeo *et al.* 2003). Several other studies highlight the importance of evaluating the psychometric properties and factor structure of well-established assessment instruments on samples that vary in age, race and gender (Rofey *et al.* 2002; Striegel-Moore *et al.* 2002; Hill and Craighead 2003).

A number of new assessment measures have been developed with promising psychometric qualities. Among the most significant is an innovative approach to measuring body size estimation with enhanced ecologic validity (Shafran and Fairburn 2002; Farrell *et al.* 2003). One of the most notable advances in the field of eating disorders assessment is the use of EMA, which reduces recall bias and enhances the accuracy of self-report. Pilot and preliminary data support the feasibility, reliability and validity of using EMA techniques with eating disorder samples (Stein and Corte 2003).

Clinical implications

Recent research findings have several important implications for clinicians. Most significantly, new instruments and modifications to old instruments will allow clinicians to expand the breadth and depth with which they can assess eating disorder constructs and populations. Recognizing that most clinicians are not able to conduct extensive interview assessments, this section will therefore focus on questionnaires. For clinical populations, data which suggest that the accuracy of the EDE-Q can be improved by adding more detailed instructions are particularly important. Additional instructions have been suggested for both adult and adolescent samples. In addition, new measures for assessing body shape checking behavior (Reas *et al.* 2002), and motivation for recovery (Cockell *et al.* 2002), will assist clinicians in assessing thoughts and behaviors that have a profound impact on the course of treatment, but may not otherwise be articulated by the patient.

For non-clinical samples, it appears that both the written and interview versions of the five-item SCOFF are able to identify individuals with clinically significant eating disorders (Morgan *et al.* 1999; Luck *et al.* 2002). Given the rates of undiagnosed and untreated eating disorders in the community, brief effective screening instruments for identifying individuals who may be suffering from an eating disorder are critically important.

Future research and considerations

Recent studies have highlighted the challenges of establishing agreement between interview and questionnaire assessment methods. Further research is required to determine ways in which both methods can yield more accurate data – for example, by adding more detailed instructions, definitions and examples to participants when they are given written self-report questionnaires (Goldfein *et al.* 2002; Passi *et al.* 2002; Celio *et al.* 2003). Although the question of whether interview methods provide more accurate data than self-report questionnaires remains unanswered, a more promising line of research should focus on when to use which type of assessment method to answer specific types of empirical questions. For example, if participants who are unfamiliar with the interviewer are more comfortable self-revealing information anonymously (Keel *et al.* 2002), telephone interviews and written questionnaires may yield more accurate data for large survey studies. However, interview methods may be more accurate for assessing change in complex variables such as binge eating in the context of treatment outcome studies.

Future studies should continue to develop and refine new technologies that can improve the accuracy of self-reported data and reduce the risk of memory biases. Although eating disorder research relies on shorter- and longer-term recall to establish diagnoses, participants often have difficulty remembering their symptoms over time (Peterson *et al*. 2001). EMA provides an important alternative, and may improve the accuracy of self-reported symptoms by reducing error in recall. The use of EMA in a wider range of studies, including treatment outcome, clearly warrants further investigation.

Future research should also focus on improving assessment methods to measure some of the most complex and multidimensional features of eating disorders, including binge eating, dietary restraint, body image, motivation, and the influence of weight and shape on self-evaluation. Assessment methods from other fields, including cognitive psychology, may be useful for measuring more cognitive constructs including self-evaluation. Research is also needed to develop measures for the assessment of eating disorder diagnostic categories that have received less empirical attention, including non-purging bulimia nervosa and eating disorder not otherwise specified. Although standard eating disorder measures may be used to study these samples, their reliability and validity have not been established. In addition, diagnostic categories that have received less empirical attention may require the development of new measures to assess features specific to these eating disorder groups.

A final consideration in the assessment of eating disorders is the degree to which investigators utilize appropriate research methods and measures that are psychometrically sound. A group of investigators recently evaluated the quality of research in the eating disorders field by comparing publications from 1980, 1990 and 2000 for both eating and anxiety disorders (Crosby *et al*. 2003; Wonderlich *et al*. 2003a). The investigators noted improvements in the quality of eating disorders research over the past 20 years, including greater reporting of reliability and validity information. However, compared with anxiety disorders, eating disorder studies were less likely to use structured diagnostic assessment (10% vs 21%) and blind raters (6% vs 16%). Therefore one of the most important considerations in the assessment of eating disorders is ensuring the widespread use of high-quality research methods and assessment. Given the importance of reliable and valid instruments, assessment of eating disorders needs to remain a top priority in research and clinical settings.

Acknowledgments

The authors would like to thank Maria Frisch and Shannon Bailey for their valuable assistance with the preparation of this manuscript. This research was supported by grants from the National Institute of Health (R01-MH59234) and the National Institutes of Diabetes, Digestive and Kidney Diseases (R01-DK61912; P30-DK50456).

Corresponding author: Carol B Peterson, PhD, Eating Disorders Research Program, University of Minnesota, 606 24th Avenue South, Suite 602, Minneapolis, MN 55454, USA. E-mail: peter161@umn.edu

References

American Psychiatric Association (1994) *Diagnostic and Statistical Manual of Mental Disorders* (4e). American Psychiatric Press, Washington, DC.

Anastasi A (1988) *Psychological Testing* (6e). Macmillan, New York.

Anderson DA and Paulosky C (2004) Psychological assessment of eating disorders and related features. In: JK Thompson (ed.) *Handbook of Eating Disorders and Obesity.* John Wiley & Sons, New York, pp. 112–29.

Beglin S and Fairburn CG (1992) What is meant by the term 'binge'? *Am J Psychiatry.* **149**: 123–4.

Black CMD and Wilson GT (1996) Assessment of eating disorders: interview versus questionnaire. *Int J Eat Disord.* **20**: 43–50.

Bryant-Waugh RJ, Cooper PJ, Taylor CL and Lask BD (1996) The use of the Eating Disorder Examination with children: a pilot study. *Int J Eat Disord.* **19**: 391–7.

Campbell M, Lawrence B, Serpell L, Lask B and Neiderman M (2002) Validating the Stirling Eating Disorders Scales (SEDS) in an adolescent population. *Eat Behav.* **3**: 285–93.

Canals J, Carbajo G and Fernandez-Ballart J (2002) Discriminant validity of the Eating Attitudes Test according to American Psychiatric Association and World Health Organization criteria of eating disorders. *Psychol Rep.* **91**: 1052–6.

Carter JC, Aime AA and Mills JS (2001) Assessment of bulimia nervosa: a comparison of interview and self-report questionnaire methods. *Int J Eat Disord.* **30**: 187–92.

Cash TF and Fleming EC (2002) The impact of body image experiences: development of the Body Image Quality of Life Inventory. *Int J Eat Disord.* **31**: 455–60.

Cassin SE, von Ranson KM, Bramfield T and Baxter AE (2003) *Validation of the Minnesota Eating Disorder Inventory: a brief measure of disordered eating.* Paper presented at the International Conference on Eating Disorders, May 29–31, Denver, CO.

Celio AA, Wilfley DE, Crow SJ, Mitchell JE and Walsh BT (2003) *A comparison of the BES, QEWP-R, and EDE-Q-I with the EDE in the assessment of binge eating disorder and its symptoms.* Paper presented at the International Conference on Eating Disorders, May 29–31, Denver, CO.

Clinton D and Norring C (1999) The Rating of Anorexia and Bulimia (RAB) interview: development and preliminary validation. *Eur Eat Disord Rev.* **7**: 362–71.

Cockell SJ, Geller J and Linden W (2002) The development of a decisional balance scale for anorexia nervosa. *Eur Eat Disord Res.* **10**: 359–75.

This paper presents a new scale designed to assess motivation for change in anorexia nervosa, entitled the Decisional Balance Scale. Factor analysis identified three factors, namely burdens, benefits and functional avoidance. The functional avoidance scale suggests that symptoms help the individual to cope with unpleasant emotions, difficulties and responsibilities. The scale demonstrates acceptable reliability.

Crosby RD, Wonderlich SA, Mitchell JE *et al.* (2003) *The state of eating disorder research publications 1980–2000: an empirical analysis. Part I (methodology).* Paper presented at the Eating Disorders Research Society Annual Meeting, October 1–11, Ravello, Italy.

de Zwaan M, Mitchell JE, Swan-Kremeier L, McGregor T, Roerig JL and Crosby RD (2003) *A comparison of different methods of assessing the features of eating disorders in post-gastric bypass patients: self-report questionnaire versus interview.* Paper presented at the Eating Disorders Research Society Annual Meeting, October 1–11, Ravello, Italy.

Fairburn CG and Beglin SJ (1994) Assessment of eating disorders: interview or self-report questionnaire? *Int J Eat Disord.* **16**: 363–70.

Fairburn CG and Cooper Z (1993) The Eating Disorder Examination. In: CG Fairburn and GT Wilson (eds), *Binge Eating: nature, assessment and treatment* (12e). Guilford, New York, pp. 317–60.

Farrell C, Shafran R and Fairburn C (2003) Body size estimation: testing a new mirror-based assessment method. *Int J Eat Disord.* **34**: 162–71.

Fichter MM, Herpertz S, Quadflieg N and Herpertz-Dahlmann B (1998) Structured Interview for Anorexic and Bulimic Disorders for DSM-IV and ICD-10: updated (third) revision. *Int J Eat Disord.* **24**: 227–49.

Fichter MM and Quadflieg N (2000) Comparing self- and expert rating: a self-report screening version (SIAB-S) of the Structured Interview for Anorexic and Bulimic Syndromes for DSM-IV and ICD-10 (SIAB-EX). *Eur Arch Psychiatry Clin Neurosci.* **250**: 175–85.

Fichter MM and Quadflieg N (2001) The Structured Interview for Anorexic and Bulimic Disorders for DSM-IV and ICD-10 (SIAB-EX): reliability and validity. *Eur Psychiatry.* **16**: 38–48.

First MB, Spitzer RL, Gibbon M and Williams JB (1995) *Structured Clinical Interview for the DSM-IV Axis I Disorders – patient edition (SCID-I/P, version 2).* Biometrics Research Department, New York State Psychiatric Institute, New York.

Franko DL, Schumann BC, Barton B *et al.* (2002) *Stability of the factor structure of the Eating Disorders Inventory in black and white adolescent girls.* Poster presented at the Eating Disorders Research Annual Meeting, November 20–23, Charleston, SC.

French SA, Peterson CB, Story M, Anderson N, Pederson Mussell M and Mitchell JE (1998) Agreement between survey and interview measures of weight control practices in adolescents. *Int J Eat Disord.* **23**: 45–56.

Ganley RM (1988) Emotional eating and how it relates to dietary restraint, disinhibition, and perceived hunger. *Int J Eat Disord.* **7**: 635–47.

Garner DM (1990) *Eating Disorder Inventory-2 Professional Manual.* Psychological Assessment Resources, Odessa, FL.

Garner DM (2002) Measurement of eating disorder psychopathology. In: CG Fairburn and KD Brownell (eds) *Eating Disorders and Obesity: a comprehensive handbook* (2e). Guilford, New York, pp. 141–6.

Garner DM (2003) *The Eating Disorders Inventory-3.* Paper presented at the Eating Disorders Research Society Annual Meeting, October 1–11, Ravello, Italy.

Garner DM and Garfinkel PE (1979) The Eating Attitudes Test: an index of the symptoms of anorexia nervosa. *Psychol Med.* **9**: 273–9.

Ghaderi A and Scott B (2002) The preliminary reliability and validity of the Survey for Eating Disorders (SEDs): a self-report questionnaire for diagnosing eating disorders. *Eur Eat Disord Rev.* **10**: 61–76.

Goldfein J, Devlin M, Kamenetz C, Wolk S, Raizman P and Dobrow I (2002) *EDE-Q with and without instruction to assess binge eating in patients with binge-eating disorder.* Poster presented at the International Conference on Eating Disorders, April 25–28, Boston, MA.

Gotestam KG and Agras WS (1995) General population-based epidemiological study of eating disorders in Norway. *Int J Eat Disord.* **18**: 119–26.

Haigh R and Treasure J (2003) Investigating the needs of carers in the area of eating disorders: development of the Carers' Needs Assessment Measure (CaNAM). *Eur Eat Disord Rev.* **11**: 125–41.

Herbozo SM, Roehrig M, Shroff H and Thompson K (2003) *The development and validation of the Verbal Commentary on Physical Appearance Scale.* Paper presented at the International Conference on Eating Disorders, May 29–31, Denver, CO.

Hill DM and Craighead LW (2003) *Gender differences in the factor structure of the Preoccupation with Eating, Weight and Shape Scale.* Paper presented at the International Conference on Eating Disorders, May 29–31, Denver, CO.

Huon GF, Piira T, Hayne A and Strong KG (2002) Assessing body and eating peer-focused comparisons: the Dieting Peer Competitiveness (DPC) Scale. *Eur Eat Disord Rev.* **10**: 428–46.

Hyland ME, Irvine SH, Thacker C, Dann PL and Dennis I (1989) Psychometric analysis of the Stunkard-Messick Eating Questionnaire (SMEQ) and comparison with the Dutch Eating Behavior Questionnaire (DEBQ). *Curr Psychol Res Rev.* **8**: 228–33.

Jackson B, Cooper ML, Mintz L and Albino A (2003) Motivations to eat: scale development and validation. *J Res Pers.* **37**: 297–318.

Johnson WG, Grieve FG, Adams CD and Sandy J (1999) Measuring binge eating in adolescents: adolescent and parent version of the Questionnaire of Eating and Weight Patterns. *Int J Eat Disord.* **26**: 301–14.

Keel PK, Crow S, Davis TL and Mitchell JE (2002) Assessment of eating disorders: comparison of interview and questionnaire data from a long-term follow-up study of bulimia nervosa. *J Psychom Res.* **53**: 1043–7.

This paper compares interview and questionnaire data in a long-term follow-up sample of women with BN. The authors found increased rates of eating disorders when assessed by questionnaire compared with interview. However, of particular interest is the finding that diagnostic agreement between questionnaire data and telephone interview data was superior to that between questionnaire data and face-to-face interview data. The authors assert that anonymous methods of assessments may yield higher rates of eating disorders because subjects are more candid.

Klump KL, McGue M and Iacono WG (2000) Age differences in genetic and environmental influences on pre-adolescent and adolescent female twins. *J Abnorm Psychol.* **109**: 239–51.

Kolotkin RL and Crosby RD (2002) Psychometric evaluation of the Impact of Weight on Quality of Life–Lite questionnaire (IWQOL–LITE) in a community sample. *Qual Life Res.* **11**: 157–71.

Kolotkin RL, Head S, Hamilton MA and Tse CTJ (1995) Assessing impact of weight on quality of life. *Obes Res.* **3**: 49–56.

Kolotkin RL, Crosby RD, Kosloski KD and Williams GR (2001) Development of a brief measure to assess quality of life in obesity. *Obes Res.* **9**: 102–11.

Le Grange D, Gorin A, Catley D and Stone AA (2001) Does momentary assessment detect binge eating in overweight women that is denied at interview? *Eur Eat Disord Rev.* **9**: 309–24.

Le Grange D, Gorin A, Dymek M and Stone A (2002) Does ecological momentary assessment improve cognitive–behavioural therapy for binge-eating disorder? A pilot study. *Eur Eat Disord Rev.* **10**: 316–28.

Leon GR, Fulkerson JA, Perry CL, Keel PK and Klump K (1999) Three- to four-year prospective evaluation of personality and behavioral risk factors for later disordered eating in adolescent girls and boys. *J Youth Adolesc.* **28**: 181–96.

Luck AJ, Morgan JF, Reid F *et al.* (2002) The SCOFF questionnaire and clinical interview for eating disorders in general practice: comparative study. *BMJ.* **325**: 755–6.

McCarthy DM, Simmons JR, Smith GT, Tomlinson KL and Hill KK (2002) Reliability, stability and factor structure of the Bulimia Test–Revised and Eating Disorder Inventory-2 scales in adolescence. *Assessment.* **9**: 382–9.

Maloney MJ, McGuire JB and Daniels SR (1988) Reliability testing of the children's version of the Eating Attitudes Test. *J Am Acad Child Adolesc Psychiatry.* **27**: 541–3.

Mazzeo SE, Aggen SH, Anderson C, Tozzi F and Bulik CM (2003) Investigating the structure of the Eating Inventory (Three-Factor Eating Questionnaire): a confirmatory approach. *Int J Eat Disord.* **34**: 255–64.

This paper used confirmatory factor analytic methods to test the factor structure of a modified version of the Eating Inventory (formerly called the Three Factor Eating Questionnaire). Previous data have proposed either three-factor or four-factor models. The results indicated that the data were a poor fit for either of these models. The

authors conclude that additional data are needed to validate the constructs thought to underlie the Eating Inventory.

Mitchell JE, Hatsukami D, Eckert E and Pyle R (1985) Eating Disorders Questionnaire. *Psychopharmacol Bull.* **21**: 1025–43.

Morey L (1991) *Personality Assessment Inventory: professional manual.* Psychological Assessment Resources, Odessa, FL.

Morgan JF, Reid F and Lacey JH (1999) The SCOFF questionnaire: assessment of a new screening tool for eating disorders. *BMJ.* **319**: 1467–8.

Nevonen L, Broberg AG, Clinton D and Norring C (2003) A measure for the assessment of eating disorders: reliability and validity studies of the Rating of Anorexia and Bulimia interview – revised version (RAB-R). *Scand J Psychol.* **44**: 303–10.

Niero M, Martin M, Finger T *et al.* (2002) A new approach to multicultural item generation in the development of two obesity-specific measures: the Obesity and Weight Loss Quality of Life (OWLQOL) Questionnaire and the Weight-Related Symptom Measure (WRSM). *Clin Ther.* **24**: 690–700.

Passi VA, Bryson SW and Lock J (2002) Assessment of eating disorders in adolescents with anorexia nervosa: self-report questionnaire versus interview. *Int J Eat Disord.* **33**: 45–54.

Perry L, Morgan J, Reid F *et al.* (2002) Screening for symptoms of eating disorders: reliability of the SCOFF screening tool with written compared to oral delivery. *Int J Eat Disord.* **32**: 466–72.

Peterson CB, Miller KB, Johnson-Lind J, Crow S and Thuras P (2001) *Recall of eating disorder and depressive symptoms: how accurate are our diagnoses?* Paper presented at the Eating Disorders Research Society Annual Meeting, November 28–December 1, Albuquerque, NM.

Pung MA, Niemeier HM and Craighead LW (2003) *Confirmatory factor analysis of the 26-item Eating Attitudes Test.* Paper presented at the International Conference on Eating Disorders, May 29–31, Denver, CO.

Reas DL, Whisenhunt BL, Netemeyer R and Williamson DA (2002) Development of the Body Checking Questionnaire: a self-report measure of body checking behaviors. *Int J Eat Disord.* **31**: 324–33.

This paper presents a new scale designed to assess body checking. The scale demonstrates acceptable reliability and validity. It is an important contribution to the literature because it targets a construct, namely weight and shape concerns, that is clinically significant but difficult to measure.

Rieger E, Touyz S, Schotte D *et al.* (2000) Development of an instrument to assess readiness to recover in anorexia nervosa. *Int J Eat Disord.* **28**: 387–96.

Rieger E, Touyz SW and Beumont PJV (2002) The Anorexia Nervosa Stages of Change Questionnaire (ANSOCQ): information regarding its psychometric properties. *Int J Eat Disord.* **32**: 24–38.

Rofey DL, Shuman ES, Corcoran KJ and Birbaum MC (2002) *Age matters: internal consistency on the EDI-2.* Poster presented at the 2002 International Conference on Eating Disorders, April 25–28, Boston, MA.

Schacter DL (1999) The seven sins of memory: insights from psychology and cognitive neuroscience. *Am Psychol.* **54**: 182–203.

Serpell L, Neiderman M, Haworth E, Emmanueli F and Lask B (2003) The use of the Pros and Cons of Anorexia Nervosa (P-CAN) Scale with children and adolescents. *J Psychosom Res.* **54**: 567–71.

Shafran R and Fairburn C (2002) A new ecologically valid method to assess body size estimation and body size dissatisfaction. *Int J Eat Disord.* **32**: 458–65.

Shibata S (2002) A Macintosh and Windows program for assessing body-image disturbance using adjustable image distortion. *Behav Res Methods Instr Comput.* **34**: 90–2.

Smeets MAM (1997) The rise and fall of body size estimation research in anorexia nervosa: a review and reconceptualisation. *Eur Eat Disord Rev.* **5**: 75–95.

Smyth J, Wonderlich S, Crosby R, Miltenberger R, Mitchell J and Rorty M (2001) The use of ecologic momentary assessment approaches in eating disorder research. *Int J Eat Disord.* **30**: 83–95.

Stein KF and Corte CM (2003) Ecologic momentary assessment of eating-disordered behaviors. *Int J Eat Disord.* **34**: 349–60.

This paper adapts a new technology, namely ecologic momentary assessment (EMA), to the assessment of eating disorders. The results indicated that this measurement technique is feasible and acceptable to women with eating disorders. Reported rates of binge eating and exercise were lower when assessed with EMA than when assessed by interview. In addition, rates of behaviors did not change significantly over the four-week assessment period.

Stice E, Telch CF and Rizvi SL (2000) Development and validation of the Eating Disorder Diagnostic Scale: a brief self-report measure of anorexia, bulimia and binge-eating disorder. *Psychol Assess.* **12**: 123–31.

Stone AA and Shiffman S (1994) Ecological momentary assessment (EMA) in behavioral medicine. *Ann Behav Med.* **16**: 199–202.

Striegel-Moore RH, Franko DL, Barton BA *et al.* (2002) *Factor structure of the Eating Disorders Inventory.* Poster presented at the International Conference on Eating Disorders, April 25–28, Boston, MA.

Stunkard AJ and Messick S (1985) The Three-Factor Eating Questionnaire to measure dietary restraint and hunger. *J Psychosom Res.* **29**: 71–83.

Sysko R, Walsh BT, Fairburn CG and Mickley D (2002). *EDE-Q as a measure of change in patients with bulimia nervosa.* Poster presented at the International Conference on Eating Disorders, April 25–28, Boston, MA.

Tanofsky-Kraff M, Morgan CM, Yanovski SZ, Marmarosh C, Wilfley DE and Yanovski JA (2003) Comparison of assessments of children's eating-disordered behaviors by interview and questionnaire. *Int J Eat Disord.* **33**: 213–24.

Tasca GA, Wood J, Demidenko N and Bissada H (2002) Using the PAI with an eating disordered population: scale characteristics, factor structure, and differences among diagnostic groups. *J Pers Assess.* **79**: 337–56.

Tasca GA, Illing V, Lybanon-Daigle V, Bissada H and Balfour L (2003) Psychometric properties of the Eating Disorders Inventory-2 among women seeking treatment for binge-eating disorder. *Assess.* **10**: 228–36.

Thelen MH, Farmer J, Wonderlich S and Smith M (1991) A revision of the Bulimia Test: the BULIT-R. *J Consult Clin Psychol.* **3**: 119–24.

Thompson JK (2004) The (mis)measurement of body image: ten strategies to improve assessment for applied and research purposes. *Body Image.* **1**: 7–14.

Vitousek KB, Daly J and Heiser C (1991) Reconstructing the internal world of the eating-disordered individual: overcoming denial and distortion in self-report. *Int J Eat Disord.* **6**: 647–66.

Wegner KE, Smyth JM, Crosby RD, Wittrock D, Wonderlich SA and Mitchell JE (2002) An evaluation of the relationship between mood and binge eating in the natural environment using ecological momentary assessment. *Int J Eat Disord.* **32**: 352–61.

Wilfley DE, Schwartz MB, Spurrell EB and Fairburn CG (1997) Assessing the specific psychopathology of binge-eating-disorder patients: interview or self-report? *Behav Res Ther.* **35**: 1151–9.

Williams GJ, Power KG, Miller HR *et al.* (1994). Development and validation of the Stirling Eating Disorders Scales. *Int J Eat Disord.* **16**: 35–43.

Wilson GT (1993) Assessment of binge eating. In: CG Fairburn and GT Wilson (eds) *Binge Eating: nature, assessment and treatment.* Guilford, New York, pp. 227–49.

Wolk SL and Walsh BT (2002) *Assessment of eating disorders in patients with anorexia nervosa: interview versus self-report questionnaire.* Poster presented at the International Conference on Eating Disorders, April 25–28, Boston, MA.

Wonderlich SA, Crosby RD, Mitchell JE *et al.* (2003a) *The state of eating disorder research publications 1980–2000: an empirical analysis. Part II (results).* Paper presented at the Eating Disorders Research Society Annual Meeting, October 1–11, Ravello, Italy.

Wonderlich SA, Crosby RD, Mitchell JE, Smyth J and Miltenberger R (2003b) *Personality traits, emotional states, and bulimic behavior: an intensive daily monitoring study.* Paper presented at the Eating Disorders Research Society Annual Meeting, October 1–11, Ravello, Italy.

8

Medical complications of eating disorders

Scott Crow

Abstract

Objectives of review. The aim of this review was to examine research on medical complications of eating disorders published during the period 2002–2003.

Summary of recent findings. Skeletal complications may be more widespread than was previously thought, affecting males as well as individuals with bulimia nervosa (BN) and eating disorders not otherwise specified (EDNOS). Effective treatments for osteoporosis in eating disorders remain uncertain. BN may have short-term but not long-term impacts on fertility, and may be associated with changes in ovarian morphology in some individuals. Psychoeducational approaches in type 1 diabetes may help to decrease eating disorder cognitions. Binge-eating disorder (BED) may increase the risk of other medical problems.

Future directions. Further research is indicated for many aspects of medical complications in eating disorders. In particular, furthering our understanding of the causes and effective management of osteoporosis will be critical. Also, in order to place BED in its proper context within the fields of eating disorders and obesity, it will be necessary to develop a definitive understanding of the medical burden associated with BED.

Introduction

Medical complications have long been thought of as prominent features of eating disorders. This is perhaps as true for eating disorders as for any mental illness. Over the past few decades, medical complications have been identified which affect essentially every organ system in the body. Although rare complications are still being identified (including some discussed below), much work in this area now involves more thorough descriptions of rates of commonly encountered complications, their pathophysiology and their appropriate management. For this review, papers examining medical complications published during the period 2002–2003 were examined. All of these papers build on a large foundation of work that has previously examined complications of eating disorders.

Literature review

Skeletal complications

The most active area of research during the period 2002–2003 is that of skeletal complications – essentially, osteoporosis. Over the last two years, three areas have been examined. Firstly, further work now describes the frequency of osteoporosis in individuals with anorexia nervosa (AN) and the clinical implications of this finding in terms of risk of fractures. Secondly, some studies have tried to elucidate correlates of and basic mechanisms accounting for bone loss. Thirdly, the results of five trials that attempted to prevent or treat such bone loss have recently become available. Two studies have examined the frequency of osteoporosis in individuals with AN. In one of these studies, the authors reported on the results of dual-energy X-ray absorptiometry (DEXA) scans performed after an 11-year follow-up in 39 individuals with AN as well as in matched controls (Wentz *et al.* 2003). They found no major differences in bone mineral density between AN subjects and controls, although there was an inverse correlation between the duration of AN and bone mineral density. A second study involved cross-sectional assessment at initial presentation of 61 adolescent girls with AN. Low bone mineral density was present in one-quarter to one-third of them, depending on the region measured (Jagielska *et al.* 2002).

A question of considerable clinical relevance is whether osteoporosis in AN actually impacts on health – for example, in terms of fracture rates. A recent study examined this question in all individuals in Denmark who were diagnosed with an eating disorder between 1977 and 1988, who were observed for varying lengths of follow-up (Vestergaard *et al.* 2002). Samples sizes were quite large (2149 AN, 1294 BN and 942 EDNOS), and a matched control group was used for comparison. As expected, AN subjects had a higher risk of fracture than control subjects (elevated approximately twofold), and this appeared to persist for some length of time. Interestingly, BN and EDNOS subjects showed increased fracture risk before eating disorder diagnosis, and for EDNOS subjects this persisted after diagnosis, although in each case the associated relative risk was more modest than that seen for AN. These very interesting results suggest that concerns about skeletal complications may cut across currently used diagnostic categories. However, some caution may be needed in interpreting the results. It is noteworthy that AN was the commonest eating disorder diagnosis, but in most population- and clinic-based studies it is the least common diagnosis. Secondly, it remains unclear whether the elevated fracture rate observed in BN and EDNOS was causally related to osteoporosis or perhaps reflected, for example, higher levels of behavioral impulsivity. Finally, it is not clear whether individuals identified as BN or EDNOS might have initially had undiagnosed AN.

A third small study examining skeletal complications reported growth retardation in 12 adolescent males undergoing treatment for AN (Modan-Moses *et al.* 2003). With continued treatment and weight restoration, the majority of these subjects showed catch-up growth, but on average they did not reach the expected growth rates.

Identifying correlates of osteoporosis in AN has also been a focus of recent work. Several correlates of low bone mineral density or levels of bone turnover markers have recently been demonstrated, including positive correlates such as height, weight and exercise (Gordon *et al.* 2002a), body mass index (BMI) (Audi *et al.* 2002) and insulin-like growth factor-1 (Audi *et al.* 2002; Gordon *et al.* 2002a). Negative correlates have included age, age at menarche, duration of illness, amenorrhea (Jagielska *et al.* 2002) and body fat percentage and dehydroepiandrosterone sulfate levels (Gordon *et al.* 2002b).

Five treatment trials for osteoporosis associated with AN were also reported in the last two years. The first of these involved assignment of patients by patient's choice (not randomly) either to menatetrenone (vitamin K_2) for, on average, 0.9 years of follow-up, or to no treatment (Iketani *et al.* 2003). In this study, 10 subjects received active medication and nine subjects did not receive any medication. Over the follow-up period, a modest decrease in bone mineral density was seen in those not receiving medications, while a smaller decrease was seen in those receiving vitamin K_2 (6.9% vs 2.8%). The authors note that there were corresponding differences in markers of bone metabolism (gamma-carboxyglutamic acid, osteocalcin and urine deoxypyridinoline). It is noteworthy that these subjects were not randomized, no blinding procedures were used, and no placebo was involved.

A second study examined oral dehydroepiandrosterone (DHEA) treatment in 61 women (Gordon *et al.* 2002b). Subjects were randomly assigned to DHEA or estrogen and progesterone thereapy. In this study, which involved one year of treatment, a similar 1.7% increase in total hip bone mineral density was seen in both treatment groups. After controlling for weight gain, no significant increase in bone mineral density was found.

A third study used human insulin-like growth factor 1 (IGF-1) and oral contraceptive therapy, alone or in combination, and there was also a placebo control group (Grinspoon *et al.* 2002). A total of 60 subjects participated, receiving nine months of treatment. IGF-1 treatment was associated with an improvement in bone mineral density. Oral contraceptive treatment did not change bone mineral density, but the co-administration of IGF-1 and oral contraceptives showed an augmented benefit (compared with IGF-1 treatment alone).

Lastly, two studies have directly examined estrogen and progesterone administration. One study enrolled 38 women with AN for one year of unblended treatment (Muñoz *et al.* 2002). Initial bone mineral density among the adolescent subjects in this trial was low, but hormone replacement therapy did lead to improved bone mineral density.

The second study also involved an unrandomized, unblinded patient choice trial in 50 women with AN, of whom 22 subjects received estrogen and progestin and 28 subjects received standard treatment (Golden *et al.* 2002). Again, dual-energy X-ray absorptiometry (DEXA) was used to measure outcome, in this instance over approximately two years of follow-up. In this trial, hormone supplementation was not associated with any benefit in terms of increased bone mineral density. Notably, the subjects who entered both of these trials already had osteoporosis. Thus it remains unclear whether early administration of hormonal supplementation prior to bone mineral loss could have a protective effect.

Reproductive system complications

A question commonly asked by patients receiving treatment for eating disorders is whether their eating disorder will impact on their later ability to have children. In recent years, two studies have examined this question over intermediate to long-term follow-up in women with BN. The first study describes the five-year follow-up of 125 women who had received treatment for BN (Carter *et al.* 2003). In this sample, 32 women (25.6%) had a baby during the follow-up period. Those who had a child had fewer symptoms at the end of treatment, and were on average older. A second study examined this question over a 10 to 15-year follow-up (Crow *et al.* 2002). In this sample of 173 women with BN, approximately 75% had been able to conceive and only 1.7% reported having attempted to conceive but being unable to do so. Taken together, these findings suggest that over the first few years following treatment, symptom status may be associated with fertility, but over longer-term follow-up, BN appears to have little if any impact on fertility.

An associated issue which has received attention in the past is the relationship between binge-eating behavior and polycystic ovaries (McCluskey *et al.* 1991). Recently, Morgan *et al.* (2002) reported on the results of follow-up ultrasonography of ovarian morphology in eight women who had received treatment for BN and for whom an initial ultrasonogram was available. At baseline, seven of the eight subjects had recent bulimia symptoms and of those seven subjects, six had polycystic ovaries and one had multifollicular ovarian morphology. At follow-up, five of the eight women had bulimic symptoms and all five of these symptomatic women had had polycystic ovaries. This was in contrast to the three women whose BN was in remission, all of whom had normal ovaries. Although this sample is small, it provides further support for the previously postulated relationship between polycystic ovaries and BN.

Diabetes mellitus

Another long-recognized association of importance to this review is the link between eating disorders and diabetes mellitus. Initially, type 1 diabetes received the most attention, with some studies finding a higher prevalence of type 1 diabetes in eating-disordered patients, while others did not. What is more consistent in those earlier studies is the finding that disordered eating, particularly insulin omission, is very common in certain diabetic individuals, and that such disordered eating appears to be linked to higher glycosylated hemoglobin levels and a greater risk of medical complications of diabetes (Crow *et al.* 1998). Whether type 2 diabetes is preferentially associated with eating disorders is less certain. Several reports have further examined these questions in recent years. The first is a study using a large primary care sample of subjects who completed the Prime MD Patient Health Questionnaire, a questionnaire that can generate diagnoses of BN and BED (in addition to other mental health diagnoses). In this sample of adults attending primary care clinics, the questionnaire identified BN diagnoses in 0.8% of subjects and BED diagnoses in 6.2% of subjects. Diabetes mellitus affected 7.8% of subjects. BED was more commonly diagnosed in those with diabetes than in those without the disorder (11.8% vs 7.6%; $P = 0.039$). BN was numerically more common among diabetic than non-diabetic subjects (12.5% vs 7.8%), but this difference was not significant (Goodwin *et al.* 2003).

A second sample examined obese subjects with and without type 2 diabetes mellitus with regard to binge-eating behavior (Mannucci *et al.* 2002). In this study, binge eating was found in a somewhat lower percentage (7.5%) of diabetic subjects than has been reported previously, and BED was actually more common in obese non-diabetic subjects than in those with diabetes. However, there was a positive correlation between Eating Disorder Examination (EDE) scores and hemoglobin A_{1C} levels among diabetic individuals. The findings stand in contrast to some but not all previous studies, and thus the relationship between type 2 diabetes and eating disorders requires further clarification.

Finally, one study has recently examined the use of a psychoeducational program in young women with type 1 diabetes mellitus (Olmsted *et al.* 2002). This issue is one of substantial significance. Although findings with regard to rates of full syndrome eating disorders have varied, disordered eating and increased risk of diabetic complications associated with such disordered eating have repeatedly been shown. In this study, 85 women were randomly assigned either to the intervention or to the group that received treatment as usual. The findings were mixed. Receiving the intervention did not result in significant changes in insulin omission or glycosylated hemoglobin levels. However, restraint and eating concern as measured by the EDE, as well as drive for thinness and body dissatisfaction as measured by the Eating Disorders Inventory (EDI), all improved in the intervention group. The use of such educational interventions in adolescents with type 1 diabetes mellitus warrants further attention.

Cardiovascular complications

Individuals seeking treatment for eating disorders frequently report chest pain, which at times is suggestive of angina. In the past, the issue of possible coronary artery disease in women with eating disorders has received limited attention. One recently published article examined carotid intima media thickness (IMT) using ultrasonography in 18 women with AN and 18 age-matched controls (Birmingham *et al.* 2003b). Carotid IMT was very similar and within normal limits for both groups – neither group demonstrated atherosclerotic plaques. These results provide some reassurance for clinicians who encounter chest pain complaints among their patients.

Refeeding hypophosphatemia

Dangerously low serum phosphate levels have long been recognized as a potential complication of refeeding in severely starved anorexic patients. Two recent reports have further expanded our understanding of this phenomenon. Firstly, Ornstein *et al.* (2003) reviewed the charts of 69 consecutive admissions to an inpatient unit for AN treatment to describe observed problems with hypophosphatemia. Four patients developed a moderately low phosphorus level (defined by the investigators as 1.0 mg/dL to 2.5 mg/dL), while 15 further patients developed mildly low phosphate levels (described by the investigators as 2.5 mg/dL to 3.0 mg/dL). More significant hypophosphatemia was associated with more severe malnourishment, and the lowest observed phosphorus levels were generally observed during the first week of hospitalization. In this sample, a total of 27.5% of subjects received phosphorus supplementation.

Although hypophosphatemia is generally considered to be a complication of inpatient treatment, a recent case report highlights the fact that it can occur outside hospital as well (Winston and Wells 2002). These authors reported a case of significant hypophosphatemia (0.2 mmol/L, reference range 0.7–1.4 mmol/L) in a male with anorexia nervosa who had begun to refeed himself with large amounts of food after a prolonged period of restriction which had resulted in a BMI of 15 kg/m^2.

Medical complications of binge-eating disorder

The diagnostic validity of BED remains controversial, and one area of controversy concerns whether BED can be differentiated from straightforward obesity by the presence of higher rates of specific or general medical complications. Rigorous data in this area are largely limited to research in the area of diabetes, but a recent report suggests that BED may be associated with higher rates of a variety of medical problems (Bulik *et al.* 2002). This study examined data from a large twin sample with regard to eating behavior, medical problems and other mental health problems. From this sample, a subset of 166 obese women were identified, and of these, slightly more than one-third endorsed a lifetime history of binge eating. Binge eating was not associated with higher BMI, but was associated with health dissatisfaction. Elevated odds ratios were seen for all medical complications examined, including hypertension, visual impairment, asthma or respiratory illness, diabetes, osteoarthritis and any major medical disorder. However, none of these elevated odds ratios reached the level of statistical significance, perhaps due to the modest sample size.

Medication abuse

One source of medical complications in individuals with eating disorders is the use and abuse of appetite suppressants, diuretics and other over-the-counter (OTC) medications. A recent survey examined the frequency of such potential risks (Roerig *et al.* 2003). This study examined self-reports of medication use in 39 consecutive patients with BN combined with a survey of local pharmacies in the area where the study was conducted. The results were striking, with 64% of patients reporting a history of diet-pill use (18% in the last month). A survey of local pharmacies yielded a total of 167 OTC products falling within this category. With regard to diuretic use, 31% of subjects reported a lifetime history of such use (21% in the last month), and 25 such products were found in local pharmacies. These results highlight the magnitude of this risk.

Brain tissue and function changes

Previous neuroimaging studies have identified changes in brain volume as a potential complication of AN. A recent study examined volume segmentation in subjects with AN before and after weight gain (Swayze *et al.* 2003). Pre- and post-treatment T1-weighted MRI scans in 17 patients with AN revealed significant reductions in total and regional white matter volume, significant increases in cerebrospinal fluid volume, and no change in gray matter volume. These changes tended to reverse with treatment. These findings confirm and extend the results of previous work in this area.

A second study (McDowell *et al.* 2003) attempted to measure the potential functional significance of cognitive changes. This study of 98 patients with AN attempted to replicate previous work showing cognitive impairment in individuals with AN, and specifically to clarify whether such cognitive changes are directly attributable to depressed mood. Using the Wechsler Adult Intelligence Scale, Revised (WAIS–R) (Wechsler 1981), these investigators showed that cognitive changes in AN were not related to ratings of mood, leaving open the possibility that such changes may result from a nutritional, stress-related or other non-affective mechanism.

Case reports of medical complications

In addition to the controlled studies and case series described above, a number of potentially important isolated reports of medical complications among eating-disordered subjects have been published in the last two years. Some may represent previously unrecognized but relatively common findings, while others may merely represent rather rare but important complications. They include the following:

1 impaired fever response to bacterial infection in AN (Birmingham *et al.* 2003a)
2 pneumomediastinum in AN (Karim *et al.* 2002)

3 respiratory muscle weakness in AN (Birmingham and Tan 2003)
4 pericardial effusion in AN (Inagaki *et al.* 2003)
5 neutropenia and bone mineral transformation in AN (Nishio *et al.* 2003)
6 hypoglycemia in AN (Yasuhara *et al.* 2003)
7 severe hyperlipoproteinemia in AN (Homma *et al.* 2002)
8 gastric dilatation in atypical AN (Holtkamp *et al.* 2002)
9 central pontine myelinolysis in AN with hypokalemia (Sugimoto *et al.* 2003).

Summary of important findings

1 An elevated risk of fractures in individuals with eating disorders was confirmed, but it remains unclear how osteoporosis in eating disorders should be treated.
2 BN may have a negative impact on short-term fertility, but this appears to abate over longer-term follow-up.
3 There may be a relationship between ovarian morphology and level of BN symptomatology.
4 Psychoeducational programs may improve eating disorder cognitions in women with diabetes mellitus.
5 The risk of hypophosphatemia appears to peak during the first week after hospitalization, but may not be solely a hospital-based phenomenon.

Clinical implications

Taken together, these findings suggest that an area of particularly useful clinical focus to discuss with patients when attempting to motivate them with regard to behavior change is the negative impact of disordered eating and abnormal weight on bone function and, in the short term, on fertility. These findings also provide some reassurance about the risk of cardiovascular disease, but on the other hand they heighten concerns about the risk of hypophosphatemia.

Future directions

Several areas are in need of further investigation. First, osteoporosis remains a very important problem in relation to eating disorders, and the study by Vestergaard *et al.* (2002) suggests that the risk of skeletal complications may not be confined to narrowly defined AN. Effective treatments for this problem are urgently required. A secondary need involves a clear definition of the medical complications of BED. Recent work suggests that BED may be associated with a higher rate of medical complications. The clear elucidation of this question would have a major impact on the ongoing debate about the diagnostic validity of BED.

Corresponding author: Scott Crow, MD, Department of Psychiatry, University of Minnesota Medical School, F290 West Building, 2450 Riverside Avenue, Minneapolis, MN 55454-1495, USA. Email: crowx002@umn.edu

References

Audi L, Vargas DM, Gussinyé M, Yeste D, Martí G and Carrascosa A (2002) Clinical and biochemical determinants of bone metabolism and bone mass in adolescent female patients with anorexia nervosa. *Pediatr Res.* **51**: 497–504.

Birmingham CL and Tan AO (2003) Respiratory muscle weakness and anorexia nervosa. *Int J Eat Disord.* **33**: 230–3.

Birmingham CL, Hodgson DM, Fung J *et al.* (2003a) Reduced febrile response to bacterial infection in anorexia nervosa patients. *Int J Eat Disord.* **34**: 269–72.

Birmingham CL, Lear SA, Kenyon J, Chan SY, Mancini GB and Frohlich J (2003b) Coronary atherosclerosis in anorexia nervosa. *Int J Eat Disord.* **34**: 375–7.

Bulik CM, Sullivan PF and Kendler KS (2002) Medical and psychiatric morbidity in obese women with and without binge eating. *Int J Eat Disord.* **32**: 72–8.

Carter FA, McIntosh VV, Frampton CM, Joyce PR and Bulik CM (2003) Predictors of childbirth following treatment for bulimia nervosa. *Int J Eat Disord.* **34**: 337–42.

Crow SJ, Keel PK and Kendall D (1998) Eating disorders and insulin-dependent diabetes mellitus. *Psychosomatics.* **39**: 233–43.

Crow SJ, Thuras P, Keel PK and Mitchell JE (2002) Long-term menstrual and reproductive function in patients with bulimia nervosa. *Am J Psychiatry.* **159**: 1048–50.

Golden NH, Lanzkowsky L, Schebendach J, Palestro CJ, Jacobson MS and Shenker IR (2002) The effect of estrogen–progestin treatment on bone mineral density in anorexia nervosa. *J Pediatr Adolesc Gynecol.* **15**: 135–43.

Goodwin RD, Hoven CW and Spitzer RL (2003) Diabetes and eating disorders in primary care. *Int J Eat Disord.* **33**: 85–91.

Gordon CM, Goodman E, Emans SJ *et al.* (2002a). Physiologic regulators of bone turnover in young women with anorexia nervosa. *J Pediatr.* **141**: 64–70.

Gordon CM, Grace E, Emans SJ *et al.* (2002b) Effects of oral dehydroepiandrosterone on bone density in young women with anorexia nervosa: a randomized trial. *J Clin Endocrinol Metab.* **87**: 4935–41.

Grinspoon S, Thomas L, Miller K, Herzog D and Klibanski A (2002) Effects of recombinant human IFG-1 and oral contraceptive administration on bone density in anorexia nervosa. *J Clin Endocrinol Metab.* **87**: 2883–91.

Holtkamp K, Mogharrebi R, Hanisch C, Schumpelick V and Herpertz-Dahlmann B (2002) Gastric dilatation in a girl with former obesity and atypical anorexia nervosa. *Int J Eat Disord.* **32**: 372–6.

Homma Y, Homma K, Iizuka S and Iigaya K (2002) A case of anorexia nervosa with severe hyperlipoproteinemia. *Int J Eat Disord.* **32**: 121–4.

Iketani T, Kiriike N, Murray BS *et al.* (2003) Effect of menatetrenone (vitamin K_2) treatment on bone loss in patients with anorexia nervosa. *Psychiatry Res.* **117**: 259–69.

Inagaki T, Yamamoto M, Tsubouchi K *et al.* (2003) Echocardiographic investigation of pericardial effusion in a case of anorexia nervosa. *Int J Eat Disord.* **33**: 364–6.

Jagielska G, Wolanczyk T, Komender J, Tomaszewicz-Libudzic C, Przedlacki J and Ostrowski K (2002) Bone mineral density in adolescent girls with anorexia nervosa. *Eur Child Adolesc Psychiatry.* **11**: 57–62.

Karim A, Ahmed S and Rossoff L (2002) Pneumomediastinum simulating a panic attack in a patient with anorexia nervosa. *Int J Eat Disord.* **33**: 104–7.

McCluskey S, Evans C, Lacey JH, Pearce JM and Jacobs H (1991) Polycystic ovary syndrome and bulimia. *Fertil Steril.* **55**: 287–91.

McDowell BD, Moser DJ, Ferneyhough K, Bowers WA, Andersen AE and Paulsen JS (2003) Cognitive impairment in anorexia nervosa is not due to depressed mood. *Int J Eat Disord.* **33**: 351–5.

Mannucci E, Tesi F, Ricca V *et al.* (2002) Eating behavior in obese patients with and without type 2 diabetes mellitus. *Int J Obes Relat Metab Disord.* **26**: 848–53.

Modan-Moses D, Yaroslavsky A, Novikov I *et al.* (2003) Stunting of growth as a major feature of anorexia nervosa in male adolescents. *Pediatrics.* **111**: 270–76.

Morgan JF, McCluskey SE, Brunton JN and Lacey JH (2002) Polycystic ovarian morphology and bulimia nervosa: a 9-year follow-up study. *Fertil Steril.* **77**: 928–31.

Muñoz MT, Morandé G, Garcí-Centenera JA, Hervás F, Pozo J and Argente J (2002) The effects of estrogen administration on bone mineral density in adolescents with anorexia nervosa. *Eur J Endocrinol.* **146**: 45–50.

Nishio S, Yamada H, Yamada K *et al.* (2003) Severe neutropenia with gelatinous bone marrow transformation in anorexia nervosa: a case report. *Int J Eat Disord.* **33**: 360–3.

Olmsted MP, Daneman D, Rydall AC, Lawson ML and Rodin G (2002) The effects of psychoeducation on disturbed eating attitudes and behavior in young women with type 1 diabetes mellitus. *Int J Eat Disord.* **32**: 230–9.

Ornstein RM, Golden NH, Jacobson MS and Shenker IR (2003) Hypophosphatemia during nutritional rehabilitation in anorexia nervosa: implications for refeeding and monitoring. *J Adolesc Health.* **32**: 83–8.

Roerig JL, Mitchell JE, de Zwaan M *et al.* (2003) The eating disorders medicine cabinet revisited: a clinician's guide to appetite suppressants and diuretics. *Int J Eat Disord.* **33**: 443–57.

Sugimoto T, Murata T, Omori M and Wada Y (2003) Central pontine myelinolysis associated with hypokalaemia in anorexia nervosa. *J Neurol Neurosurg Psychiatry.* **74**: 353–5.

Swayze VW II, Andersen AE, Andreasen NC, Arndt S, Sato Y and Ziebell S (2003) Brain tissue volume segmentation in patients with anorexia nervosa before and after weight normalization. *Int J Eat Disord.* **33**: 33–44.

Vestergaard P, Emborg C, Stoving RK, Hagen C, Mosekilde L and Brixen K (2002) Fractures in patients with anorexia nervosa, bulimia nervosa and other eating disorders – a nationwide register study. *Int J Eat Disord.* **32**: 301–8.

Wechsler D (1981) *Wechsler Adult Intelligence Scale, Revised.* The Psychological Corporation, New York.

Wentz E, Mellstrom D, Gillberg C, Sundh V, Gillberg IC and Rastam M (2003) Bone density 11 years after anorexia nervosa onset in a controlled study of 39 cases. *Int J Eat Disord.* **34**: 314–18.

Winston AP and Wells FE (2002) Hypophosphatemia following self-treatment for anorexia nervosa. *Int J Eat Disord.* **32**: 245–8.

Yasuhara D, Deguchi D, Tsutsui J, Nagai N, Nozoe S and Naruo T (2003) A characteristic reactive hypoglycemia induced by rapid change of eating behavior in anorexia nervosa: a case report. *Int J Eat Disord.* **34**: 273–7.

9

Psychological trauma and eating disorders

Timothy D Brewerton

Abstract

Objectives of review. The aim of this chapter is to review research published during the period 2002–2003 on the relationship between traumatic experiences and the development of eating disorders.

Summary of recent findings. Recent reviews and an 18-year longitudinal study confirm that childhood sexual abuse (CSA) is a significant but non-specific risk factor for the development of eating disorders, especially bulimia nervosa (BN) and other eating disorders with bulimic symptomatology. New cross-sectional research further demonstrates significant associations between sexual and other forms of abuse and bulimic disorders in adults, as well as in adolescent girls and boys. The scope of abusive experiences has also been widened to include bullying, racial discrimination, dating violence, date rape, physical neglect and emotional abuse.

Future directions. Further research is needed on the effect of psychological trauma and post-traumatic stress disorder (PTSD) on the long-term course and prognosis of the eating disorders. Randomized controlled treatment trials in bulimic patients with abuse histories and trauma-related comorbidity, such as PTSD, are a logical future step. Finally, future research is likely to further elucidate the psychobiologic underpinnings of abuse, eating disorders and comorbidity, which may lead to better prevention and treatment strategies.

Introduction

The relationship between traumatic experiences, such as sexual, physical and emotional abuse, and the eating disorders continues to be of great scientific and clinical interest, and has been the subject of a number of research publications over the last two years, which will be the focus of this review. However, a brief summary of the knowledge base on this topic is in order before these new data are presented. The conclusions from the comprehensive review on the role of childhood sexual abuse (CSA) by Wonderlich *et al*. (1997) remain essentially uncontested to this day, and can be briefly summarized as follows.

1 CSA is associated with bulimia nervosa (BN).
2 CSA is more strongly associated with BN than with anorexia nervosa (AN).
3 CSA is not a specific risk factor for eating disorders.
4 CSA is not associated with greater severity of the eating disorder.
5 Particular features of CSA are associated with eating disorder symptoms, including decreased social competence, poor maternal relationships, unreliable parenting, severity of the CSA, and presence of lifetime post-traumatic stress disorder (PTSD).
6 CSA is associated with psychiatric comorbidity in subjects with eating disorders.

More recent research since this study was published has largely substantiated these conclusions. In addition to CSA, other data have linked sexual assault and physical assault during adulthood, as well as resultant PTSD, to BN (Dansky *et al*. 1997). In this large, national, representative sample of adult women in the USA (National Women's Study), over half (54%) of this non-treatment-seeking, non-clinical sample of women with BN reported experiences of rape, molestation or aggravated assault (compared with 31% in non-bulimic subjects), and 37% met the criteria for a lifetime prevalence of PTSD (compared with 13% in non-bulimic subjects). Other studies have reported that histories of childhood physical abuse or severe corporal punishment are associated with bulimic symptomatology in children and adolescents. These data have been summarized elsewhere (Brewerton 2002, 2004).

Literature review

This literature review employed the following methodology. A MEDLINE search was conducted for all indexed articles published during the years 2002 and 2003 and during January 2004, using all possible combinations of two sets of keywords cross-referenced with each other. The first set of keywords included 'eating disorders,' 'bulimia,' 'anorexia nervosa,' 'binge-eating disorder,' and 'eating disorder not otherwise specified' (EDNOS), while the second set of keywords included 'sexual abuse,' 'sexual assault,' 'sexual harassment,' 'physical abuse,' 'physical assault,' 'emotional abuse,' 'child abuse,' 'neglect,' 'victimization,' 'trauma,' 'PTSD' and 'dissociation.' Particular attention was given to articles with new data and to review articles, although a few case reports that illustrate new concepts or relationships have been included.

Comprehensive reviews

Smolak and Murnen (2002) reported their results of a meta-analysis of the relationship between CSA and eating disorders using 53 data-containing articles and book chapters. They focused on two specific objectives. The first was to assess the extent and consistency of the relationship between CSA and eating disorders, and the second was to examine the methodological factors that contribute to the heterogeneity of this relationship. The studies examined were categorized into two basic types: (1) those comparing individuals with CSA with those without CSA in terms of eating disorder incidence (30 studies), and (2) those comparing individuals with an eating disorder (usually BN) with those without an eating disorder in terms of CSA experiences (23 studies). A small but statistically significant positive relationship between CSA and eating disorders emerged for both types of studies ($r = 0.18$, $P < 0.001$ and $r = 0.12$, $P < 0.01$, respectively). In the second type of study (CSA with or without eating disorder) the positive relationship between CSA and eating disorders was marked by statistically significant heterogeneity ($P < 0.01$) in that the effect sizes were largest when the Eating Attitudes Test (EAT) or the Eating Disorders Inventory (EDI) was used as the primary eating disorder measure ($r = 0.284$, $P < 0.05$), as opposed to a specific measure of BN. Effect sizes also varied significantly by participant's age in these studies, and were largest when participants were in their twenties ($r = 0.24$, $P < 0.05$), compared with when they were in their teens ($r = 0.11$) or aged 30 years or over ($r = 0.12$).

In the first type of study (eating-disordered subjects with or without CSA) there was also a statistically significant relationship ($P < 0.01$). Effect sizes were largest when comparison groups consisted of normal controls ($r = 0.2$) as opposed to when they consisted of psychopathology controls ($r = 0.08$, $P < 0.05$). The age of participants did not predict a difference in r-values between groupings in this subsample of studies. Across all studies from both groups, the overall effect size was calculated to be $r = 0.1$ ($P < 0.01$), thereby indicating a small effect with significant heterogeneity. Interestingly, studies that used CSA status as the independent variable showed an effect size greater than twice that of studies which used eating-disorder status as the independent variable, and this disparity appeared to be primarily accounted for by important methodological differences across studies. One of the most notable was the variation in definitions used to define an eating disorder. The CSA-focused studies, which had an effect size of $r = 0.284$, were much more likely to use the EAT or the EDI as eating disorder measures than the eating-disorder-focused studies. In addition, the nature of the comparison group was quite important in terms of explaining heterogeneity. Within eating-disorder-focused studies, those that compared a clinical eating disorder group with a non-clinical group had an effect size of $r = 0.21$, whereas those that compared a clinical eating disorder group with other clinical patients yielded an effect size of $r = -0.12$. The authors concluded that future models of CSA and eating disorder need to specify more clearly what aspects of eating disorder (e.g. body image or eating) are most influenced by which types of CSA. A reason not cited by the authors that might account for the difference in effect sizes between the two types of studies is a disturbance in memory. It is possibly easier for already identified CSA subjects to remember and report whether they had an eating disorder or eating disorder symptoms than it is for eating-disordered subjects to remember and report whether or not they were victims of CSA. In a large, representative sample of adult women in the USA, forgetting traumatic events was associated not only with CSA, but also with BN and purging behavior independent of a BN diagnosis (Brewerton *et al.* 1999).

Jacobi *et al.* (2004) recently published a systematic and rigorous review of risk factors, including sexual abuse, for the *onset* of eating disorders, including AN, BN and BED. These investigators used the recently described rigorous definitions of risk factors by Kraemer *et al.* (1997, 1999) as the basis of their review. They found only one study that supported the classification of sexual abuse as a retrospective correlate for the development of AN, and they called for more replication studies. However, there was much more data for BN, and they concluded that there is strong evidence to support the notion that sexual abuse is a non-specific retrospective correlate as well as a variable risk factor of medium potency for the development of BN. In terms of BED, they noted the paucity of studies to date, yet concluded that sexual abuse and physical neglect were non-specific variable risk factors for BED. In addition, perceived paternal neglect was noted to be a retrospective correlate of medium potency with BED.

New longitudinal prospective studies

Johnson *et al.* (2002) published results from the most comprehensive longitudinal study to date on the association between childhood adversities, including CSA, physical abuse and neglect, and the subsequent later development of eating- or weight-related problems, including eating disorders. The authors studied a large community-based sample of mothers and their offspring (*n* = 782) followed over an 18-year period. Information about sexual abuse and physical neglect was obtained from structured interviews of both child and mother. Of the total sample of offspring, 6.6% received an eating-disorder diagnosis during adolescence or adulthood, with female offspring having a rate of 11% and male offspring having a rate of 2% (odds ratio (OR) = 5.2). Individuals who had experienced sexual abuse or physical neglect during childhood were at elevated risk for subsequent eating disorders (OR: sexual abuse = 4.82; physical neglect = 5.11). The great majority of the eating disorders identified in this study were characterized by bulimic symptomatology (BN, BED or EDNOS with purging), and only one case of AN (in a boy) was identified. In addition, both sexual abuse and physical neglect predicted recurrent fluctuations in weight, strict dieting and self-induced vomiting, while physical neglect predicted obesity, irrespective of the presence of an eating disorder. It is notable that all of the significant relationships reported in this study were manifested *after* controlling for age, difficult temperament, childhood eating problems and parental psychiatric disorders. Another key finding that is important to emphasize is that offspring who had experienced three or more kinds of maladaptive paternal behaviors were three times more likely to have eating disorders. This lends credence to the hypothesis that repeated traumatic events are more specific to the development of eating disorders with bulimic symptomatology (see below). The results of this pivotal and impressive research indicate that maladaptive paternal behavior may play a more important role than maladaptive maternal behavior in the development of eating disorders in progeny. Previous work has focused much more on the mother's role and has relatively neglected the father's role. In terms of physical abuse and its derivatives, there were several findings. Physical abuse predicted low body weight (OR = 4.71, P < 0.01) but not a diagnosis of AN. High levels of peer aggression predicted use of medication to lose weight (OR = 3.85, P < 0.01), and harsh maternal punishment (OR = 4.82, P < 0.01) and loud arguments between parents (OR = 6.15, P < 0.01) predicted obesity (independent of an eating disorder). Although sexual abuse and physical neglect were found to be non-specific and variable risk factors in this study, its longitudinal design clearly established these factors as significant contributors to the development of eating disorders and related eating problems, particularly those involving bulimic symptoms.

New studies of abuse and eating disorders in adults

Leonard *et al.* (2003) evaluated associations between childhood physical and sexual abuse and eating disturbances, psychiatric symptoms, and the probability of later abuse in adulthood. In total, 51 outpatient bulimic women and 25 age- and BMI-matched 'normal-eater' college women, who had no history of eating disorders according to the Eating Disorders Examination (EDE) and no psychiatric history, took part in the study. In addition to the EDE, the Eating Attitudes Test (EAT), Childhood Trauma Interview (CTI), Trauma Assessment for Adults (TAA), Dimensional Assessment of Personality Pathology Basic Questionnaire (DAPP-BQ), Center for Epidemiological Studies Depression Scale (CES-D), Barrat Impulsivity Scale (BIS) and Dissociative Experiences Scale (DES) were administered to all subjects in order to measure eating symptoms, comorbidity, and childhood and adulthood abuse. Bulimic women reported significantly higher levels of CSA, childhood physical abuse and combined childhood sexual and physical abuse compared with the 'normal-eater' women. Bulimic women not only demonstrated more psychopathology than non-bulimic women, but they also showed an association between the presence and severity of trauma and the severity of concomitant psychopathologic symptoms. As might be expected, dissociation and submissiveness were positively associated with the severity of prior abuse. An important finding of this study is that abuse during adulthood was almost always preceded by previous childhood abuse. Only one (6.7%) of the 15 bulimic women who reported abuse during adulthood did not report some form of previous childhood abuse. These findings suggest an association between certain psychopathologic traits and the likelihood of abuse (especially when it occurred both in childhood and in adulthood). Observed associations could implicate causal effects of childhood abuse on personality development, influences of personality traits in heightening the risk of abuse, or both. These data add to the findings of other investigators that multiple episodes of abuse are particularly relevant to the development of BN.

Striegel-Moore *et al.* (2002) reported results from an interview-based assessment of a community sample of 162 women with BED, 107 psychiatric comparison subjects and 251 healthy controls, all of whom were matched for age, ethnicity and level of education. Two questions were examined in this study – firstly, whether sexual and physical abuse, bullying by peers and ethnicity-based discrimination were associated with an increased risk of developing BED, and secondly, whether any such increased risk is specific to BED. Caucasian women with BED reported significantly higher rates of all forms of abuse, including sexual and physical abuse, bullying and racial discrimination, compared with healthy controls. Only discrimination rates were significantly higher in Caucasian women with BED than in psychiatric comparison subjects. In black women with BED, all forms of abuse except discrimination were significantly higher than in healthy controls. In addition, black women with BED reported sexual abuse rates that were significantly higher than those reported by psychiatric comparison subjects. These results are consistent with the findings of previous research that investigated patterns of risk for psychiatric disorder, in that the authors discovered both ethnic similarities (physical abuse and bullying by peers) and differences (sexual abuse and discrimination) in the risk for BED.

New studies of abuse and eating disorders in children and adolescents

Fonseca *et al.* (2002) examined a number of familial factors, including sexual abuse, in relation to extreme weight control measures in a large group of adolescents (n = 9042) using a comprehensive health survey of Connecticut students (seventh, ninth and eleventh grades). Extreme dieters, who intentionally vomited or took diet pills, laxatives or diuretics in order to lose weight, were compared with adolescents who reported none of these behaviors (using logistic regression controlling for body mass index (BMI) and age). Extreme weight control behaviors were reported in almost 7% of adolescents. Risk factors for boys included sexual abuse history (OR = 2.8, $P < 0.001$) and high levels of parental supervision/monitoring, while protective factors included high parental expectations, maternal presence, and connectedness with friends and other adults. For girls, the only significant risk factor besides BMI (OR = 2.17, $P < 0.002$) was a history of sexual abuse (OR = 1.45, $P < 0.001$), while protective factors included family connectedness, positive family communication, parental supervision/monitoring and maternal presence. These findings confirm an association between sexual abuse and extreme weight control behaviors, primarily involving purging, in both girls and boys, even when a formal eating disorder diagnosis has not been made. The authors noted that sexual abuse as a predictive factor and connectedness to family members, other adults and friends as a protective factor, further establish the importance of the interrelationships between extreme weight control behaviors and interpersonal interactions at a family and social level. It is notable that purging, not bingeing, is what characterized the eating-disordered group, and that it was these behaviors which were linked to sexual abuse. This link with purging rather than bingeing behaviors has been noted previously in a large representative sample of adult women in the USA (Dansky *et al.* 1997; Brewerton *et al.* 1999, 2003).

Ackard and Neumark-Sztainer (2002) assessed the prevalence of date rape and date violence in adolescents, as well as the associations between these events and disordered eating behaviors and psychopathology, in a very large sample ($n = 81\ 247$) of boys and girls in ninth and twelfth grades in Minnesota using the 1998 Minnesota Student Survey. Approximately 9% of girls and 6% of boys reported experiencing date rape or violence. More specifically, 4.2% of girls and 2.6% of boys reported date violence, while 1.4% of girls and 1.2% of boys reported date rape. In total, 3% of girls and 2.2% of boys reported both types of experiences on a date. Significant differences were found by grade in school for girls (but not for boys), with girls in the twelfth grade reporting the highest rates of date-related violence (11.5%). Racial differences were also found, with white girls reporting the highest rates of date violence and combined date violence and date rape, and Mexican-American girls reporting the highest rates of date rape alone. The authors found that both date violence and date rape were associated with higher rates of eating-disordered behaviors in both girls and boys. Date violence and/or rape were also associated with suicidal thoughts and attempts, as well as lower scores on measures of self-esteem and emotional well-being, especially in girls. Controlling for both age and race, those adolescents who experienced both date violence and date rape were more likely to use laxatives (OR: girls = 5.76; boys = 28.22), to vomit (OR: girls = 4.74; boys = 21.46), to use diet pills (OR: girls = 5.08; boys = 16.33), to binge eat (OR: girls = 2.15; boys = 5.80) and to have suicidal thoughts or attempts (OR: girls = 5.78; boys = 6.66) than their non-abused peers. These odds remained significant, albeit weakened, after other abusive experiences involving adults had been controlled for. In particular it should be noted that a higher percentage of girls and boys who reported an abusive dating experience also reported repeat victimization (physical or sexual abuse perpetrated by an adult) compared with their peers who had not had an abusive dating experience. Because of the cross-sectional nature of this study, any statement about causality cannot be made with certainty, but the authors speculated that normal developmental processes are likely to be disrupted by abusive experiences during dating relationships. Examples of such normal developmental processes that might be disrupted include the development of a stable self-concept and an integrated body image during adolescence. Fornari and Dancyger (2003) expounded eloquently on this important topic in a recent overview of psychosexual development and eating disorders. They noted that potential adaptations to such trauma might include anxiety about and avoidance of adult intimacy, as well as sexually provocative 'acting-out' behaviors.

In another paper, Ackard and Neumark-Sztainer (2003) used the same dataset described above (the Minnesota Student Survey) to examine associations between multiple forms of sexual abuse (including date rape, sexual abuse by an adult non-family member and sexual abuse by an adult family member) and eating-disordered behaviors and psychological health among adolescents in Minnesota. After controlling for grade and race, girls with multiple forms of abuse were found to have significant odds ratios for the following behaviors: vomiting (OR = 4.1), laxative abuse (OR = 5.1), diet pill abuse (OR = 4.3), bingeing (OR = 2.2), fasting (OR = 2.3) and thinking about/attempting suicide (OR = 6.12). Boys with multiple forms of abuse had the following statistically significant odds ratios: vomiting (OR = 24.2), laxative abuse (OR = 29.2), diet pill abuse (OR = 17.3), bingeing (OR = 5.6), fasting (OR = 2.3) and thinking about/ attempting suicide (OR = 9.5). Of particular interest in this study is the finding that boys and girls with multiple forms of sexual abuse reported similar rates of bingeing (42.6% vs 41.1%), taking diet pills (22.3% vs 26.5%) and vomiting (18.7% vs 23.3%), but boys who had been sexually abused in multiple ways had higher rates of laxative abuse than girls (22.4% vs 7.4%). The authors note that sexual abuse may be a particular risk factor for disordered eating behaviors among boys. It is also notable that the odds ratios for purging behaviors are much more robust than those for binge eating, thereby linking sexual abuse experiences more closely to purging than to bingeing, particularly when there are multiple forms or occurrences. These data also confirm links between sexual abuse experiences and comorbidity, such as suicidality, which are often associated with bulimic symptomatology.

In another study by Ackard, Neumark-Sztainer and Hannon (2003) using a different data-set, the prevalence of adolescent dating violence and its associations with behavioral and mental health problems, including eating-disorder-related behaviors, were investigated in a nationally representative sample of 3533 high-school students in grades 9–12 using the Commonwealth Fund Survey of the Health of Adolescent Boys and Girls. The authors also looked at the percentage of adolescents who remain in potentially harmful relationships because of fear of being hurt if they leave. The authors found that dating violence for both girls and boys was associated with dieting, binge eating and purging, as well as alcohol consumption, drug use, cigarette smoking, suicidal thoughts, depression and low self-esteem. Girls and boys who endorsed both physical and sexual abuse reported higher rates of dieting (girls: 70.4% vs 56.4%; boys: 50.0% vs 22.5%) and binge–purge behavior (girls: 47.4% vs 13.7%; boys: 48.4% vs 4.7%) than their non-abused peers. These differences persisted after controlling for race, socioeconomic status and BMI. Among girls who had ever binged and purged, dating violence during adolescence was associated with bingeing and purging at least several times a week. Notably, 100% of boys with a history of sexual abuse and 95% of boys with a history of both sexual and physical abuse reported bingeing and purging several times a week, compared with 57% of non-abused boys. The parallel results for girls were not as striking, but were nevertheless higher in those reporting sexual abuse (63%) and combined sexual and physical abuse (64%) than in girls who denied abuse (45%). One major limitation of this study is that the enquiry about 'bingeing and purging' was presented as one question rather than as two separate questions, so that respondents who engaged in either bingeing or purging, but not both, would have to give a negative response. Nevertheless, this study adds to the growing body of literature linking sexual and physical abuse to bulimia. These results also highlight the importance of abuse in the development of bulimic symptomatology in boys, an area that has often been overlooked in previous studies.

Sherwood *et al.* (2002) reported the results of administration of a 225-item questionnaire to 5163 seventh, ninth- and eleventh-grade female public school students with the aim of examining the factors associated with eating disorders among girls involved in weight-related sports. Eating-disorder symptoms were found in almost one-third of girls involved in both weight-related and non-weight-related sports. However, after controlling for a number of factors, including grade, race, socioeconomic status and study-design effect, girls in weight-related sports were found to be 51% more likely to have eating-disorder symptoms than girls in non-weight-related sports. Of relevance to this review is the finding that girls in weight-related sports who had eating disorders had experienced more physical abuse (OR = 3.29) and sexual abuse (OR = 3.87) than girls in weight-related sports without eating disorders. These results may be useful in future efforts to identify subpopulations of girls at higher risk for developing eating disorders.

Comorbidity and clinical features associated with trauma

Grilo and Masheb (2002) examined the association between childhood maltreatment and personality disorders (PDs) in 116 adult outpatients with DSM-IV-defined BED. All patients completed the Childhood Trauma Questionnaire (CTQ) to assess childhood maltreatment in five specific areas, namely sexual abuse, physical abuse, emotional abuse, physical neglect and emotional neglect. In addition, patients were administered the Diagnostic Interview for DSM-IV Personality Disorders (DIPD-IV). Overall, some kind of childhood maltreatment was reported in 82% of BED patients, and cluster C PDs were by far the commonest type of PD (27% cluster C vs 6% cluster A and 7% cluster B). Of all the types of abuse and PDs examined, only emotional abuse was significantly associated with the presence of a cluster C PD in this sample of BED patients. Patients with cluster C PDs had experienced significantly more clinically significant emotional abuse (74%) than those without cluster C PDs (45%, $P < 0.009$). Specific cluster C PDs were tested for an association with emotional abuse, and only avoidant PD showed a significant link. Emotional abuse histories were reported in 81% of those with avoidant PD compared with 46% of those without avoidant PD. Finally, the authors performed a logistic regression analysis to examine the contributions of the five different forms of abuse in predicting PDs. Taken together, the five scales of the CTQ resulted in the correct classification of a PD in 71.3% of cases ($P < 0.01$), and only emotional abuse independently contributed to a correct classification ($P < 0.001$).

The study by Dohm et al. (2002) evaluated rates of self-harm and substance use in women with either BN or BED, and assessed whether differences in self-harm and substance use are related to sexual or physical abuse. Alcohol abuse, self-harm, and use or abuse of various illicit drugs were evaluated in a sample of 53 women with BN and 162 women with BED. Self-harm and substance use generally did not differentiate BED and BN cases, but rates of self-harm and substance use were elevated among women with a history of sexual or physical abuse compared with women without such a history. Elevated rates of self-harm and substance use may not be related uniquely to BN diagnostic status, but may be related to a characteristic shared by women with BN and BED, such as a history of sexual or physical abuse.

Schoemaker et al. (2002) addressed the complicated role of child abuse as a risk factor for BN from the perspective of the self-medication hypothesis. This hypothesis asserts that, in abused BN cases, binge eating becomes a primary means of coping with the disturbances in anxiety and/or mood that originate from the abuse. In a population-based study (n = 1987), DSM-III-R diagnoses were assessed using the Composite International Diagnostic Interview (CIDI). Differences in rates of exposure to child abuse between BN cases and healthy, psychiatric, substance use and dual-diagnosis controls were employed to test the self-medication hypothesis. A history of psychological or multiple abuses was found to be a specific risk factor for dual-diagnosis disorder (cases with psychiatric and substance use disorders) and for BN. Nearly all BN cases who experienced multiple or psychological child abuse also showed comorbid anxiety and/or mood disorders. The authors concluded that their findings provide tentative support for the self-medication hypothesis.

Hartt and Waller (2002) examined the relationship between the severity of four forms of reported child abuse (emotional abuse, neglect, physical abuse and sexual abuse) and bulimic psychopathology in a sample of 23 bulimic women (15 women with BN, five with AN, binge-purge type, and three with BED). In addition, the authors investigated the association between abuse, dissociation and core beliefs in these patients, who completed a number of standardized self-report measures of child abuse (Child Abuse and Trauma Scale, CATS), dissociation (Dissociative Experiences Scale II, DES-II), core beliefs (Young Schema Questionnaire, YSQ) and bulimic symptomatology (Bulimic Investigatory Test – Edinburgh, BITE). Patients also kept diaries of daily bulimic behaviors over a period of two weeks. The results indicated no dimensional relationship between any of the four forms of child abuse and bulimic pathology. However, a positive correlation was found between overall abuse severity and DES-II scores (r = 0.4, $P < 0.05$), with neglect and sexual abuse accounting for the majority of the variance. The authors also found that a subset of core beliefs was associated with child abuse, and that there were different cognitive profiles associated with each type of trauma. Emotional abuse was correlated with beliefs about defectiveness/shame, emotional inhibition, mistrust/abuse and vulnerability to harm, while neglect was associated with beliefs about emotional inhibition, mistrust/abuse and vulnerability to harm. Sexual abuse was correlated with beliefs about emotional deprivation, emotional inhibition, mistrust/abuse and subjugation, while physical abuse was only correlated with a belief about emotional deprivation. Overall, the severity of abuse was correlated with six core beliefs, including defectiveness/shame, emotional deprivation, emotional inhibition, mistrust/abuse, subjugation and vulnerability to harm. Although these results should be interpreted with care because of the small and heterogeneous sample used, they call for further research involving larger, homogenous samples in order to investigate their generalizability and establish whether particular abusive experiences and core beliefs need to be addressed therapeutically in such cases. In addition, future research should consider the relationships between abuse, core beliefs and other impulsive behaviors.

Waller *et al.* (2003) explored the role of somatoform dissociation in eating disorders and disturbed eating behavior in relation to the well-established link between disturbed eating and psychological dissociation. They argue that the concept of psychological dissociation is limited to cognitive and emotional disruption that interferes with integration and processing, thereby resulting in absorption, amnesia, depersonalization and derealization, all of which involve an escape from awareness. The concept of somatoform dissociation expands this concept to include the physiologic component, including neurophysiologic reactivity and blunted autonomic nervous system responses in reaction to perceived threatening stimuli. While psychological dissociation has been linked to all forms of abuse and neglect, somatoform dissociation has been particularly linked to physical abuse and contact sexual abuse, both of which have been reported to occur at significantly higher rates in individuals with bulimic eating disorders. The authors postulated that the rates of both forms of dissociation would be higher in women with a bulimic disorder than in women with the restrictive form of AN. The sample that they studied consisted of 131 women with DSM-IV-defined eating disorders (21 AN-restricting subtype, 40 AN-binge/purge subtype, and 70 BN) and 75 women without an eating disorder. All of the participants completed measures of psychological dissociation (DES-II), somatoform dissociation (Somatoform Dissociation Questionnaire-20) and bulimic attitudes/behaviors (BITE). The results revealed that scores on measures of both psychologic and somatoform dissociation were higher in eating-disordered women with a bulimic component (BN, AN-binge/purge subtype) than in the non-clinical or non-bulimic eating-disordered women (AN-restrictor subtype). Somatoform dissociation showed especially robust associations with the specific bulimic behaviors of laxative abuse, diet pill abuse, diuretic abuse and excessive exercise, as well as with bulimic attitudes. The authors stressed that the diagnostic formulation and treatment of patients with bulimic features are likely to be enhanced by the assessment of both psychologic and somatoform dissociation. These data raise the question of whether the rate of DSM-IV-defined somatoform disorders may be higher in patients with eating disorders, but this is an area in which very little research has been done to date.

Lieb *et al.* (2002) report their results from a prospective epidemiological study on the natural course of somatoform disorders using a representative sample ($n = 2548$) of respondents from Munich, Germany. They studied this large group of adolescents and young adults at baseline and at follow-up (on average 3.5 years later). The follow-up incidence, stability and selected baseline risk factors for somatoform disorders and syndromes, including psychopathology and trauma exposure, were examined using the standardized Munich-Composite International Diagnostic Interview (M-CIDI). Over the duration of the follow-up interval, the incidence of any somatoform diagnosis was 25.7%, while the stability was 48%. One of the predictors of this stability or chronicity was the presence of an eating disorder, while female gender, lower social class, the experience of any substance use, anxiety and affective disorder, as well as the experience of traumatic sexual and physical threat events, predicted new onsets of somatoform conditions. These data add somatoform disorders and syndromes to the list of trauma-related comorbid disorders associated with eating disorders.

In the paper by Paul *et al.* (2002), the authors determined lifetime and six-month occurrence and phenomenology of self-injurious behavior in patients with eating disorders. Women ($n = 376$) in inpatient treatment for an eating disorder (119 subjects with AN, 137 subjects with BN and 120 subjects with EDNOS) were assessed for self-injurious behavior and also completed the Traumatic Life Events Questionnaire (TLEQ), the Dissociative Experience Scale (DES), the Barratt Impulsiveness Scale (BIS) and the Yale–Brown Obsessive-Compulsive Scale (YBOCS). Self-injurious behavior occurred in 34.6% of the total sample of eating-disordered women at some point in their lifetime, and in 21.3% during the previous six months. The highest lifetime occurrence rates were found in subjects with AN-binge/purge type (41.7%), EDNOS (35.8%) and BN (34.3%). The onset of the self-injurious behavior began after the onset of the eating disorder in 49.2% of cases, before the onset of the eating disorder in 25.4% of cases, and simultaneously in 25.4% of cases. Multivariate comparisons were computed for the factors of self-injurious behavior and diagnostic subgroup. Patients with self-injurious behaviors reported a significantly higher number of traumatic events, showed significantly higher dissociation scores, and exhibited significantly more obsessive-compulsive thoughts and behaviors than those without self-injurious behaviors. These findings strongly support the contention that patients with eating disorders are at risk for self-injurious behavior, and they point to the necessity for a routine screening for self-injurious behavior as well as histories of abuse and comorbid dissociative phenomenology.

Psychobiology

Although not directly related to eating disorders and trauma or PTSD, this study by Muck-Seler *et al.* (2003) deserves recognition, given its relevance to the role of serotonin (5-HT) in the pathophysiology of PTSD, depression and associated appetite disturbance. This research focused on platelet serotonin (5-HT) concentration and symptoms of comorbid depression in outpatient war veterans with or without PTSD. PTSD and depression were evaluated using the Clinician-Administered PTSD Scale (C-APTSDS), the Davidson Trauma Scale (DTS), the Montgomery-Asberg Depression Rating Scale (M-ADRS) and the Hamilton Anxiety Scale (HAS). A total of 65 male drug-free war veterans (48 subjects with PTSD and 17 subjects without PTSD) and 65 age- and gender-matched healthy controls were studied. Comorbid depression occurred in 54% of war veterans with PTSD and 31% of war veterans without PTSD. Although platelet 5-HT concentration was not significantly different between the groups of depressed and non-depressed war veterans with or without PTSD and healthy controls, the platelet 5-HT concentration differed between war veterans with various degrees of appetite loss. A positive correlation was observed between severity of appetite loss and platelet 5-HT concentration in war veterans with PTSD, while there was no such relationship between platelet 5-HT concentration and the severity of other symptoms of PTSD or depression. War veterans with PTSD had a high incidence of comorbid depression, which was not related to platelet 5-HT concentration. The marked relationship between platelet 5-HT concentration and severity of appetite loss is consistent with a wealth of previous evidence that the 5-HT system is involved in the regulation of appetite and satiety (Brewerton *et al.* 1994; Brewerton 1995;

Brewerton and Steiger 2004). This may be important to the future understanding of the biological mechanisms underlying the onset of eating disorders following trauma and PTSD.

Treatment aspects

A small number of articles published over the last two years have addressed treatment issues. Bell (2002) published a review of findings concerning which prognostic clinical factors might influence outcome following treatment for BN. Among the factors considered was a history of childhood sexual abuse. Of the studies noted, some have supported a link between CSA and poorer outcome, while others have not. No studies specifically looking at the impact of PTSD on treatment outcome were identified. The authors did find evidence that the comorbid diagnosis of borderline personality disorder (BPD) is a negative prognostic factor for BN. BPD has been associated with childhood sexual abuse, neglect and PTSD, so it is unclear to what extent these or other factors, such as impulsivity, account for this effect. However, the authors noted that 'modifying BN treatment for abuse survivors makes good clinical sense, but this decision is theoretically rather than empirically based.' This area of research is in its infancy, and much work remains to be done.

In a study by Murray and Waller (2002), the hypothesis that shame serves as a mediator of the relationship between reported sexual abuse and bulimic attitudes and behaviors was examined. A non-clinical sample of female under-graduates ($n = 214$) completed standardized measures of experiences of sexual abuse, internalized shame and bulimic psychopathology. Regression analyses were used to test for the mediating role of shame. The findings were compatible with a model in which levels of shame partially account for the relationship between any history of reported sexual abuse and bulimic psychopathology, but entirely account for the link between intrafamilial abuse and bulimic attitudes. The experience of shame appears to be important in understanding the relationship between reported sexual abuse and bulimic attitudes. Where individuals report a history of sexual abuse, particularly intrafamilial abuse, it may be clinically useful to focus on shame as a psychological consequence of that experience.

Summary of important findings

During the last two years, a number of advances in the clarification and understanding of the links between psychological trauma and eating disorders have been made. The available data support the conclusion that CSA is a significant risk factor, albeit a non-specific one, for the development of eating disorders, especially BN and other eating disorders with bulimic symptomatology in adults and adolescents of both sexes. The scope of abusive experiences has been widened to include bullying, racial discrimination, dating violence, date rape, physical neglect and emotional abuse, and bulimic disorders and symptoms have also been associated with multiple forms or episodes of abuse. Comorbid conditions and clinical features that appear to be associated with traumatic histories and bulimic disorders include dissociative disorders and symptoms, somatoform disorders, somatoform dissociation, self-injurious behaviors, substance abuse disorders and personality disorders. Appetite loss in PTSD patients is highly correlated with platelet 5-HT concentrations, which suggests that 5-HT may play a role in the mechanisms linking trauma, PTSD and associated eating disturbances.

Clinical implications

The clinical implications of these data are immense and they influence several areas, including the evaluation, treatment, etiology, course, comorbidity and prevention of eating disorders, particularly those with bulimic symptomatology. Given the increasing strength of the scientific basis for psychological trauma as a risk factor for bulimic disorders, it can now be more persuasively argued that the standard of care for a comprehensive psychiatric or psychologic evaluation of eating-disordered patients or clients involves the careful assessment of previous experiences of abuse and neglect. In fact, one could argue that this should be part of the psychiatric or psychologic evaluation of any patient or client.

From a clinical perspective, a brief discussion of the issue of specificity of eating-disorder risk factors is in order. It is often assumed that because CSA or other forms of abuse are 'only' non-specific risk factors for the eating disorders, they are therefore not important. However, non-specific risk factors in other types of disorders have been found to be very significant. A useful analogy in medicine is cigarette smoking as a risk factor for lung cancer. It is indeed a highly validated risk factor for lung cancer, but despite its importance in the development of this lethal condition, it is nevertheless a non-specific risk factor for this disease. Cigarette smoking is also a risk factor for a variety of pulmonary disorders, such as emphysema, bronchitis and asthma, as well as for cardio-vascular and neurologic disorders, such as myocardial infarction and stroke. Does the fact that smoking is a risk factor for these other conditions detract from its importance in causing lung cancer? There is no doubt that other factors (i.e. genetics) contribute to lung cancer, but can it be denied that helping individuals to stop smoking and preventing others from smoking in the first place reduces the eventual development of lung cancer and ultimately saves lives? Such is the situation with regard to psychologic trauma and the development of eating disorders. Focusing treatment and prevention efforts on child abuse/neglect and interpersonal violence in general could have enormous therapeutic effects, not only on eating disorders themselves but also on related comorbidity.

These findings also have important treatment implications that extend beyond evaluation into the realm of treatment. Effective, comprehensive evaluation leads to accurate and more complete diagnosis, which in turn leads to more specific and comprehensive treatment. In other words, diagnosis guides treatment. The effectiveness and specificity of treatments for PTSD and related disorders have advanced greatly over the last few years, including manualized CBT with prolonged exposure, eye movement desensitization reprocessing (EMDR) and pharmacotherapy. Eating-disorder specialists may benefit from recognizing and treating trauma-related conditions in these complex comorbid cases. Finally, it is incumbent upon clinicians who treat traumatized eating-disordered patients to understand the forensic aspects that are potentially involved and to counsel their patients or clients intelligently about these matters.

Future directions

Although recent research has further substantiated the links of BN and related comorbid disorders with histories of abuse, the links with PTSD remain relatively unresearched. There is a need for further study of the role of childhood maltreatment, as well as of PTSD, in the long-term course, prognosis and treatment response of the eating disorders. Childhood abuse and PTSD have been found to be poor prognostic indicators for depression, anxiety and substance use disorders (Zlotnick *et al.* 1997, 1999; Ouimette *et al.* 1998; Breslau 2001). If abuse is linked to BN with comorbidity, and if comorbidity indicates a worse prognosis compared with a single disorder, then abuse may be linked to treatment resistance and poorer outcome in abused bulimic patients with comorbidity (Brewerton 2004). However, this hypothesis needs to be confirmed by future follow-up studies. If this is shown to be the case, randomized controlled treatment trials in bulimic patients with abuse histories and trauma-related comorbidity, such as PTSD, are a logical and necessary future step for the field.

Future research is likely to elucidate further the psychobiologic underpinnings of abuse and neglect, PTSD, eating disorders and other related comorbid disorders using modern technological methods such as brain imaging and molecular biology techniques. Once the genetic vulnerability factors have been clarified, it will be necessary to understand how environmental factors, such as abuse, trigger and interact with susceptibility genes and what the cascade of neurophysiologic events involves. This may allow for the development of novel pharmacologic interventions.

Corresponding author: Timothy D Brewerton, MD, Department of Psychiatry and Behavioral Sciences, Medical University of South Carolina, Charleston, USA. Email: tbrewerton1@comcast.net

References

Ackard DM and Neumark-Sztainer D (2002) Date violence and date rape among adolescents: associations with disordered eating behaviors and psychological health. *Child Abuse and Neglect.* **26**: 455–73.
Using one of the largest sample sizes (*n* = 81 247) of any previous study related to abuse and eating disorders, this study examined the rates of self-reported date rape and date violence in high-school girls and boys, and convincingly demonstrated the

association of these events with eating-disordered behaviors, particularly purging behaviors, in both sexes.

Ackard DM and Neumark-Sztainer D (2003) Multiple sexual victimizations among adolescent boys and girls: prevalence and associations with eating behaviors and psychological health. *J Child Sex Abuse.* **12**: 17–37.

Ackard DM, Neumark-Sztainer D and Hannan P (2003) Dating violence among a nationally representative sample of adolescent girls and boys: associations with behavioral and mental health. *J Gender-Specific Med.* **6**: 39–48.

Bell L (2002) Does concurrent psychopathology at presentation influence response to treatment for bulimia nervosa? *Eat Weight Disord.* **7**: 168–81.

Breslau N (2001) Outcomes of post-traumatic stress disorder. *J Clin Psychiatry.* **62(Suppl. 17)**: 55–9.

Brewerton TD (1995) Towards a unified theory of serotonin dysregulation in eating and related disorders. *Psychoneuroendocrinology.* **20**: 561–90.

Brewerton TD (2002) Bulimia in children and adolescents. *Child Adolesc Psychiatry Clin North Am.* **11**: 237–56.

Brewerton TD (2004) Eating disorders, victimization and comorbidity: principles of treatment. In: TD Brewerton (ed.) *Clinical Handbook of Eating Disorders: an integrated approach.* Marcel Dekker Inc., New York, pp. 509–45.

Brewerton TD and Steiger H (2004) Neurotransmitter dysregulation in anorexia nervosa, bulimia nervosa and binge-eating disorder. In: TD Brewerton (ed.) *Clinical Handbook of Eating Disorders: an integrated approach.* Marcel Decker Inc., New York, pp. 257–81.

Brewerton TD, Murphy DL and Jimerson DC (1994) Test meal responses following m-chlorophenyl-piperazine and L-tryptophan in bulimics and controls. *Neuropsychopharmacology.* **11**: 63–71.

Brewerton TD, Dansky BS, Kilpatrick DG and O'Neil PM (1999) Bulimia nervosa, PTSD and 'forgetting': results from the National Women's Study. In: LM Williams and VL Banyard (eds) *Trauma and Memory.* Sage Publications, Durham, pp. 127–38.

Brewerton TD, Dansky BS, O'Neil PM and Kilpatrick DG (2003) *Relationship between 'purging disorder' and crime victimization in the National Women's Study.* Ninth Annual Meeting of the Eating Disorders Research Society, 1–4 October, Ravello, Italy.

Dansky BS, Brewerton TD, O'Neil PM and Kilpatrick DG (1997) The National Women's Study: Relationship of crime victimization and PTSD to bulimia nervosa. *Int J Eat Disord.* **21**: 213–28.

Dohm FA, Striegel-Moore RH, Wilfley DE, Pike KM, Hook J and Fairburn CG (2002) Self-harm and substance use in a community sample of black and white women with binge-eating disorder or bulimia nervosa. *Int J Eat Disord.* **32**: 389–400.

Fonseca H, Ireland M and Resnick MD (2002) Familial correlates of extreme weight control behaviors among adolescents. *Int J Eat Disord.* **32**: 441–8.

Fornari V and Dancyger IF (2003) Psychosexual development and eating disorders. *Adolesc Med State Art Rev.* **14**: 61–75.

Grilo CM and Masheb RM (2002) Childhood maltreatment and personality disorders in adult patients with binge-eating disorder. *Acta Psychiatr Scand.* **106**: 183–8.

Hartt J and Waller G (2002). Child abuse, dissociation and core beliefs in bulimic disorders. *Child Abuse and Neglect.* **26**: 923–38.

Jacobi C, Hayward C, de Zwaan M, Kraemer H and Agras WS (2004) Coming to terms with risk factors for eating disorders: application of risk terminology and suggestions for a general taxonomy. *Psychol Bull.* **130**: 19–65.
Although this review is not specifically focused on abuse, it is a superb overview and critical analysis of all known risk factors, including sexual abuse, for the development

of AN, BN and BED. Despite its rigor, sexual abuse is identified as a variable risk factor for all of the eating disorders.

Johnson JG, Cohen P, Kasen S and Brook JS (2002) Childhood adversities associated with risk for eating disorders or weight problems during adolescence or early adulthood. *Am J Psychiatry.* **159**: 394–400.

This unique prospective longitudinal study conducted over an 18-year period is one of the best (if not *the* best) studies to date on the role of abuse in the development of eating disorders. These results further establish sexual abuse as an important predictor of BN and other bulimic disorders. In addition, the role of physical neglect in forecasting disturbed eating behaviors was elucidated, thereby widening the scope of psychologic trauma to neglect, a relatively under-researched area.

Kraemer HC, Kazdin AE, Offord DR, Kessler RC, Jensen PS and Kupfer DJ (1997) Coming to terms with the terms of risk. *Arch Gen Psychiatry.* **54**: 337–44.

Kraemer HC, Kazdin AE, Offord DR, Kessler RC, Jensen PS and Kupfer DJ (1999) Measuring the potency of risk factors for clinical or policy significance. *Psychol Med.* **4**: 257–71.

Leonard S, Steiger H and Kao A (2003) Childhood and adulthood abuse in bulimic and nonbulimic women: prevalences and psychological correlates. *Int J Eat Disord.* **33**: 397–405.

Lieb R, Zimmermann P, Friis RH, Hofler M, Tholen S and Wittchen HU (2002) The natural course of DSM-IV somatoform disorders and syndromes among adolescents and young adults: a prospective longitudinal community study. *Eur Psychiatry.* **17**: 321–31.

Muck-Seler D, Pivac N, Jakovljevic M, Sagud M and Mihaljevic-Peles A (2003) Platelet 5-HT concentration and comorbid depression in war veterans with and without post-traumatic stress disorder. *J Affect Disord.* **75**: 171–9.

Murray C and Waller G (2002) Reported sexual abuse and bulimic psychopathology among nonclinical women: the mediating role of shame. *Int J Eat Disord.* **32**: 186–91.

Ouimette PC, Brown PJ and Najavits LM (1998) Course and treatment of patients with both substance use and post-traumatic stress disorders. *Addict Behav.* **23**: 785–95.

Paul T, Schroeter K, Dahme B and Nutzinger DO (2002) Self-injurious behavior in women with eating disorders. *Am J Psychiatry.* **159**: 408–11.

Schoemaker C, Smit F, Bijl RV and Vollebergh WA (2002) Bulimia nervosa following psychological and multiple child abuse: support for the self-medication hypothesis in a population-based cohort study. *Int J Eat Disord.* **32**: 381–8.

Sherwood NE, Neumark-Sztainer D, Story M, Beuhring T and Resnick MD (2002) Weight-related sports involvement in girls: who is at risk for disordered eating? *Am J Health Promotion.* **16**: 341–4.

Smolak L and Murnen SK (2002) A meta-analytic examination of the relationship between child sexual abuse and eating disorders. *Int J Eat Disord.* **31**: 136–50.

Using a meta-analysis of 53 research studies, this comprehensive review demonstrated that childhood sexual abuse is indeed a risk factor for eating disorders, particularly BN or those with bulimic symptoms. This conclusion was true whether or not the study examined the rates of eating disorders in CSA victims or the rates of CSA in eating-disorderd subjects.

Striegel-Moore RH, Dohm FA, Pike KM, Wilfley DE and Fairburn CG (2002) Abuse, bullying, and discrimination as risk factors for binge-eating disorder. *Am J Psychiatry.* **159**: 1902–7.

This is an important, well-controlled study involving three cells (BED patients, general psychiatric patients and controls) that not only extends the concept of abuse or trauma to bullying and racial discrimination, but also carefully teases out racial differences. This study also demonstrates the specificity of certain risk factors involving abuse, i.e. the rates of racial discrimination in white women with BED and sexual abuse in black women with BED, both of which were significantly higher than in matched psychiatric comparison subjects.

Waller G, Babbs M, Wright F, Potterton C, Meyer C and Leung N (2003) Somatoform dissociation in eating-disordered patients. *Behav Res Ther*. **41**: 619–27.

Wonderlich SA, Brewerton TD, Jocic Z, Dansky BS and Abbott DW (1997) The relationship of childhood sexual abuse and eating disorders: a review. *J Am Acad Child Adolesc Psychiatry*. **36**: 1107–15.

Zlotnick C, Warshaw M, Shea MT and Keller MB (1997) Trauma and chronic depression among patients with anxiety disorders. *J Consult Clin Psychol*. **65**: 333–6.

Zlotnick C, Warshaw M, Shea MT, Allsworth J, Pearlstein T and Keller MB (1999) Chronicity in post-traumatic stress disorder (PTSD) and predictors of course of comorbid PTSD in patients with anxiety disorders. *J Traumat Stress*. **12**: 89–100.

10

Classification of eating disorders 2002–2003

B Timothy Walsh and Dana A Satir

Abstract

Objectives of the review. This review provides a summary of the literature published during the period 2002–2003 focusing on issues related to the classification of eating disorders. The major topic of recent interest has been binge-eating disorder (BED). In addition, several articles have addressed the possible need for changes in the criteria for the more established diagnoses, anorexia nervosa (AN) and bulimia nervosa (BN).

Summary of recent findings. Although some recent studies of BED suggest that it is a distinct and clinically useful category, debate continues as to whether the available information is sufficient to merit BED's 'official' recognition. Studies related to AN and BN have focused on the substantial number of individuals who present with clinically significant eating disturbances, but who do not fully meet the current diagnostic criteria for AN or BN.

Future directions. For a number of reasons, defining what constitutes an eating disorder remains among the critical issues facing the field. The literature on this topic continues to be interesting and provocative, but additional data-based studies are needed to resolve current diagnostic challenges.

Introduction

The classification of eating disorders remains a topic of interest and concern to both clinicians and researchers. The two major disorders, anorexia nervosa (AN) and bulimia nervosa (BN), are well established. Diagnostic criteria for both were provided in DSM-III (American Psychiatric Association 1980), and the current, DSM-IV (American Psychiatric Association 1994) criteria are widely used. However, difficult problems persist concerning the precise location of the boundary between these disorders and other less well-characterized disturbances of eating behavior, and the need for and interpretation of specific criteria. Of greater concern is the broad category of e5ating disorder not otherwise specified (EDNOS). A substantial fraction (and in some clinics, the majority) of individuals who present for treatment of an eating disorder do not meet the criteria for either AN or BN, and must therefore be formally categorized in the DSM-IV system as having EDNOS. DSM-IV suggested that binge-eating disorder (BED) might be a useful new category for many individuals currently grouped within EDNOS, and provided provisional criteria in an appendix. Debate about the utility and validity of BED as a category continues.

We shall review articles published in the last two years (2002–2003) that focus on the diagnosis of eating disorders. There is little question that the topic of BED has continued to generate the greatest interest. In 2003, a supplement to the *International Journal of Eating Disorders* offered a scholarly and timely review of the current status of BED. In this brief summary, we shall first focus on BED, highlighting the summaries provided in the *International Journal*, and reviewing several other recent articles related to BED. We shall then review the smaller recent literature that focuses on AN and BN, and the broad category of EDNOS.

Literature review

Binge-eating disorder

Although the syndrome was first described nearly half a century ago (Stunkard 1959), BED did not receive significant attention until diagnostic criteria were first proposed for possible inclusion in DSM-IV. Ultimately, BED was included in DSM-IV in two ways – as an example in the broad category of EDNOS and as a proposal in Appendix B, with specific diagnostic criteria, among a number of possible new categories suggested for further study. The debate as to whether BED should become a new 'official' category continues.

In the supplement to the *International Journal of Eating Disorders*, Devlin et al. (2003) provide a comprehensive update of the current nosological status of BED. They propose and evaluate four models of how to conceptualize BED: (1) as a distinct disorder unto itself; (2) as a variant of BN; (3) not as a disorder, but as a behavioral subtype of obesity; and (4) not as a disorder, but as a behavioral feature associated with other psychopathology. Within each model, Devlin et al. (2003) summarize the relevant literature and evaluate whether or not these models satisfy the criteria for reliability and validity sufficiently to warrant categorical status. For example, they cite evidence which suggests that individuals with BED differ significantly from individuals classified as having the purging subtype of BN on demographic characteristics, treatment responsiveness, and eating behavior in the laboratory, but note the uncertainty about where to classify individuals with non-purging BN. Their review also suggests that it might not be useful simply to consider BED as a subtype of obesity, because most studies to date do not indicate that obese individuals with BED differ greatly from similar individuals without BED in their response to obesity treatment. Overall, Devlin et al. (2003) conclude that it is not possible at present to reach at a clear conclusion about where BED should be formally located within the diagnostic system.

Although most of the other articles in the *International Journal of Eating Disorders* supplement expressed similar concerns about a number of unresolved issues related to BED, an interesting range of opinion was voiced. Notably, Stunkard, who first clearly described the phenomenon, suggested that because of the difficulty of clearly defining the diagnostic criteria for BED and the substantial psychopathology with which this disorder is associated, the greatest value of BED may be as a behavioral marker for psychological symptoms associated with obesity, rather than as a separate diagnostic category (Stunkard and Allison 2003). Cooper and Fairburn (2003) also noted the difficulties of diagnosis surrounding BED, and suggested changes in the diagnostic criteria for BED and BN in order to clarify the border between these two syndromes. Among the most sympathetic to the utility of BED as a diagnostic entity were Wilfley *et al.* (2003), who argued that the distinctive psychopathology of BED, its co-occurring psychiatric and physical morbidities and its association with obesity 'constitute an eating disorder of clinical severity and a significant public health problem' (p. S36). Yanovski (2003) emphasized the potential importance of addressing BED in therapeutic attempts to address the growing epidemic of obesity.

In the *International Journal of Eating Disorders* supplement, Walsh and Boudreau (2003) reviewed laboratory studies of eating behavior focusing on BED, including three published in the last two years (Anderson *et al.* 2001; Geliebter *et al.* 2001; Guss *et al.* 2002). Such studies are of potential relevance to the diagnostic validity of BED, as they provide objective information about the eating behavior of individuals with BED, which is purportedly different from that of otherwise comparable individuals without the disorder. Walsh and Boudreau concluded that virtually all laboratory studies conducted to date have found that individuals with BED consume more food during both binge and non-binge meals than do comparable controls. Individuals with BN appear to consume more food when binge-eating, but less food when not binge-eating, than do those with BED. Walsh and Boudreau suggested that these laboratory studies support, but do not conclusively demonstrate, the validity of BED as a unique diagnostic category.

A more recent study (Hsu *et al.* 2002) examined eating behaviors and other characteristics of 37 severely obese individuals (BMI $\geq$ 40 kg/m^2) awaiting gastric-bypass surgery. Nine subjects met partial or full criteria for BED and differed from the other individuals in several ways, including the consumption of a significantly greater number of calories while being provided with ad lib liquid food for 24 hours. The authors indicated that their results supported the validity of BED within this group of severely obese individuals.

Although not as directly related to the issue of diagnosis, other articles in the *International Journal of Eating Disorders* supplement provide useful summaries of the current state of knowledge about BED, including reviews of epidemiology (Striegel-Moore and Franko 2003), psychologic and pharmacologic treatment (Carter *et al.* 2003; Wonderlich *et al.* 2003), the medical morbidity of BED (Bulik and Reichborn-Kjennerud 2003) and the occurrence of BED among children and adolescents (Marcus and Kalarchian 2003).

A novel approach by Williamson *et al.* (2002) to examining the validity of BED as a diagnostic category has used taxometric methods. These authors first conducted a factor analysis to analyze symptoms among 341 women, most of whom had an eating disorder. The three factors identified, namely binge eating, fear of fatness/compensatory behaviors and drive for thinness, were then examined using taxometric analyses. These techniques are a group of statistical procedures used, in this instance, to determine whether the three factors identified varied along a continuum or suggested the presence of latent classes. The taxometric analysis indicated that AN, BN, EDNOS and BED cannot be understood in terms of a strictly dimensional model – they emerged as qualitatively distinct, not just quantitatively different, from non-obese individuals without eating disorders. Secondly, when the disorders were examined separately, the results suggested the presence of discrete syndromes for all but AN. Although this study was not focused solely on BED, the results suggest that the symptom constellation of individuals with BED is relatively distinct, and add support to the validity of the syndrome.

A large (*n* = 385) study by Crow *et al.* (2002) also supported the distinction between BED and the other major eating disorder diagnoses. These researchers obtained extensive interview and self-report measures of general psychopathology and eating-disorder symptoms. Using step-wise discriminant analyses, they found clear differences between subjects with AN, with BN and with BED. However, it was not possible to distinguish full and partial syndromal BED, highlighting the persistent difficulty of knowing where the diagnostic thresholds should be defined.

Anorexia nervosa

The core diagnostic criteria for AN have persisted with only minor changes since the publication of DSM-III. Major concerns about these criteria involve the threshold for considering an individual underweight (85% of the weight expected for age and height, according to the DSM-IV guideline), and whether amenorrhea should be required for female subjects with the disorder. Most of the modest literature on these issues pre-dates the two-year time-frame (2002–2003) covered by this review. However, a major change introduced by DSM-IV was the delineation of two subtypes within AN, namely the binge-eating/purging (AN-B/P) subtype and the restricting (AN-R) subtype (for review, *see* DaCosta and Halmi 1992), and several empirical studies comparing the characteristics of the two subtypes have appeared in recent years.

Casper and Troiani (2001) obtained information from a self-report measure of perceived family function from 22 adolescents with AN, 45 control adolescents and their families. The authors report significant differences between the perceptions of the AN-R and the AN-B/P groups, including the provocative observation that the AN-R patients perceived themselves to be better functioning than did either the AN-B/P patients or the controls. Limitations include the small sample size, the self-report nature of the measure, and the fact that the numbers of AN-R and AN-B/P patients were not provided.

Eddy *et al.* (2002) also compared AN subtypes, and included the important dimension of change in subtype over time. Over an eight-year period, the authors collected data (at 6- to 12-month intervals) from treatment-seeking women, of whom 51 subjects were initially classified as AN-R and 85 subjects were classified as AN-B/P. At intake, AN-R patients had a significantly shorter duration of illness, lower percentage of ideal body weight and greater likelihood of having been hospitalized than did AN-B/P patients. However, there were no significant differences between patients with the AN-B/P or AN-R subtype in terms of frequency of borderline personality diagnosis, history of suicide attempts or gestures at intake, or rates of recovery, relapse or mortality. In addition, after eight years of follow-up, 62% of AN-R women met the criteria for AN-B/P, while only 12% of the patients in the sample reported an absence of regular binge- eating and purging behaviors.

Like most other studies that have addressed the issue, this study noted significant clinical differences between AN subtypes. However, unlike most other studies that have compared AN subtypes, Eddy *et al.* did not detect differences on measures of impulsivity between the subtypes. Importantly, the study documents the fact that a substantial number of individuals who originally meet the criteria for AN-R will develop binge eating and/or purging, and therefore change diagnostic subtype over time.

Ward *et al.* (2003) provided an exploratory analysis of psychosocial and biologic characteristics among a small group of women who had recovered from AN. The authors compared subjects with a history of AN-R ($n = 13$), subjects with a history of AN-B/P ($n = 5$) and female controls ($n = 18$). At the time of assessment, on several measures of psychopathology (both non-specific and eating related), the women with a history of AN-B/P had significantly higher scores than did the women with a history of AN-R. Although the findings suggest the possibility of enduring differences between subtypes, the small number of subjects limits the confidence with which these findings can be interpreted.

Amenorrhea was not required for the diagnosis of AN by DSM-III, and was introduced as a formal criterion in DSM-III-R (American Psychiatric Association 1987). The DSM-IV Work Group formally considered the elimination of this criterion, but because of the lack of empirical evidence to support a change, the criterion was maintained. Since the publication of DSM-IV, several studies have examined the characteristics of patients with AN with and without amenorrhea.

A recent investigation by Watson and Andersen (2003) compared the characteristics of patients who met the full criteria for AN with those of patients with 'atypical AN,' defined as individuals who met all of the other DSM-IV criteria but failed to meet the amenorrhea criterion for three months and/or weighed more than 85% of the matched mean population weight (MMPW). The authors reviewed the charts of 588 inpatients who had been admitted for treatment of an eating disorder, and identified 230 patients who met the full DSM-IV criteria for AN and 67 others who fell into the following categories: amenorrhea and > 85% MMPW ($n = 18$); irregular menses and > 85% MMPW ($n = 21$); irregular menses and < 85% MMPW (n = 28). There were many similarities between the characteristics of patients who meet the full criteria and those of the atypical group. However, in addition to having higher weight, the atypical group had a shorter duration of illness, fewer previous hospitalizations, a higher level of reported history of sexual and physical abuse, and higher bone mineral density. The authors felt that the subgroup of atypical patients who were below 85% MMPW but reported some menstrual function most closely resembled the patients who met the full AN criteria, and suggested that modification of both the amenorrhea and weight criteria should be considered.

Bulimia nervosa

Little of the recent literature has focused on the diagnostic criteria for BN. However, the challenging question of what constitutes an episode of binge eating continues to receive attention. Keel *et al.* (2001) directly addressed this issue by comparing 30 women who met the full DSM-IV criteria for BN ('objective bulimia nervosa,' OBN) with 24 women who met all of the criteria except that their binge meals were characterized by a sense of loss of control but *not* by the consumption of an objectively large amount of food ('subjective bulimia nervosa,' SBN). Women with OBN were significantly older than women with SBN, reported binge eating and purging twice as frequently as women with SBN, and scored significantly higher on the Bulimia Test-Revised (BULIT-R) and on measures of impulsivity. In addition, a significantly higher proportion of women with OBN had received psychologic treatment. However, on most measures of psychopathology there were no significant differences between groups. These data suggest that there are clinically significant differences between women with OBN and SBN, implying that requiring the presence of objectively large binge episodes to meet the diagnostic criteria for BN has some utility. On the other hand, this study also suggests that women with SBN have significant psychological symptoms, implying the potential benefit of a more specific category than EDNOS for such individuals.

The study by Crow *et al.* (2002), noted above, also compared full-syndrome BN cases (n = 87) with partial-syndrome BN cases (n = 57). Partial-syndrome BN cases included patients who met all of the DSM-IV criteria for BN except the criterion requiring overconcern with weight and shape and patients who met all of the criteria except for reporting that the frequency of binge-eating episodes was more than once a month but less than the DSM-IV criterion of twice a week. Using step-wise discriminant analysis, Crow *et al.* found that full-syndrome BN could be distinguished from subthreshold BN by the presence of significantly higher total scores on the Yale-Brown-Cornell Eating Disorder Scale (YBC-EDS). However, on virtually all other demographic characteristics and measures of eating disorders and other psychopathology, the two BN groups were not distinguished.

These two studies, as well as previous investigations, suggest that the characteristics of many individuals who meet most but not all of the current DSM-IV criteria for BN resemble the characteristics of individuals who meet all of the criteria. However, what is less clear is precisely how to restructure the diagnostic boundaries of BN and EDNOS in ways that will enhance the coverage of significant clinical problems but not make BN overly inclusive.

Night eating syndrome

Virtually all of the literature on diagnostic classification and EDNOS published in 2002 and 2003 focused on BED and is reviewed above.

In addition, night eating syndrome (NES), another disorder linked to obesity and also originally described by Stunkard *et al.* (1955), was usefully summarized by Stunkard and Allison (2003). NES is characterized by morning anorexia, evening hyperphagia and insomnia, and may be viewed as a combination of an eating disorder, a sleep disorder and a mood disorder. NES appears to be distinguished from BED by a greater frequency of small nocturnal eating episodes and a lower intensity of body-image disturbance, and may be less responsive to non-specific interventions than is BED. Stunkard and Allison note that pharmacologic and psychotherapeutic studies are under way, and call for additional research on NES.

Summary of important findings and clinical implications

Recent publications on the diagnosis of eating disorders reflect the continuing debate as to the validity of BED and how best to specify the diagnostic criteria for AN and BN. A consensus does not yet appear to have formed in the field regarding the wisdom of formally designating BED as an eating disorder. On the other hand, there appears to be growing support for eliminating the requirement for amenorrhea from the diagnosis of AN. Directly or indirectly, these issues highlight the broad concern that a substantial number of individuals who present for treatment of an eating disorder must currently be classified as having an EDNOS. Although there is consensus about the existence of this problem, data on the utility of additional diagnostic schemes, other than BED, are scarce.

This ongoing debate should remind clinicians that diagnostic criteria must be regarded more as guidelines than as rigid rules. A major purpose of diagnostic categories is to guide clinicians to information that is relevant to prognosis and useful treatment interventions. It is likely that individuals who 'almost' meet diagnostic criteria for a category will respond to treatments in a similar fashion to individuals who more fully satisfy the diagnostic criteria, and may therefore for clinical purposes deserve to be described as having the disorder in question.

Future directions

Diagnostic categories play an impressive role in determining the research agenda and in guiding clinical treatment. The eating disorders field would benefit from clarification of the status of BED and from the development of additional data-based diagnostic schemes to describe the large number of individuals in the EDNOS category.

Corresponding author: B Timothy Walsh, MD, New York State Psychiatric Institute-Unit 98, 1051 Riverside Drive, New York, NY 10032, USA. Email: btw1@columbia.edu

References

American Psychiatric Association (1980) *Diagnostic and Statistical Manual of Mental Disorders* (3e). American Psychiatric Association, Washington, DC.

American Psychiatric Association (1987) *Diagnostic and Statistical Manual of Mental Disorders* (3e, revised). American Psychiatric Association, Washington, DC.

American Psychiatric Association (1994) *Diagnostic and Statistical Manual of Mental Disorders* (4e). American Psychiatric Association, Washington, DC.

Anderson DA, Williamson DA, Johnson WG and Grieve CO (2001) Validity of test meals for determining binge eating. *Eat Behav.* 2: 105–12.

Bulik CM and Reichborn-Kjennerud T (2003) Medical morbidity in binge-eating disorder. *Int J Eat Disord.* S34: S39–46.

Carter WP, Hudson JI, Lalonde JK, Pindyck L, McElroy SL and Pope HG Jr (2003) Pharmacologic treatment of binge-eating disorder. *Int J Eat Disord.* S34: S74–88.

Casper RC and Troiani M (2001) Family functioning in anorexia nervosa differs by subtype. *Int J Eat Disord.* 30: 338–42.

Cooper Z and Fairburn CG (2003) Refining the definition of binge-eating disorder and nonpurging bulimia nervosa. *Int J Eat Disord.* S34: S89–95.

Crow SJ, Agras WS, Halmi K, Mitchell JE and Kraemer HC (2002) Full syndromal versus subthreshold anorexia nervosa, bulimia nervosa, and binge-eating disorder: a multi-center study. *Int J Eat Disord.* 32: 309–18.

Several studies have compared full- and partial-syndrome eating disorders, but this paper is the first to include BED as part of the analyses. The results are important because they indicate that full cases of AN and BN, as well as BED, cannot be meaningfully distinguished from their subthreshold counterparts. This study, like others before it, calls into question the discriminant nature of the current diagnostic criteria because of the similarities between full and subthreshold cases.

DaCosta M and Halmi KA (1992) Classifications of anorexia nervosa: question of subtypes. *Int J Eat Disord.* 11: 305–13.

Devlin MJ, Goldfein JA and Dobrow I (2003) What is this thing called BED? Current status of binge-eating disorder nosology. *Int J Eat Disord.* S34: S2–18.

This paper is a comprehensive review of diagnostic features, as well as theoretical considerations, in the classification of binge-eating disorder (BED). The authors provide an up-to-date review and analysis of different conceptualizations of the disorder.

Eddy KT, Keel PK, Dorer DJ, Delinsky SS, Franko DL and Herzog DB (2002) Longitudinal comparison of anorexia nervosa subtype. *Int J Eat Disord.* 31: 191–201.

This study utilizes a useful longitudinal design, and notes a high cross-over rate from AN-R to AN-B/P, suggesting that AN-R might represent a phase of AN rather than a distinct subtype.

Geliebter A, Hassid G and Hashim SA (2001) Test meal intake in obese binge eaters in relation to mood and gender. *Int J Eat Disord.* 29: 488–94.

Guss JL, Kissileff HR, Devlin MJ, Zimmerli E and Walsh BT (2002) Binge size increases with body mass index in women with binge-eating disorder. *Obes Res.* **10**: 1021–9.

Hsu LKG, Mulliken B, McDonagh B *et al.* (2002) Binge-eating disorder in extreme obesity. *Int J Obes Rel Metab Disord.* **26**: 1398–403.

Keel PK, Mayer SA and Harnden-Fischer JH (2001) Importance of size in defining binge-eating episodes in bulimia nervosa. *Int J Eat Disord.* **29**: 294–301.

This is one of the few studies comparing women who meet all of the criteria for BN except for the size of their binge eating with full-threshold BN cases.

Marcus MD and Kalarchian MA (2003) Binge eating in children and adolescents. *Int J Eat Disord.* **S34**: S47–57.

Striegel-Moore RH and Franko DL (2003) Epidemiology of binge-eating disorder. *Int J Eat Disord.* **S34**: S19–29.

Stunkard AJ (1959) Eating patterns and obesity. *Psychiatr Q.* **33**: 284–95.

Stunkard AJ and Allison KC (2003) Binge-eating disorder: disorder or marker? *Int J Eat Disord.* **S34**: S107–15.

This is an interesting commentary expressing concerns about BED as a diagnostic category by the investigator who first described the syndrome.

Stunkard AJ, Grace WJ and Wolff HG (1955) The night-eating syndrome: a pattern of food intake among certain obese patients. *Am J Med.* **19**: 78–86.

Walsh BT and Boudreau G (2003) Laboratory studies of binge-eating disorder. *Int J Eat Disord.* **S34**: S30–38.

Ward A, Campbell IC, Brown N and Treasure J (2003) Anorexia nervosa subtypes: differences in recovery. *J Nerv Ment Dis.* **191**: 197–201.

Watson TL and Andersen AE (2003) A critical examination of the amenorrhea and weight criteria for diagnosing anorexia nervosa. *Acta Psychiatr Scand.* **108**: 175–82.

Wilfley DE, Wilson GT and Agras SW (2003) The clinical significance of binge-eating disorder. *Int J Eat Disord.* **S34**: S96–106.

Williamson DA, Womble LG, Smeets MA *et al.* (2002) Latent structure of eating disorder symptoms: a factor analytic and taxometric investigation. *Am J Psychiatry.* **159**: 412–18.

This study represents an innovative approach to the topic of classification through the use of taxometric analyses. The results of this study support the categorical distinction of eating disorders as discrete syndromes, in favor of a dimensional model that has been suggested by some researchers.

Wonderlich SA, de Zwaan M, Mitchell JE, Peterson C and Crow S (2003) Psychological and dietary treatments of binge-eating disorder: conceptual implications. *Int J Eat Disord.* **S34**: S58–73.

Yanovski SZ (2003) Binge-eating disorder and obesity in 2003: could treating an eating disorder have a positive effect on the obesity epidemic? *Int J Eat Disord.* **S34**: S117–20.

Index

Page numbers in italics refer to tables.